God's
Vitamin "C"™

for the Spirit

Compiled by
Kathy Collard Miller
and **D. Larry Miller**

STARBURST PUBLISHERS

P.O. Box 4123, Lancaster, Pennsylvania 17604

Kathy Collard Miller and **D. Larry Miller** speak nationally and internationally, both as individuals and together, at couple's retreats and other events. Also, Larry speaks at men's events and Kathy at women's. Larry has been involved in law enforcement for over 25 years and currently works for an Orange County, California, law enforcement agency.

Kathy is the author of 15 books, including *Healing the Angry Heart, Help for Hurting Moms, Your View of God . . . God's View of You, Sure Footing in a Shaky World,* and the *Daughters of the King* Bible study series. She has written over 100 published articles for *Decision, L.A. Times, Christian Parenting Today, Today's Christian Woman, Virtue,* and many other magazines. She is a contributing editor for *The Christian Communicator* and teaches at writers' seminars. As a part of the teaching staff of Christian Leaders, Authors, Speakers Seminar (CLASS), Kathy offers techniques and skills for effective communication on the platform.

Kathy and Larry have told their exciting and dynamic story of a healed marriage on numerous radio and TV programs. In addition, Kathy has shared on the 700 Club and many other radio and TV programs about being delivered from being an abusive mother.

They can be reached for scheduling speaking engagements at P.O. Box 1058, Placentia, California 92670 (714) 993-2654.

To schedule Author appearances write:
Author Appearances, Starburst Promotions, P.O. Box 4123
Lancaster, Pennsylvania 17604 or call (717) 293-0939

Credits:
Cover by David Marty Design
Illustrations by Bill Dussinger
Unless otherwise noted, or paraphrased by the author, all Scripture quotations are from the King James Version of The Holy Bible.

We, the Publisher and Authors, declare that to the best of our knowledge all material (quoted or not) contained herein is accurate, and we shall not be held liable for the same.

First Printing, January 1996
Second Printing, January 1996
Third Printing, February 1996

ISBN: 0-914984-83-7
Library of Congress Catalog Number 95-71943
Printed in the United States of America

Table of Contents

God's Vitamin "C" for The Spirit is a collection of inspirational Stories, Quotes, Cartoons, and Scriptures by many of your favorite Christian speakers and writers. It will motivate your life and inspire your spirit. You will find them to be both heart-tugging and thought-provoking.

Be sure to read **God's Chewable Vitamin "C" for the Spirit:** *A Dose of God's Wisdom, One Bite at a Time* (see page 302 for ordering information), a collection of Quotes and Scriptures from many of the same speakers and writers found in **God's Vitamin "C" for the Spirit.**

1

Christian Living

Therefore, my beloved brethren, be ye steadfast, unmoveable, always abounding in the work of the Lord, forasmuch as ye know that your labour is not in vain in the Lord.

1 Corinthians 15:58

"Make Me Like Joe!"

Joe was a drunk who was miraculously converted at a Bowery mission. Prior to his conversion, he had gained the reputation of being a dirty wino for whom there was no hope, only a miserable existence in the ghetto. But following his conversion to a new life with God, everything changed. Joe became the most caring person that anyone associated with the mission had ever known. Joe spent his days and nights hanging out at the mission, doing whatever needed to be done. There was never any task that was too lowly for Joe. There was never anything that he was asked to do that he considered beneath him. Whether it was cleaning up the vomit left by some violently sick alcoholic or scrubbing the toilets after careless men left the men's room filthy, Joe did what was asked with a smile on his face and a seeming gratitude for the chance to help. He could be counted on to feed feeble men who wandered off the street and into the mission, and to undress and tuck into bed men who were too out of it to take care of themselves.

One evening, when the director of the mission was delivering his evening evangelistic message to the usual crowd of still and sullen men with drooped heads, there was one man who looked up, came down the aisle to the altar, and knelt to pray, crying out for God to help him to change. The repentant drunk kept shouting, "Oh God! Make me like Joe! Make me like Joe! Make me like Joe! Make me like Joe!"

The director of the mission leaned over and said to the man, "Son, I think it would be better if you prayed. 'Make me like *Jesus!*' "

The man looked up at the director with a quizzical expression on his face and asked, "Is he like Joe?"

—Tony Campolo

You Can't Outgive the Lord!

My dad was the original soft touch to those who were hungry. He was an evangelist who journeyed from place to place to hold revival meetings. Travel was expensive and we never seemed to have much more money than was absolutely necessary. One of the problems was the way churches paid their ministers in those days. Pastors received a year-round salary but evangelists were paid only when they worked. Therefore, my father's income stopped abruptly during Thanksgiving, Christmas, summer vacation, or any time he rested. Perhaps that's why we were always near the bottom of the barrel when he was at home. But that didn't stop my father from giving.

I remember Dad going off to speak in a tiny church and coming home ten days later. My mother greeted him warmly and asked how the revival had gone. He was always excited about that subject. Eventually, in moments like this she would get around to asking him about the offering. Women have a way of worrying about things like that.

"How much did they pay you?" she asked.

I can still see my father's face as he smiled and looked at the floor. "Aw . . ." he stammered. My mother stepped back and looked into his eyes.

"Oh, I get it," she said. "You gave the money away again, didn't you?"

"Myrt," he said, "the pastor there is going through a hard time. His kids are so needy. It just broke my heart. They have holes in their shoes and one of them is going to school on these cold mornings without a coat. I felt I should give the entire fifty dollars to them."

My good mother looked intently at him for a moment and then she smiled. "You know that if God told you to do it, it's okay with me."

Then a few days later the inevitable happened. The Dobsons ran completely out of money. There was no reserve to tide us over. That's when my father gathered us in the bedroom for a time of prayer. I remember that day as though it were yesterday. He prayed first.

"Oh Lord, you promised that if we would be faithful with you and your people in our good times, then you would not forget us in our time of need. We have tried to be generous with what you have given us, and now we are calling on you for help."

A very impressionable ten-year-old boy named Jimmy was watching and listening very carefully that day. *What would happen?* he wondered. *Did God hear Dad's prayer?*

The next day an unexpected check for $1,200 came for us in the mail. Honestly! That's the way it happened, not just this once but many times. I saw the Lord match my dad's giving stride for stride. No, God never made us wealthy, but my young faith grew by leaps and bounds. I learned that you cannot *outgive* God!

—James Dobson

Do you know about the father whose little son had always been in junior church and was about to graduate to the worship services, so during the week his daddy took him to visit the big sanctuary and get acquainted with it?

"Here's the pulpit where the pastor preaches to us," he said. " And here are all the pews where the people sit. And, Freddie, here in front is our service flag, where we show a star for each person in this church who's in the service."

Freddie asked, "And what are the gold stars, Daddy?"

"Well, son, the gold stars represent the men and women who have died in the service."

"Which service, Daddy," asked Freddie, "morning or evening?"

The Birdbath

The solid gold-plated birdbath
    stands strongly and patiently
    in front of the apartment dwelling.
    Filled to the brim with water,
    it glistens in the evening haze of the setting sun.

It stands like a silent sentinel,
    awaiting to welcome weary-winged travelers
    and always ready to wash and renew them.
    Yet it simply stands,
    ready and waiting.

I hear You speak, Lord,
    through the silent and sturdy birdbath.
    Am I to learn, too, to stand solid in You,
    and always be ready to give an answer
    of the hope that's in me
    to any pilgrim who may ask.

Is the perpetual presence of the birdbath
    a reminder to me to stand like a guard in constant prayer,
    always ready and waiting
    and filled with Your water of life?
    Lord, make me like the birdbath.
    It never traps the birds
    nor keeps them any longer than they want to stay.

But it lets the birds fly free
and never forces them to wash in its water.
It simply remains standing, ready and waiting;
freely offering refreshing revival
and renewing rest and replenishment.

Oh my patient, Lord,
please make me like the birdbath!

—Virgean L. F. Bosworth

Be Alert

A Spirit-led boldness will often prod at unexpected moments. Be aware of those divine appointments that God sets up for you. Even if you resist, God will often keep working. One hectic Sunday taught me that lesson.

Not liking to be alone, sit alone, or ride in airplanes or shuttle buses alone, I tend to make new friends every trip I take. But this particular Sunday, I had no time to make friends. I had to get off the plane, collect my luggage, grab a taxi or shuttle, and dash to the hotel where I would check in, get ready for church, and catch a taxi to take me across town. All that in an hour and a half!

My plans fell apart from the onset. First, the plane took off thirty minutes late. Then, when I got to the baggage-claim area, only two of my three bags came off the carousel. Having previously experienced "lost luggage syndrome," I knew I had one hope to make it to church: Run to the Delta baggage counter and have them call the baggage handlers who unloaded the plane. They could check for my bag before it took off for its next destination. I began to pray like crazy, "Oh, Lord, help me, please!"

I ran, talked fast, ran back to the baggage return . . . and sure enough, a lone carry-on bag toppled off the belt. It was mine! I snatched it up and waved to the amazed Delta agent as I dashed off.

Now I was more than fifty minutes behind schedule. As soon as I stepped out into the ground transportation area, I had more timely decisions to make. Spotting a shuttle-bus driver, I hurried over to him. He assured me that the next bus would be departing in five to seven minutes. Hurrah! I hopped on and proceeded to wait fifteen minutes.

Now I was beginning to grow not only impatient but angry

that I had been misled about the departure time. If I had known about the delay, I could have easily taken a taxi. I left my spacious front-row seat, got off the bus, and questioned the driver once again regarding the estimated time of arrival at my hotel. He assured me that I would get downtown to my hotel in twenty minutes, just barely enough time to make it to church, but I could still do it.

With some reservation, I considered whether to get my bags off the bus and head for a taxi. Slowly I reboarded the bus, only to find my front-row seat occupied. To the back of the bus I headed.

I sat down next to a business-looking woman. I was too preoccupied with trying to meet my schedule to even say hello. I tapped my fingers on the seat ahead of mine, looked at my watch every other minute, and sighed deeply.

Finally, the shuttle door closed and off we went at an excruciatingly slow, southern pace. Just then the driver listed seven hotels he had to stop at. I almost "died!" Now frustrated, I looked around. The occupants in each set of seats had struck up a conversation, and for once (and it's rare), I didn't even feel like talking. Within a matter of seconds, however, I asked the woman next to me what line of work she was in."

"Sales and marketing," she responded. Then she inquired, "Why are you in such a hurry?"

Well," I said, "there's this really great preacher in Atlanta, Dr. Charles Stanley, that I've always wanted to hear in person, and I'm only in town tonight. He is on national television and has a radio ministry. I've been looking forward to hearing him, but the service begins at 6:30! I don't want to miss it. He really is a great preacher."

Because of my past experience with conversations like this, I knew that this could make her uncomfortable.

Instead, she asked, "What kind of church is it? What does he talk about? Why are you so determined to hear him?" I told her about his style of preaching, his monthly magazine, and how encouraging I find his words.

Then she asked, "What hotel are you leaving from? Could I join you?"

As it turned out, the Hilton where I was staying was right across the street from the Marriott where she had a reservation. We planned to meet out front of my hotel at 6:00 P.M.

I was amazed at God's providence. The lost piece of luggage, the delay, and the bumped seat had put me exactly in the right place for God's timing in both of our lives!

To top it off, a friend spotted me at the hotel as I was attempting to hail a taxi and offered us a ride to church. And a wonderful couple in front of us at church safely returned us to our hotels.

What an adventure! But I knew it had only begun. I asked if she would like to share dinner, thinking I could be someone to either listen, advise, evangelize, or pray with her— wherever God would lead. We did it all! Although it took a lot of prodding, God finally alerted me to this wonderful opportunity to share him with someone new.

—Becky Tirabassi

The Ripple Effect

Recent surveys of pastors reveal that a startling percentage of them are not convinced they are having any real impact on *anyone*. This is particularly regrettable because *making a difference* is the very reason most pastors go into the ministry.

A Sunday school teacher named Edward Kimball wasn't always sure his life had much consequence, either. In 1858, he at least was able to lead a shoe clerk to Christ. The clerk, Dwight L. Moody, became an evangelist, and in 1879 Moody awakened an evangelistic zeal in the heart of F. B. Meyer, the pastor of a small church in New England. Meyer, preaching on a college campus, won a student named J. Wilbur Chapman to Christ.

While Chapman was engaged in YMCA work, he employed a former baseball player named Billy Sunday to help with evangelistic meetings. Sunday held a series of services in the Charlotte, North Carolina area, and a group of local men were so enthused by the meetings that they planned another campaign. This time they brought preacher Mordecai F. Ham to town.

During one of his meetings, a young man named Billy Graham yielded his life to Christ. Since then, millions have heard the gospel through Graham's ministry. *Kimball had started quite a ripple effect!* So can you.

In fact, you're probably already making a greater impact than you think.

—Jim Buchan

Every Talent Counts

She wore a plain blue housedress and dark shoes, and her dull blond hair was tied in a bun above her collar. When she stepped into the front of the bus, I remembered her. I had been away from my home church for eight years, but I couldn't forget her shyness. One-on-one contact had been difficult for her.

A quiet smile of recognition crossed both our faces as she walked to the back of the bus.

I wondered why she had boarded and where she was going.

Ten miles later, my questions were answered. As she walked off the bus at the next stop, she placed a piece of folded paper on each unoccupied seat. I picked up one of the papers and read about Christ's salvation, and how to obtain this gift of God.

I thought, "So this is how she witnesses for her Savior. She knows the excitement of a daily walk with Christ. Yet shyness prevents a one-on-one evangelism. She is zealous, thankful, and caring, and is using a talent God gave her to share Christ's love with others."

I knew that when she returned home she would again leave the tracts and pray that the Holy Spirit would touch those who read them.

—Dick Hagerman

"Neither Would I"

One day as the famed Nobel Peace Prize winner Mother Teresa was working in the slums of India dressing the wounds of a dying leper, an American tourist observing her asked permission to take a photograph. When permission was granted the tourist, observing the tenderness with which the sainted Mother dressed the bloody, smelly gaping hole where the leper's nose used to be, said in mingled awe and repulsion, "Sister, I wouldn't do what you are doing for ten million dollars!"

"Neither would I, my friend," was Mother Teresa's reply, "neither would I."

—Nancy L. Dorner

There was a dear black saint of God who happened to enter a fashionable church. After the service, he approached the preacher and told him that he wanted very much to join the church. The pastor knew that his consent to such a request would certainly not meet with the approval of the official board of the church and of the congregation. At the same time he did not want to appear cruel and harsh. So he said to this man, "John, go home and pray for two weeks for the Lord to guide you definitely whether He wants you to join this church." Accordingly, humble John took this advice and went home. When the two weeks were up, he came again to the church, and after the service the preacher said to him, "John, what was the guidance of God?" "Sir," John replied, "God told me that He has been trying to get in here for the past fifteen years, and He hasn't succeeded, so I had better give up trying where God cannot find entrance."

Mama, Tell Me

When I was just a child of four, I'd ask my Mama
   questions galore!
Like, "Mama, tell me, tell me true, will I grow up to be like
   you?"
She'd say, "Child, you have the ability to be anything you
   want to be!
Just remember always, in all you do, to let your Jesus shine
   through you."
Now, those words were special as words should be, but not
   the last for Mama and me.

It wasn't long till I went to school with hopes of learning
   the Golden Rule,
When I said to Mama, "Mama, tell me true, can't *you* come
   to school with me, too?
I just don't know what I'll ever do if I have to be apart from
   you!"
Her advice was simple to understand as she said, "Trust in
   God, he'll help you stand,
and please remember, Child, in all you do, let your Jesus
   shine through you."

Well, years flew by as they often do, with glasses and braces
   and clumsiness, too.
I sprained my ankle at the county fair, and Kenny Johnson
   was standing right there!
I said, "Mama, do you think I'll ever shine, like ladies who
   are proper and fine?"
Well, by now you know what Mama said, and by now she'd
   say it while shaking her head.

She said, "Just remember in all you do, to let your Jesus
    shine through you! "

Well, somehow I made it through graduation, even went on
    to higher education!
Then Kenny Johnson proposed to me, and I just knew it
    was meant to be!
But, you know me, to Mama I flew, "Oh, Mama, tell me,
    what will I do?
We're getting married, me and Kenny! I'll wear satin,
    pearls, and a good-luck penny!"
She said, "A lucky penny will never do, but trust your Jesus,
    He'll see you through!"

Again the years flew by as they often do, with blessings
    abundant, some heartaches, too.
With Kenny, two girls, one dog, and one boy, and being a
    Grandma brought Mama such joy!
And when sweet Mama died at eighty-two, there was a
    smile on her face for her God so true!
But, if she were here know what she'd do? She'd be giving
    advice to me and you . . .
She'd say, "Mothers, daughters, and grandpas, too, just let
    your Jesus shine through you!"

—Dori Drabek

Who'll Cry at Your Funeral?

Our children were young—one preschooler and one elementary age. The business finally started to do reasonably well. People who before wouldn't give me the time of day suddenly acted friendly.

The mail started to bring invitations to join organizations and attend functions—community chest groups, societies, dinner parties, service organizations. Money was always involved. I couldn't believe the pressure we felt to join up. How do we pick? On what basis do we prioritize our yeses and nos? For a long time I said yes to just about everything.

We were about to buy into a network of shallow relationships built on the sole foundation of commercial gain. Time with our kids, who needed us most and whom we loved most, was about to go into remission.

My wife, Patsy, the proverbial woman of intuition, saw what was happening first, but I was blind as a bat, thinking, "We've arrived!" "Yes," Patsy added, "but at the wrong place."

One evening, as we reviewed our calendar and a stack of time-consuming opportunities, the thought came, "Why not prioritize everything we do on the basis of who's going to be crying at our funeral?" We did it. The results saved our family.

This simple question—"Who's going to be crying at our funeral?"—cuts out time wasters with the accuracy of a laser beam. Why should you and I give ourselves to people who don't love us, at the expense of those who do?

—Patrick M. Morley

Unknown Results

I was driving to an appointment when, while stopped at a light, I flipped the radio on and began listening. The true story was being told about an ordinary man by the name of George Smith. As you can tell, even his name was ordinary. He had aspirations of becoming a great missionary. For several years he planned and prepared. Finally the big day came—he was going to a village that had never had the Gospel in any form.

Mr. Smith shared his very soul with these people in this far-away land. He worked hard but didn't seem to be making any headway in the work. He grew weary after a number of years of struggling that appeared to reap almost no results. The only measurable success for all his years of labor was one young man who was studying the Bible with him daily. The intensity of his discouragement grew so strong that he finally admitted failure and made plans to return to his homeland. His young student was given a Bible and encouraged to continue learning how to live by its principles. George Smith was so heartbroken and felt so defeated that it soon affected his health and within months he died.

A few years later a church organization sent a delegation to the village where George Smith had gone to determine the viability of sending a missionary team there. You can imagine their surprise when they saw a huge church in the center of the village. What amazed them even more was learning that there were thirty-one satellite churches in the surrounding villages and that the overwhelming majority of the people were actively serving God. They asked, "How can this be?" The answer was simple: it all began with that one Bible and a young man who developed a passion for sharing his faith with those around him.

Immediately I thought, "Oh, if only George could have known

what a difference he made." Then the truth hit me like a bolt of lightning: Wasn't I giving my time and talent in ministry? Wasn't I questioning that my efforts mattered to anyone? Wasn't I feeling defeated and ineffective? Wasn't I perhaps more concerned about measurable results than just being available to God? Could it be that, if I didn't adjust the direction of my thinking, I might have the same perspective as George Smith? What could I do to prevent the occurrence of such a tragedy?

Months later, during my devotions the thought came that answered those questions. All I needed to do was begin every day by focusing on this one question: *What would Jesus do?*

Immediately, peace made a cocoon about my heart. No longer was I overcome with fear of not seeing the results of my efforts—it was enough to know that I was daily making myself available to God with the purpose of honoring Him with my life.

—Betty J. Price

Thanks For Nothing

My brother once said that the trouble with being an atheist is that when your motorcycle plunges off a cliff into the Colorado River and you aren't killed, there's no one to thank. I'm a Christian, but sometimes I forget to thank God for the things that haven't happened. Not this year.

I'm grateful for the accidents I wasn't involved in, the illnesses that never developed, and the times I could have been mugged, but wasn't.

I'm thankful my house didn't burn down when I left the iron on for five hours. I'm thankful that when we left the garage door up all night, nothing was taken. I thank God for the time our neighbors found the convicted rapist outside our bathroom window before he could get into the house.

I'm thankful that the phone call in the middle of the night was a wrong number and not someone calling to tell us about a death in the family.

I'm thankful for the times my husband insisted we talk our problems out when I didn't want to, when it would have been easier to run away. I'm thankful I don't have to work outside my home, that I'm available when my children's friends need a place to come or a friend to talk to. Although living on one of the most dangerous earthquake faults in the world has increased my faith, I thank God we don't have to worry much about avalanches, tornados, volcanoes, mudslides, or floods.

I'm grateful now that God kept us from overseas missions, and for showing me that Southern California is a mission field, too.

I thank God for all the times I've tripped over my son's book bag or couldn't find a place for the margarine in the fridge door because my daughter had filled it with bottles of nail polish because these remind me that I have a family that's made me very happy.

I'm thankful for the night the baby wouldn't let me sleep, when his sobs finally quieted, my exasperation turned to peace, and we rocked sleepily together in the moonlight, his downy head against my cheek.

I'm thankful that I did not know how to drive when I was a young mother, when it took all morning to walk a toddler to the grocery store and back. I thank God for the caterpillars and colored pebbles I wouldn't have noticed if my son hadn't pointed them out.

I'm grateful my mother didn't live near enough to help, that I wrote to her instead; preserving memories of every new frustration and delight with my children, memories otherwise forgotten.

Ever since my daughter nearly sheared off her finger tip in the bathroom door, I'm thankful for every uneventful day.

I'm glad I have Someone to thank.

—Jessica Shaver

Plant Your Garden Today

First, plant three rows of peas
   Patience
   Promptness
   Prayer

Next, plant three rows of squash
   Squash gossip
   Squash indifference
   Squash criticism

Then, five rows of lettuce
   Let us obey the Lord
   Let us be loyal
   Let us be true to our obligations
   Let us be unselfish

Finish with four rows of turnip
   Turn up when needed
   Turn up with a smile
   Turn up with a vision
   Turn up with determination.

—**Author Unknown**

Unguarded Places

Each morning at precisely 8:25 AM I would walk my very scared and reluctant kindergartner from our car to her classroom. We faced this routine each day, going through the same reassuring gestures: a big hug, a confident smile and a firm handshake. All to convince my scared little kitten that "Mommy will return."

I wasn't alone in this ritual. In the beginning, there were many shaky legs and teary-eyed five-year-olds facing a terrifying three hours. One by one these children grew braver and soon the group had diminished to a crowd of two—my Amy and a towhead of a little guy, Jeffy.

Jeffy was escorted to class each morning by his Sachs-Fifth-Avenue-looking father. You know the type: square jaw, designer suits, and a perfect smile that would cut through any heart in a flash.

As it happened, Jeffy's father and I found ourselves walking to our cars together day after day. From the very start, I was aware of his cordial attitude toward Amy as well as his attentiveness to me. We chatted very briefly at first. It wasn't long until the small talk grew into full-grown conversations. Was he likable? Yes. Handsome? For sure. Wooing? Most definitely!

I admit I began to feel uneasy. But as is common, I convinced myself we were not doing anything wrong. Each time we spoke, my feelings of guilt weakened.

I enjoyed his friendship, this new attention, the secret feelings. I told myself again and again, "This is only a friendship; nothing is going on."

Then one morning a light came on inside. I realized where I was headed and it was not to Bible study. I found myself deliberately getting up earlier so I could spend more time with my hair and makeup. I wanted to look my best for . . . just a friend? At 7:30 in the morning?

I knew I liked being with him. I enjoyed his attention far too much for this to remain a safe place. I was coward and decided to just disappear. I changed the time I was bringing Amy to school and even came late for a few days, just to be sure I'd miss him. In order to be accountable, I told my husband about the entire situation. I asked the Lord for forgiveness and thanked Him with a grateful heart for opening my eyes in time.

—Pamala Kennedy

Easy to Grab, Hard to Let Go

The zoo where I worked had a thirteen-foot giant that to me seemed to be the embodiment of evil. He had a scar over his left eye that made him look mean and, more significantly, kept him from shedding his skin in a normal fashion. At least twice a year we would get the dreaded phone call from the reptile house: "The king cobra shed his skin last week, but the eye cap didn't come off. Looks infected. Suppose you and the doc could come down and clean it?"

A snake's skin includes a clear scale over the eye to protect it from sand and foreign objects. Snakes have no eyelids, so have no way to blink for protection. Since the snake's scar prevented a normal shed, the eye cap needed to be surgically removed.

Only two people at the zoo could take responsibility for grabbing the more deadly snakes, and this was the most deadly. (This snake's venom glands contain enough poison to kill one-thousand adults.)

The next day the curator of reptiles was assigned to grab the head. Two reptile keepers were to steady the body. When the snake was subdued, the veterinarian would begin the delicate surgery. His arena kept him inches from a lethal injection. My job was to furnish scalpel, sponge, hemostat, and anything else to expedite the procedure.

The five of us carefully took our positions: the two keepers on either side of the large cage door, the curator in front of the door, about six feet away. The vet and I stood on either side of the curator, about ten feet from the door. The keepers' only defense was sheer bird nets with two-foot handles.

With a nod of his head, the curator signaled for the door to be opened. Seconds later the king cobra appeared. As soon as he saw us, he stopped, spread his cape, and raised to full stature.

The cage was two feet off the ground, so we were all looking at him at eye level.

The cobra was trembling with excitement as he, in turn, stared at each of his five enemies. He seemed to be choosing who would be his prey. The curator was chosen, and with shocking quickness the snake lunged forward, hissing and growling with malevolent rage. With lightning speed, the skilled keepers placed the sheer nets over the snake's head. And as he pushed to get through, the curator firmly grasped his neck just behind his venom sacs. The keepers grabbed the writhing body, then the curator nodded and said, "Let's get this over with."

The pressure was incredible. The vet's hands were trembling and beads of sweat began to run down the curator's forehead. The curator turned to me and said, "Do you have any cuts or scratches on your hands?"

I looked and said, "No."

"Get a wad of paper towels, quick," he followed in a strained voice. I did so,

"Now, put it in the cobra's mouth."

The king watched the paper towels as they were carefully positioned to allow him to bite them. He bit down violently and began to chew. The towels became yellow with venom until they began to drip.

The curator continued, "Did you know that several elephants die every year from king cobra bites? A man could never survive a bite from a full load of venom. That's why I'm having you drain his venom sacs. My hands are sweaty and my fingers are cramping. When I let him go, it may not be quick enough. More people are bitten trying to let go of snakes than when they grab them. You get weak quick!"

There are many situations in life that are parallels—easy to grab, hard to let go—so it pays to think twice before you grab them. Indebtedness, vengeance, lying, adultery, drugs, alcohol, pornography, promiscuity—these and many more are serpents that will drain your strength.

—Gary Richmond

2

Faith & Trust

But without faith it is impossible to please him: for he that cometh to God must believe that he is, and that he is a rewarder of them that diligently seek him.

Hebrews 11:6

Altars

"Altars of Remembrance" our pastor calls them—those moments when God lands in the middle of everyday life. I remember the time I asked God to give our daughter, Keri, a blessing. Instead she got an altar.

When you're the smallest kid in junior high, with a noncompetitive nature and no passion for academics, having two older sisters who overachieve is no bonus.

Each program Keri set out to join—from basketball to yearbook—resulted in "maybe next time." Still the following year she came back strong. "Mom, I've decided to go out for every sport until I make one."

As Keri's mother, I could see her strong points. She frequently consoled struggling friends. She could blend colors, shapes and textures. Her humor melted tense situations with a single comment. Though I knew God would eventually show her the value of her special gifts, I wanted her to experience a smidgen of success without more rejection.

That year we took several long walks to the gym door where Keri's name wasn't posted. Then she informed us she was going out for volleyball.

"Volleyball!" I moaned to my husband. "Her nose barely reaches the bottom of the net." We were in for a long season.

What she lacked in size and power, Keri made up for in effort. After two hours of organized practice each day, she then hounded her sisters, her father, and occasionally me, to toss balls at her. To our surprise, she managed to escape first cuts. Unfortunately, there was one more obstacle.

The night before final cuts, Coach Harris called. "Mrs. Smith, I just wanted to tell you how impressed I've been with Keri's attitude. I've never had a student work any harder." I braced myself for what I felt was coming. "Though I can't use her on A-team," she continued, "I would like to put Keri on B-team if she would be willing."

Being the only eighth grader on the team, Coach Harris pointed out, Keri would practice and play at different times than her friends. Also, she said, her picture in the yearbook with the younger second stringers while her pals were on first string might be embarrassing.

Knowing I couldn't make this decision, I turned the phone over to Keri. When she came out of her room, I could tell by her puffy eyes the coach had been right. This wasn't going to be easy.

"Coach Harris says that if I play on B-team, I'll be the team captain and play in every game." She sighed, "So-o-o, I guess I'm playing."

Even with all the warning, adjusting to B-team was hard for Keri. Still she seemed excited—that is, until the evening before the first game when she bolted through the door.

"I'm awful," she sobbed. "I can't spike. I can't return. I can't even get the ball over the net. Mom, I'm not even captain. A seventh grader is captain. I don't want to play!"

I'm not even captain. It was obvious Keri's distress had more to do with position than performance. The title "Team Captain" had given dignity to an awkward situation.

"I understand how you feel," I responded, "and I won't make you play." But when I got home from work the next day, Keri was dressed in her uniform. Though her mood was still somber, she had decided to remain on the team.

"Keri," I said, "I need to tell you something. All day I've prayed about this. I don't understand why this is happening, and I don't like it. But Keri," I continued, "I've asked God to somehow bless you through it, and I believe He will."

"It doesn't matter, Mom. I just want to get this over," Keri replied.

By the time I got to the school, B-team had taken the court to warm up. Keri intently chewed her bottom lip as she watched the opponents go through their drills. "They're supposed to be real good," I recalled her saying.

Indeed they were. My stomach tightened as I watched. Each girl was allowed four practice serves. All four of Keri's failed to make it over the net.

"Dear God, please," I moaned as the game began and a well-hit ball sailed right at her. To my delight, Keri slammed it back across the net. Within seconds, another volley had begun, and again, Keri saved the point. A Hollywood script writer could not have created a more unbelievable scene. Whenever the ball came near her, she managed to break a serve or save a point.

Then it was Keri's turn to serve. She scored five points before someone broke her streak. After one particularly good play, a woman next to me said, "That little kid is good, isn't she?" I nodded.

Soon everyone in the gym knew to watch "the little kid." When the final whistle blew, B-team had soundly trounced their opponents. The bleachers erupted in cheers and Keri's team hoisted her off the court.

I waited awhile before I worked my way across the gym, where the congratulating was still going on. I needed the time to reflect on what God had just done for Keri. I wondered if she even realized it. It didn't take long to find out.

"You're incredible! We need you on A-team," Keri's friend Jennifer squealed.

"I'll tell you what, you're some volleyball player." The school principal pumped Keri's hand.

"Should we go before you have to start signing autographs?" I teased.

Keri turned toward me, huge pools spilling from her green eyes. She knew. She knew she had never played volleyball like that before. She knew she would probably never play like that again, but it didn't matter. For now Keri knew that the all-knowing, all-powerful God cared enough for the littlest kid in junior high to reach down and build her an altar of remembrance.

—**Patricia Smith**

The Father to the Fatherless

Eight-year-old Amy was thin, with scraggly blond hair and a dirty face. But she had a brilliant smile and earnest blue eyes. Amy was one of the seven girls assigned to my cabin when I was a counselor at a Christian summer camp for underprivileged children. When all the girls first arrived at the cabin, we went around the circle each telling something about ourselves. When it came to Amy's turn, she told us quietly that her mother had been murdered.

Later, when I had a chance to ask her about it, she told me that her mother had been on drugs and was murdered by a man that had been a friend of hers. That was all the details that Amy knew. I asked her if she had a dad, and she told me that she didn't know who her dad was. Then, she was quiet. "Oh," she said, as if she had forgotten something. "I do have a dad in heaven."

I wasn't sure which was worse for this little girl—not to know who her dad was or to have had a dad and lost him. "Oh," I said, "did you have a dad who died?"

"No," she answered, looking at me indignantly, "God!"

I had to laugh at my own blunder as I looked into her young freckled face. After all, wasn't I the one who was supposed to be teaching her?

—Teresa Vining

A Prayer Experiment Brings Astonishing Results

My first dramatic experience of answered prayer concerned a lost cat. Our five-year-old son Jeff had been given a darling black and white kitten with a curly tail, which we named "Kinky." Jeff loved her very much. He bought a pretty red leather collar with fake "jewels" on it for Kinky to wear. When we went on vacation we handed Kinky over to the little girl next door to care for while we were away. When we returned we learned she had let the kitten out and it had run away!

Jeff was broken-hearted. But I reassured him, "Don't worry, Honey, we'll find Kinky. She couldn't have gone very far. We'll search the entire neighborhood and knock on every door until we find her."

So we went from door to door, leaving our telephone number in case someone should find the lost kitten. No one had even seen her. Ads in the newspaper and on the radio also proved fruitless.

The following Saturday morning we were eating breakfast when we heard our own ad on the local radio station. Jeff began to cry, "Mommy, we'll never find Kinky. She's gone forever."

I stopped short. I had forgotten to pray about the lost kitten. That should have been the first thing I did, but I was a new Christian and not yet accustomed to letting God help me with life's problems. So right then and there, Jeff and I bowed our heads and prayed that God would return Kinky to us.

We had no sooner opened our eyes and raised our heads than the telephone rang. It was a lady who lived all the way across town.

"I've found a kitten and I just heard your ad on the radio," she said. "It doesn't match your description, but I thought if you hadn't found yours, your little boy might like to have this one. Would you like to come and see it?"

I explained the situation to Jeff. Would he like to at least go take a look at this kitten? He decided he would look at it—but he really wanted only Kinky. So we got in the car and drove to the lady's home on the other side of town.

The kitten she had found was nothing like our Kinky. Jeff was not taken with it at all. So we got back in the car and started for home. We had gone just a few blocks when Jeff started to cry again. "Mommy," he said, "Maybe I should take that kitten. It would be better than no kitten at all. I don't think we're ever going to find Kinky."

So I pulled off to the side of the road and gave him a hug, wiping his eyes and nose with a tissue. Jeff said, "Let's pray once more, Mommy, and then if God doesn't bring Kinky back right away, we'll go get that little gray kitten."

So once more we bowed our heads and Jeff, in his little boy quaking voice, asked God to either send his kitten back *right away*, or he would go back and get the other one.

When we opened our eyes, Kinky was sitting on the pavement not ten feet away from our car! Jeff jumped out of the car and ran to her but I was virtually paralyzed with shock! We were still a long way from home.

How that kitten came to be there God only knows; I certainly don't. But it was without a doubt our kitten; it had the same curly tail and the little red patent leather jeweled collar and the exact markings. I was stunned, and so shaken I could hardly drive home.

All the way home I pondered this amazing answer to prayer and the sequence of events that had brought it about. Had we not gone to see the gray kitten on the other side of town we would never have been driving down that particular street at that particular time.

Had God used that telephone call to put us where we needed to be in order to find Kinky? Had God picked up the kitten from wherever it was and set it down in front of us? Or was it just a very strange coincidence? I decided then and there to make prayer my first resource instead of my last resort from then on.

—Nancy L. Dorner

Roller Skates With Pink Wheels

I can't move . . . I can't talk . . . I can't pray . . . I can't breathe . . . I hear voices far away, echoing out of proportion. "She's lost all reflexes. Move her to the Intensive Care Unit quickly and incubate her. Set the respirator at 5."

My words to my friend at lunch yesterday flit through my mind. I said, "I'm so frustrated in caring for our three small children. My husband has a busy career and my life doesn't have a purpose or sense of direction."

Medical staff hover over me. "I don't know exactly what the problem is but she's lost her whole central nervous system."

I need to bake the birthday cake . . . 6 candles . . . roller skates with pink wheels . . . balloons . . . party hats . . . ice cream.

"She's incontinent. We should perform a spinal tap in the next hour."

I'm in a slightly downhill rocky tunnel. I shiver as I reach the bottom and notice two large doors next to one another. One is closed and locked with a huge brass padlock. The second door is open and Jesus stands in the doorway. The light radiating from inside which lights up the darkness of the tunnel seems to say, "Welcome my child to your heavenly home."

Instead, Jesus stands with his arms folded across his chest. "Go back. Dig in with your fingers and toes and climb out of here. You have a husband, three small children and other family and friends on earth who still need you. Your time on earth is not done."

I fight. I'm so tired. I struggle and dig until my fingernails are caked with dirt and I lie panting and exhausted at the mouth of the tunnel.

I'm still alive. I open my eyes to see my husband's worried and tired face. He squeezes my hand and I struggle to communicate.

As the nurse gently wipes my nose, I think of the many times I've wiped little runny noses. My thoughts are trapped by the respirator tube. I want to tell the world that I saw Jesus and my heart swells with renewed purpose.

I close my eyes. The HISS-HISS-HISS of the respirator lulls me to rest. My body relaxes. I feel at peace. I know that when my time on earth is over, I will go through the heavenly doors and Jesus will say, "Welcome my child."

I will use a wheelchair the rest of my life, but I can still focus on roller skates with pink wheels.

—Marcia Van't Land

Still She Smiles

There she goes down the road
    in her old black wheelchair.
Watching children run and play,
    something she will never do again.
    Still she smiles.
Why does she keep on going through
    her pain and agony?
She keeps on going for her children and her husband.
    Still she smiles.
When she goes into the hospital,
    she is very sad indeed.
She is weak and tired with tubes
    and IV's in her body.
    Still she smiles.
She has had her disease
    for twelve years.
Yet, her friends show her love and comfort.
    Still she smiles.
Even though she wants to jump up and run
    from all her sorrows
    she cannot go.
I don't want my mom's life to end.
    Still she smiles.
When will the road ever end?
I hope it's a long road,
    for I don't want her life to end.
    Still she smiles.

—Ruth Van't Land (Marcia Van't Land's teenage daughter)

His Eye Is On The Parakeet

It happened one rainy Sunday afternoon. My son Sammy's baby parakeet, Jinx, flew into a hard-back chair and broke a "blood" feather. Of course, the entire feather did not completely dislodge upon impact; thus the tiny bit of remaining root allowed Jinx's blood to flow freely. Big drops.

I suggested the conservative "wait and see" approach to Sammy. A few minutes later, a phone call to our local pet store informed us Jinx could bleed to death if we did not pluck out the remaining bit of feather. Not the blood-and-guts type, plucking feathers is rather repugnant to me. Sammy's blue eyes swimming in tears before me questioned, "You're not going to let her bleed to death, are you Mom?"

Of course not. What '90s mother would allow such a thing? Thus, fifteen minutes later we found ourselves seated in the waiting room of the pet emergency hospital.

The bird only cost me $9.95 and the emergency room visit would set me back a minimum of $35.00. Even though mathematically impaired, my mental calculations told me the math did not add up; I would lose money on this.

A $35.00 gouge later, little Jinx was back in her cage, Sammy's tears were dried, and my eyes were itching; no, burning actually. A look in the mirror confirmed my suspicion that my eyes were swelling with hives. With my luck, I had probably sat in a chair in the waiting room at the pet hospital previously occupied by a cat. The next morning, my eyes were still puffy. A visit to the family doctor that afternoon confirmed that, indeed, sitting in cat hair and rubbing my eyes contracted a case of allergy-related hives.

So . . . adding a doctor's visit and anti-hive medication to the already "forked-over" $35.00, all for a ten dollar bird: I know now I have gone crazy!

But, my child had faith I could make things right for his parakeet. I saw the very real sorrow Sammy felt when faced with losing his pet. What parent wouldn't try to make this right?

Our parakeet experience reminds me of God, our Heavenly Father, who hears our prayers uttered in fear, sorrow, and frustration, and Who, at great cost to Himself through His Son's sacrifice, makes things right for us. The "math" doesn't come out right for Him either, yet He willingly paid the price.

—Jeri Chrysong

Early one summer, city workers in Hamilton, Ontario, were trimming limbs from trees along the streets. In one tree marked for cutting they found a nest of baby robins. The workers decided not to touch the limb until the young birds had flown away.

Later, when the nest was abandoned, they examined it and discovered in the bottom a little scrap of paper. The robins had used it, along with the dried twigs, to build their nest. On the paper were these words: "We trust in the Lord our God."

—Susanne E. George
(from her Valedictorian Address)

Time Will Tell

I was in grade three at the time and the wristwatch I wanted for Christmas was pictured in the Eaton mail order catalog. Instead of a plain black strap it had a gold expansion bracelet which seemed infinitely more attractive to my young eyes. Since I did not have doting grandparents who could lavish such expensive gifts upon their little granddaughter, I knew if I got the watch at all, it would have to come from my parents' meager farm income.

My dreams were big, but my hopes were slim. Grade four, five, six—every year, when the Christmas catalog arrived in the mail, I took a pencil and circled the watch of my choice. I never said a word, but the not-so-subtle reminder invoked a certain amount of guilt nonetheless. I knew such extravagant expectations were beyond the bounds of the family budgets and I had no way of earning any spending money. Yet still I dreamed and prayed. *God, You know I want to give You first place in my life, but that oval wristwatch with the gold expansion bracelet is running a close second. What are we going to do about it, God?*

Year after year there were parcels under the tree which had distinct possibilities in terms of size and shape. I always waited until last to open them, savoring the delicious anticipation, trying hard to hide my disappointment when the small, neat, package turned out to be a bar of soap or a fat box of crayons, but never the watch.

And then came grade seven. Far too grown up to circle things in the Christmas catalog, I made up a list of suggestions I hoped would be of some help when my mother sent off her next order to Eatons. As I carried the envelope to the post office, I could not resist holding it up to the sunlight. She had ordered a watch, all right, but not the one I wanted. She had ordered the one with the plain black strap, and who could blame her? After all, it was cheaper by a $1.49.

As the postmaster hoisted the bags of mail into the train baggage car that day, I wished I had torn up the entire order form. After waiting so long, settling for second best was too disappointing to contemplate.

The days dragged by. There were Christmas exams, report cards, a turquoise dress to be sewn for the school concert, hours of practice, and no parcel from Eatons. Maybe it really did get lost in the mail. Did wishful thinking ever come true?

On Christmas morning there was the usual assortment of mittens and scarves and books, and as usual, one parcel had distinct possibilities in terms of size and shape. In spite of myself, I could feel the old hopes rising, and I waited to open it until last. As I tore off the gift wrap, I could see the anxiety on my mother's face.

"It isn't quite what I ordered," she apologized. "But I hope you like it anyway."

Like it? I *loved* it—an oval wristwatch *with a gold expansion bracelet.*

Tucked into the lid of the blue velvet box was a familiar mail order note:

"Dear Customer: We regret that we were unable to fill your order as requested. We have therefore substituted with merchandise of equal value or better. Goods satisfactory or your money cheerfully refunded. The T. Eaton Company Limited."

A small thing, perhaps, but to this very day I believe it was more than store policy which moved an unknown clerk to substitute watches; more than mere coincidence that she chose the very one I liked. I believe God understood my yearnings, and in His providential plan, He knew I would wear that watch for many years as a symbol of His willingness to give if only I would put Him first. Psalm 37:4 came true for me that day: *Delight thyself also in the LORD; and he shall give thee the desires of thine heart.*

—**Alma Barkman**

Heart Attack!

"You're okay."

I opened my eyes to see a nurse bending over me, patting my hand.

Something's wrong! I wanted to shout. *Something's gagging me!* My whole body retched involuntarily.

"Calm down. It's just a ventilator tube. Your heart stopped and we had to put a tube down your throat to help you breathe."

What had happened? I blinked and looked around at six or seven people scurrying around my bed. The lights seemed un-usually bright as I tried to remember the events of the past few hours.

Earlier that evening my husband, Dave, and I had had dinner with our twelve-year-old son, Dan. Our nine-year-old daughter, Rebekah, was away at camp for the week. After dinner, we had attended a 40th birthday party for some friends, then I went on to a meeting for mountain bike enthusiasts. Mountain biking was a sport I really enjoyed. I didn't know many 40-year-old women who had the stamina or determination to do mountain biking.

When I arrived at the meeting, there was standing room only. I stood near the back, grateful to be near the open door. After a couple of minutes I began to feel strange. My chest felt tight, my lower arms ached, and it was hard to breathe. It wasn't excruci-ating, but it didn't feel normal.

Something told me I needed to get home, and foolishly, I decided to drive myself. The two-mile drive seemed to take an eternity. Every driver seemed to be out for a pleasure drive, every light signal seemed doomed to "catch" me. As I drove, I began to wonder if I was going to make it home.

I finally pulled into the driveway and honked the horn, bursting into tears as soon as I saw Dave and Dan. "Something's wrong," I whimpered. "I can't breathe very well, and my chest and arms hurt."

I could see the color drain from their faces as Dave climbed into the driver's seat. As he drove me to the emergency room, I hung my head out the window, praying my nausea would stop. I berated myself for being so melodramatic. It was probably nothing but indigestion.

Arriving at the hospital, I was wheeled right in and doctors started putting patches and wires all over me. After they did an EKG, I was told, "We don't think it's your heart, but we're going to run some tests."

Inwardly, I began to criticize myself. *Well, that's just great! I was stupid to come here. Here I was worried it might be a heart attack. Now they'll think I'm a hypochondriac.*

I watched as an assortment of nurses and doctors paraded by taking blood samples, checking blood pressure, and running various tests. I resigned myself to waiting, praying only that *if* there was something wrong, they'd find it quickly. As one doctor prepared to check the oxygen in my blood, he seemed to swim before me.

"I feel really dizzy," I mumbled. Then everything went black.

That was the last thing I remembered. Now, as I looked around, I felt frightened.

The nurse patted my hand and tried to reassure me. "Your heart stopped for about 45 seconds and we had to use the shock paddles to bring you back. We're going to keep you here for some more tests. It's a good thing your husband brought you right in. If your heart had stopped when you were at home, you probably wouldn't be alive right now."

I was shocked! But, I knew there had been some cholesterol-related heart problems in my family. That is why I had been careful about my diet and exercise. At barely 40 years old, I felt awfully young to be having heart trouble.

Over the next several days, I learned that I had had a coronary artery spasm, a relatively rare occurrence, however, in my case they could find no definite cause. All my tests showed I was in good shape, with no blockage in my arteries. "We rarely get to see such clean arteries," the nurse commented after my heart catheterization. I was finally sent home after six days.

So what did it all mean? Why did God allow this seemingly meaningless traumatic experience? Looking back on those events of four years ago, I am able to see a few lessons God had for me.

When I first went home, the doctor ordered me to cut down on my activities. That's very hard for me. I thrive on being busy. But God taught me that I don't have to be constantly busy to know He loves me. He loves me because I'm me. God loved me enough to spare my life. He was in complete control as my world seemed to be collapsing. Even his timing was perfect. My heart could have stopped at anytime, anyplace. Instead, I was already hooked up to heart machines when the cardiac arrest occurred. And, I was surrounded by people who were trained to handle just such an emergency.

Shortly after my heart attack, God brought Psalm 116 to my attention. Perhaps it best answers the question Why? *For you, O LORD, have delivered my soul from death, my eyes from tears, my feet from stumbling, that I may walk before the LORD in the land of the living . . . How can I repay the LORD for all his goodness to me?* (verses 8,9,12 NIV).

—Karin Lindholtz Fite

A House for Christmas

"Are we going to find a house before Christmas?" Janet, our five-year-old, asked my husband and me as we returned home from our new jobs.

"And will we have a Christmas tree?" Patty, the three-year-old, chimed in. A tree was very important to her. Our six-year-old boy just wanted a room of his own.

"We're still looking," I reassured them. "God said that if we asked, He would provide. You know we have all been praying."

And indeed we had. We had been in Arizona for three weeks and still were unable to find a furnished house within our budget. Coming in December, we had arrived at the same time as the winter visitors (lovingly called "snowbirds") and housing was scarce. We had moved to Arizona because of my husband's health and we knew it was God's will, but we couldn't stay with our friends indefinitely.

While driving home from work each night, looking at the majestic mountains and flaming Arizona sunsets, I gained strength. I felt assured that if God wanted us to come here, He would help us find a house—before December 25.

But Christmas was getting closer, and we all were getting more and more discouraged. One day after returning home from househunting, I told my husband about a four bedroom place I had found. Although I had talked the landlady out of the last month's rent in advance and the security deposit, my husband insisted we still could not afford the high rent. It was three times what we had paid in Michigan, plus we would have to buy furniture.

Finally my husband agreed to look at it. We were just getting ready to walk out the door when the telephone rang. A friend's voice from church said, "Our daughter and family have decided to move to New York and wondered if you would like to look at their house."

The rent was unusually low and the place was furnished, and had a piano and a basement. It seemed made to order. But there was one drawback. "We won't be moving till January 15," our friend's daughter explained, "so we don't want to say anything to the landlord yet."

January 15! Three and a half weeks more with our friends, who also had three children. No home of our own for Christmas. "Lord, you promised," I prayed desperately, and took new hope.

On December 23rd the phone rang again. "We've decided to move tomorrow instead of waiting till January," the voice said.

"I know," I replied.

"How could you know? We just decided ourselves."

"Because the Lord promised us a house before Christmas," I told her confidently.

However, there was another obstacle. "You have to go talk to the landlord. We just called and told him and he said others are also interested."

We learned that she was right. As I marched into the real estate office and announced we wanted to rent the house our friends were vacating, the landlord laughed. "You and about twenty others." He held up a long list of names. My heart sank.

"Sit down," he invited. "I'll check these out."

He began calling: "too high," "too low," "wrong neighborhood," "too small," "needs too much work," "already found a place." Finally he checked off the last name and said, "You must have someone looking out for you. The place is yours."

As I wrote out the check he added, "I'll make the receipt out to begin December 28. That's when their rent is up." Four days of free rent!

As we moved into the house on December 24 (we moved in through the back door as the occupants were carrying their possessions out the front), we noticed several boxes in the storage room. "Can you use any of these things?" the man asked. "If not, just throw them out."

When we left our home in Michigan, we sold most of our belongings, including many of the children's toys. One that was hard for our son to part with was his oversized plastic bowling set (with one pin missing). "We'll buy you a new set in Arizona," I promised. And now, here was a set in the storage room . . . with all ten pins.

Is God . . . *able to do exceeding abundantly above all that we ask or think* . . . (Ephesians 3:20)? Most definitely, for another item our friend's daughter left for us in the corner of the living room, in answer to a three-year-old's prayers, was a Christmas tree—completely decorated.

—**Donna Clark Goodrich**

A woman who was a very faithful church-goer had just received her drivers license. Before putting the key in the ignition for her first solo trip, she prayed for a safe journey: "Lord, please guide my hands to steer this car properly." Then she began to drive, but soon she found herself in an emergency situation behind the wheel: a garbage truck was approaching from the rear, seemingly out of control; and a collision appeared imminent.

Inexperienced and panic-stricken, the woman didn't know how to react, so she threw her arms in the air and cried out, "Lord, You take the wheel!"

The Ugly Puppling

My roommate's Chihuahua, Chica, had her second litter right before Fourth of July weekend. I watched the blind, squirming, baby-fuzzed little puppies grope for mom and caught my eye on the biggest one of all. It was *ugly*.

She had yellow baby fuzz. Not just *any* old yellow—it was dried up, dirty, 1960s-awful mustard yellow. She had gray baby fuzz. Not just *any* old gray. It was smoggy, dark, grit-and-soot gray. And the colors didn't blend. Plus, she had ugly white patches on her head. Poor thing, she looked like a misshapen field rat. I called her "Ugly" right from the start.

Friends and neighbors would come over and see the puppies. There was the dark gray one, the black and white one, and "the field rat." I watched every day to see how they would turn out.

Well, the first week went by, then the second. They grew quickly as developmental changes surged through their little puppy bodies. The gray one began to develop a shorter snout, like the dad. The black and white one grew longer, wavy hair like cowlicks and started looking like a jersey cow. "Ugly," however, didn't get uglier—she started getting *cute*. What a surprise!

Her ugly disparate baby fuzz colors began to blend together. I didn't even know when it happened. I just noticed one day that she was a speckled, lovely light tan color like windswept beach sand. And those ugly white patches formed distinct markings like the markings on the face of an Alaskan Husky—a bigger, lovelier, more noble dog. She seemed to take more initiative to explore their little puppy cage and was first to discover that she could yap. No longer could I call her Ugly. I began to call her Husky.

One quiet evening as I sat cuddling her on my lap, I thought about how I used to call her Ugly and how she turned out quite cute—indeed, the cutest one in the bunch. I remembered how grainy and dirty her yellow and gray fur had looked. Suddenly God's Spirit led my mind down a different corridor.

Remember her yellow and gray fur? He seemed to ask. *Yellow and gray don't go together. Yet that puppy, like the Ugly Duckling, became quite handsome in its time as the colors blended in. All she needed was time.*

You once thought that you were not acceptable physically because you were racially mixed. Yet you are, because that is how I chose to make you. You're blending just the way I want you to. The way one starts is not always the way one ends up.

You berate yourself constantly for not being able to "grow up already" from all your emotional wounds and scars. Give yourself time. In My time, you'll be grown up and lovely, inside and out. It's not time yet, but it will be time soon. My good work in you will be perfect. I made this puppy to be a picture just for you.

With a soft smile and dripping eyelashes, I picked up the wriggling puppy and set her on my shoulder, under my chin. Puppy Therapy never felt so good.

—Glenda Gordon

Do You Want Mountain Moving Faith?

Some people think faith comes from miracles, but others know miracles come from faith.

A small congregation in the foothills of the Great Smokies built a new sanctuary on a piece of land willed to them by a church member. Ten days before the new church was to open, the local building inspector informed the pastor that the parking lot was inadequate for the size of the building. Until the church doubled the size of the parking lot they would be unable to use the new sanctuary.

Unfortunately, the church with its undersized parking lot had used every inch of their land except for the mountain against which it had been built. In order to build more parking spaces, they would have to move the mountain out of the back yard.

Undaunted, the pastor announced the next Sunday morning that he would meet that evening with all members who had "mountain moving faith." They would hold a prayer session asking God to remove the mountain from the back yard and to somehow provide enough money to have it paved and painted before the scheduled opening dedication service the following week.

At the appointed time, two dozen of the congregation's 300 members assembled for prayer. They prayed for nearly three hours.

At ten o'clock the pastor said the final "Amen." "We'll open next Sunday as scheduled," he assured everyone. "God has never let us down before, and I believe He will be faithful this time, too."

The next morning as he was working in his study there came a loud knock at his door. When he called "come in," a rough-looking construction foreman appeared, removing his hard hat as he entered.

"Excuse me, Reverend. I'm from Acme Construction Company over in the next county. We're building a huge new shopping mall over there and we need some fill dirt. Would you be willing to sell us a chunk of that mountain behind the church? We'll pay you for the dirt we remove and pave all the exposed area free of charge, if we can have it right away. We can't do anything else until we get the dirt in and allow it to settle properly."

The little church was dedicated the next Sunday as originally planned—and there were far more members with "mountain moving faith" on opening Sunday than there had been the previous week!

Would you have shown up for that prayer meeting? Some people say faith comes from miracles. But others know: *miracles come from faith!*

—Nancy L. Dorner

A little boy was overheard talking to himself as he strode through his backyard, baseball cap in place and toting ball and bat. "I'm the greatest baseball player in the world," he said proudly. Then he tossed the ball in the air, swung and missed. Undaunted, he picked up the ball, threw it into the air and said to himself, "I'm the greatest player ever!" He swung at the ball again, and again he missed. He paused a moment to examine the bat and ball carefully. Then once again he threw the ball into the air and said, "I'm the greatest baseball player who ever lived." He swung the bat hard, and again missed the ball.

"Wow!" he exclaimed. "What a pitcher!"

—Robert Schuller

Pants With No Pockets

I have a close friend in the ministry who traveled across country for a week of meetings. The only problem was, his baggage didn't make it. He really needed a couple of suits. So he went down to the local thrift shop and was pleased to find a row of suits. When he told the guy "I'd like to get a couple of suits," the salesman smiled and said, "Good, we've got several. But you need to know they came from the local mortuary. They've all been cleaned and pressed, but they were used on stiffs. Not a thing wrong with 'em; I just didn't want that to bother you." My friend said, "No, that's fine." So he hurriedly tried some on and bought a couple for twenty-five bucks apiece. Great deal!

When he got back to his room, he began to get dressed for the evening's meeting. As he put one on, to his surprise there were no pockets. Both sides were all sewed up! Though surprised, he thought, *Why of course! Stiffs don't carry stuff with 'em when they depart.* The suits looked as if they had pockets, but they were just flaps on the coat. The minister was reminded all week long that life is temporal. And he probably preached all the better for that thought!

—**Charles Swindoll**

Peace of Mind

We knew a man in England who had no child—He and his wife had prayed long and hard that God would grant them a little one to brighten their days. The man lived in a depressed area of Britain and worked in a huge industrial plant. The work at the plant was greatly influenced by a Communist-dominated union, and most of the man's fellow-workers were of that particular political persuasion. Because the man was a Christian, he didn't have an easy time of it. Then one day his wife told him that she was pregnant! Their joy knew no bounds, and somehow the man's work in this hostile environment took on a whole new perspective. It was easier now to bear the snide remarks, or even the silent treatment meted out as a favorite way of punishing a worker who wouldn't conform to the popular pattern.

The time came for their baby to be born, and you can imagine the shock, when the baby girl was born mongoloid. Now the couple had to face the fact that their long-awaited child was not perfect and would require a life of service and sacrifice on both of their parts. But this was not the only sorrow they had to grapple with. The wife knew she needed to tell unbelieving relatives, and the man thought of the people he would have to face at work. How could he go back and tell his workmates what had happened? What would they say? But even that unpleasant thought paled into insignificance beside the nagging doubts that wouldn't go away concerning the heart of his God. *Were he and his wife truly loved?* How could a God who loved them truly allow such tragedy to come into their lives? With much still unresolved in his mind, he returned to work. His fears had been justified, as the men gathered around to cruelly tease and terribly taunt him.

"How is it, you serve God, and He gave you 'half a child,'" they asked him gleefully. "And how is it, we don't even believe

God exists, and our children are healthy and beautiful!" Standing there in the midst of that arena of arrogant atheism the man bowed his head. Shame filled his heart, for he knew that those voices were but an echo of his own doubts. But for that hour he had been given the Holy Spirit, whose work it was to assure him he was truly loved whatever happened to him.

Suddenly the man looked up, and his tormentors were amazed at the change in his face. He smiled and was content. A hush fell, as quietly the man said, "I'm so glad, *so* very glad, my God gave her to me and not to you!" In his great personal trouble, he refused to doubt the love of God and made this determination in the face of apparent disaster. *I will mention the lovingkindness of the Lord, and the praises of the Lord, according to all that the Lord hath bestowed on us . . . .* (Isaiah 63:7).

—Jill Briscoe

The Ladies Club

When I was young "The Ladies" came to play bridge at our house. They were the mothers of my school friends. The moms did this about once a month and they moved from house to house. Each girl was eager to have her mother host the game. This insured that the candy and exotic nuts in the little silver or china bowls set on the card table would be available to "sneak a few." But the best thing about having your mom be the hostess was that if you hurried home from school and were sly and quiet you could overhear the gossip.

When The Ladies came for bridge at our house the gossip was good. I knew it was of high quality because while they tried to keep their voices low they were too excited and emphatic to do so. *Loramanda is pregnant! Again! The* women shook their heads mournfully and with disapproval while concentrating on cards and bidding.

The timbre of the voices and the sound of shock and horror frightened me. I loved Mrs. Britts. She was definitely a fun mom. She gave the best birthday parties. She didn't even need a party to think of some great new game. With six kids, she was a clever and enthusiastic mom who could make things stretch to make ends meet.

She was going to have a seventh child and I was afraid it would kill her. After all, as The Ladies kept reminding each other, she was at the advanced age of 42! And it had been nine years since the last one.

Sitting at the Britts' dinner table is where I first learned that you could pray by just talking to God. They didn't say a memorized grace. They bowed their heads and spoke to God; even the kids! So I gave it my best shot and begged God not to let her die. It was the first time I really prayed for something. Months later she gave birth to David and she and David lived. A miracle, I thought.

The memory of it came back the other day as I drove past the Britts' house. Mrs. Britts died last year. The big church was packed for the funeral. Mr. Britts has Alzheimer's. Several blocks away, I saw him headed home and knew I didn't have to worry about him getting confused on the rest of his journey. There beside him, with a bag of groceries held by one arm and the other steadying and guiding his father, was David. They were both smiling and laughing, fully engaged in their conversation. I wish The Ladies could have seen it.

—Carol Wolff

Tyler's Story

It started at conception. A genetic defect that would profoundly alter three lives—four, include mine, too.

The seeds of tragedy, pain, and victory were born in a tiny little boy named Tyler Lee on May 22, 1984. I held him for the first time when he was not quite 12 hours old. His parents were—and are—my two best friends. And now I had a third best friend, this perfect miracle, this baby boy.

By the time he was six months, we all noticed something wrong. He wasn't sitting up. He had trouble rolling over. Constant constipation plagued him. At eight months, his parents took him to a specialist.

Emotional, uncertain days and many tests later, their doctor told them, "I'm very sorry. Your baby has Hoffman-Werding disease. It's the most virulent form of muscular dystrophy." Into the silence that followed his words, the doctor added, "Tyler will never walk, probably never sit up. He probably won't live much beyond the age of 2." The tests clearly confirmed the terrible diagnosis. Tyler had almost no muscle development. Not even his intestines could work properly.

That night we sat silently together, sharing our tears, holding and cherishing their little Tyler. The pain was too new, too raw.

They called me on Sunday to say they were having a prayer meeting with friends and the elders from their church Monday night. They were going to anoint Tyler with oil and ask for God's healing—in faith that no matter what the answer was, God knew best and loved Tyler even more than they did.

Of course, I'd be there, even though absolutely nothing in my conservative background had ever considered such a bold assault on Heaven.

Monday evening the deacons from their church and their closest friends gathered in the family room with Tyler. Heart joined heart in prayers both silent and verbal as we approached the throne of heaven for Tyler's healing. There was one focus, one accord, one hope in God our heavenly Father.

The next day, Tuesday, Tyler had another appointment with the specialist. His parents called me the moment they reached home. "He's healed—completely! God gave us our miracle!"

God instantly, miraculously, divinely healed Tyler Lee Roark that night. Where there had been no muscle function, now every muscle function in his body tested absolutely normal that Tuesday morning.

"It's a miracle," his doctor said, "I can't explain it. He's a perfectly normal eight-month-old baby. Take him home."

Today, Tyler is a healthy, active, 11-year-old who gave his heart to Jesus as Savior five years ago. Tyler holds national long-distance track titles and state records in both Iowa and Oklahoma. Untrained and uncoached, Tyler's running ability is a gift. He started setting state records when he was 9; his first national title came as a 10-year-old.

He has a room filled with trophies and ribbons . . . and a humble spirit that lets him enjoy running—whether he wins or loses. He's the first to congratulate others and be happy for them if they win. He knows that winning isn't the only reason he's there. He knows that his ability is a gift from God and that he's there to glorify his Father by running, by doing his best, and showing others Christ in him.

God has chosen to give Tyler a tremendous athletic ability that has brought him media attention, both TV and newspaper. And in every interview his parents joyfully give God the glory and tell how Tyler was healed.

—Mary Nelson

A group of botanists were searching in the Alps for rare flowers. A very fine specimen was spotted on a small ledge of rock that could only be reached with a lifeline. The job was far too dangerous for the inexperienced botanists so they summoned a local shepherd boy who was familiar with the terrain. They offered him several gold coins to climb down the rope and retrieve the rare specimen.

Although the boy desperately wanted the coins, he feared that the job was too dangerous. Several times he peered over the edge of the cliff, but he couldn't see any safe way of getting to the flower. Besides, he would have to place his trust in the hands of strangers who would be holding his lifeline. Suddenly, the boy had an idea. He left the group for a few moments, then returned holding the hand of a much older man. The shepherd boy then ran excitedly to the edge of the cliff and said to the botanists, "You can tie the rope under my arms now. I'll go into the canyon, as long as you let my *father* hold the rope."

3

Family Life

And thou shalt love the LORD thy God with all thine heart, and with all thy soul, and with all thy might. And these words, which I command thee this day, shall be in thine heart: And thou shalt teach them diligently unto thy children, and shalt talk of them when thou sittest in thine house, and when thou walkest by the way, and when thou liest down, and when thou risest up.

Deuteronomy 6:5–7

Truths For Our Families

ONE
Despite all the changes that disrupt families, God is in control.

TWO
Even though divorce rates are high, most marriages stay intact.

THREE
No family is without problems and periodic crises.

FOUR
All parents make mistakes, but most kids survive very well.

FIVE
It is possible to have healthy families even in a chaotic and immoral society.

SIX
We can raise kids successfully even if we don't have all the answers.

SEVEN
The majority of families are not seriously dysfunctional.

EIGHT
Even good parents sometimes have rebellious kids.

NINE
Even bad parents sometimes have healthy adjusted kids.

TEN
God loves our families.

—**Gary R. Collins**

Please Uplift Your Personal Belongings

It had been a long and difficult twenty-two-hour airplane trip for my daughter, Susan, who was traveling alone from Los Angeles, California, to Sydney, Australia, with two very active toddlers. Finally the children had worn out and were sound asleep, but not until just before the scheduled landing. As the airplane made it's final approach, Susan looked around and began to gather together all the paraphernalia that was needed when one tries to keep a 2 and 4-year-old occupied, quiet and reasonably happy in such confined quarters. She was exhausted, already her patience had worn thin, and the prospect of two weeks of traveling with toddlers was hanging heavy on her mind.

The flight attendant stepped to the microphone and began the disembarking announcements. "The crew of Air New Zealand wants to be the first to welcome you to Australia." After explaining the passport and custom procedures, she finished with the admonition: "Please be sure to look around your seat and *uplift* all your personal belongings."

As Susan turned to look around, her eyes lit on Elizabeth and Andrew, still sleeping peacefully. She thought about how easy it is, when one is tired, to be impatient and cranky. She knew that often reflected in her reactions to the children, "her personal belongings."

The flight attendant's word, "uplift," strange to an American, who would say "pick up," took on a new meaning for her. She vowed right then, that during the next two weeks, whenever she was tempted to be cross or cranky, she would remember to "uplift her personal belongings," those precious children that God had entrusted to her care.

—Betty Southard

"KP" Duty

I was standing at the kitchen sink, working so diligently on dinner preparations, my mind totally committed to the task at hand—peeling potatoes. In the army they call it "KP" duty. I think that's a good title for the task, but in my home it stands for "Kid Pleasing." Mashed potatoes are one of their favorite foods.

As I was busy with my "KP" duty, my middle son, three-year-old Steven, was playing nearby. Being a conscientious mother, my ears were tuned to my son and my eyes focused on the pile of potatoes. Within a few moments I felt a tug on my skirt proceeded by the words, "Mommy . . ." I nodded in agreement, giving some brief verbal acknowledgments as well. There were more tugs on my skirt and more little words, "Mommy . . ." Again, I'd give a brief verbal comment and yet stay right on task at my "KP" duty. After all, I was working so hard to perform that all important, kid-pleasing task.

Five minutes passed. Steven continued to chatter and then I felt those tugs on my skirt again. This time the tugs seemed harder and more persistent. I finally put my potatoes down in the sink and bent down to my son. Steven took my face in his two little chubby hands, turning me directly to his line of vision and said, "Mommy, will you listen to me with your eyes?"

Fourteen years later I am still learning to listen with my eyes. Then I was the one bending down. Now they bend down to me and listen with their eyes!

—Star Paterson

Blue Ribbons Are For Mothers

It was an afternoon of mother-daughter harmony.

My six-year-old daughter, Inga, sat in my lap at the sewing machine as I guided her in sewing the edges of a pre-printed stuffed animal. She wanted to enter it in the youth division at the county fair.

"I'll sew lots when I grow up," she insisted, echoing words I had told my own mother.

My mother had been an excellent seamstress. She began sewing in her Depression-era childhood, hand-hemming flour sacks for dishtowels. Then came marriage and two daughters, and she filled our closets with home-sewn dresses, play clothes, formals, and coats. She tailored Dad's wool suits and fashioned my older sister's wedding gown. Patchwork quilts graced our beds. Later she indulged my sister's two children with multitudes of little outfits pulled out of scraps.

Mother became so mentally absorbed in sewing that once she pulled into a service station and asked the attendant for "three yards of gas." It was a family joke for years.

With that for heritage, my sister and I should have also incurably loved uniting fabric and thread. But when mother died at 59 of cancer, neither of us had progressed beyond the basic sewing of high school home economics. Perhaps mother left us no need to sew. Or maybe we despaired of achieving her proficiency.

My father died of a heart attack six months after mother. As I sorted and disposed of their belongings, I realized again how sewing dominated mother's life. Boxes crammed my old bedroom turned-sewing room. My sister took some. With tears, I saved out the wedding satin mother bought for me "in hopes"—but now at 32 I was still unmarried. Then I heaped tables with piles of yardage, large bags of scraps, hundreds of buttons, and dozens of patterns, selling Mother's "someday" projects to strangers.

Perhaps we disappointed Mother as seamstresses. But in our own ways we became what the Psalmist called *daughters . . . like pillars carved to adorn a palace* (Psalm 144:12b NIV). Mother died satisfied that she'd passed to us the torch of faith in Christ.

My sister became an elementary teacher before marriage and motherhood. I became a newspaper reporter. Still, Mother's seamstress's shadow hung over me. With one of my first paychecks I bought a sewing machine. I think that pleased her, but I sensed her taking note of the flaws whenever I showed her my super-simple projects. In short time, many ended up in thrift store drop-offs.

Yet, the little girl inside me yearned for mother's smile of approval. I'd gotten it in sixth grade, when my matching skirt and blouse won a blue ribbon in the Camp Fire Girls exhibit hall. But I'd sewn it with mother at my elbow for every stitch.

When we would meander through the economics building at the fair, I would wonder why mother never entered her sewing into this competition.

Newlywed (at age 34) budgeting got me sewing again. My results were full of mistakes, but each shirt or nightie or curtain got a little better. In a few years I had a son and daughter to clothe. People who knew that I sewed, and that I welcomed scraps and remnants, happily sent them my way.

Among them was mother's best friend Ruth. Early one summer she sent huge boxloads of her sewing room cleanout with a note of encouragement, "I *know* you can do something with this." To prove her right, I started sewing the next day.

By the end of the summer one thought kept coming to me: "put your sewing in the county fair." My rational side objected, *My sewing? A beginner's bunglings?* Yet one September afternoon I loaded two garment bags and drove to the fairgrounds. Fighting embarrassment, I handed the fair clerk my entries. One by one she tagged my projects—from blouses to little girls' dresses, snowsuits, and blankets.

A few days later our family returned to the fair. My daughter beamed to find a blue ribbon on her stuffed animal. Then we went to the home economics building. Red and white ribbons marked my patchwork bedspread and baby blanket. I went to the rack for clothing. From each of my garments, a blue ribbon flashed. Nine of them. Amazement and satisfaction filled my heart.

After the fair, I felt there was unfinished business. I'd sewn many of the blue-ribbon items from Ruth's cleanout fabric. She'd be pleased to know. But there was something else. A neighbor and long-time family friend, she'd also grieved when my parents died. But with incredible compassion, she'd come alongside me with comfort, motivation, and practical help as I emptied the house and struggled through probate.

I filled an envelope with those blue ribbons, then wrote, "Dear Ruth, Remember your fabric? It went to the fair—all sewn up. These blue ribbons are for Mother. I want you to have them on her behalf."

My little daughter Inga, proudly possessive of her own blue ribbon, couldn't fathom why I'd give mine away.

I just smiled. Motherhood perfects the "giver" in us. It asks us to relinquish our selfish agendas for our children's talents. When we do, we'll gain even more. *Cast your bread upon the waters,* wrote the Preacher, *for thou shall find it after many days* (Ecclesiastes 11:1). Mother didn't raise replicas of herself. But in releasing us to be ourselves, she left her worthy thumbprint on our hearts.

That's the prize of surrendering your blue ribbons—your best—to the Lord.

—Jeanne Zornes

My Best Friend

I have a very special best friend. She has moved hundreds of miles away from me, but the distance hasn't made any difference in our friendship. When I have a problem she listens quietly on the telephone and never tries to give me advice. She just sympathizes and lets me know she cares that I am having a bad time.

If I ask her to pray about a specific situation, she always remembers to ask me about it later, so that I know she has continued to be concerned about me.

When I buy an item that I think is exciting, she asks me questions about it and gets excited, too. She'll tell me she can't wait until the next time she visits so she can see it. She doesn't jump in before I am finished talking to tell me about something bigger or better that she has just purchased. Then when she visits, she remembers to find new things in my house and raves about them, even though sometimes I know they are things she never would have personally bought. If something makes me happy, it makes her happy, too.

My friend never tries to top my good news with a story of her own that is better. When I'm sick, she listens to me moan and groan about my aches and pains and doesn't tell me she has worse ones, and if I'm complaining about my financial situation she doesn't begin a list of her own expenses.

I think my friend must be the world's best listener. She understands that feelings can't be brushed off or waved away. They have to be talked about before they dissipate.

But the very best part about this friend, is that twenty-eight years ago she arrived in my life as my brand new baby daughter!

—June Cerza Kolf

Help! I'm A Stepmother

My pastor-husband died on my thirtieth birthday, leaving me with three small children. I soon realized I was not cut out for the single life. But available men weren't growing on trees, especially men who were willing to take on a ready-made family.

Desperately wanting a daddy they could call their own, my kids began praying that God would send just the right man into our lives. I was struck with the awesome responsibility of not only finding someone else I could love, but of insuring that this future "someone" would also be good for my children.

After two lonely years of widowhood, God answered our prayers, sending us the man of my dreams and the daddy the kids needed. With His great sense of humor, God also sent along four more kids for me to raise—it seems our new man for the job, Jack Harvey, was also given the responsibility of finding a good stepmother for his brood when their mother died of a brain tumor.

When we went out for our first date, neither of us could find sitters for our Terrible Twos so we brought them along. The restaurant was packed with men for a Rotary Club luncheon. The maitre d' escorted us to a table in the dining room where the Rotarians were meeting, making our kids the only rowdies in the restrained atmosphere of a business luncheon.

Shortly after we were seated, Jeff whispered, "Mommie, I hafta go to the bafroom."

I hurriedly deposited Jeff at the men's room door because he refused to use the women's "bafroom."

Suddenly, Jeff's voice bellowed, "Mommie! Come wipe me!" My face flamed as polite snickers grew into loud guffaws. Jack reached across the table and patted my hand. "Don't worry, I'll take care of it." I began to fall in love with him at that moment, and we were soon married.

The wedding was a corporate merger, with his four lined up on one side of the aisle and my three on the other. When the organist hit the triumphant chords of Mendelssohn's recessional, the kids were to fall in line two by two behind us, signifying the union of the two families. But our two toddlers, awed by the pomp and circumstance, chose to play with the altar flowers. We each hoisted a squirming little boy to our shoulder and proceeded down the aisle—the bride and groom each carrying a Terrible Two, followed by five other kids of assorted sexes and sizes. Before long, folks began seeing us as a unit, not as two badly mismatched families struggling to live under the same roof.

After a time of melding our two families into one, we discovered we were going to have another to add to the number! The Bible says *A merry heart does good like a medicine,* and Jack's great sense of humor saved the day. In those days Zero Population Growth was the big thing, and our large family was the butt of many jokes. We figured if people were laughing at us anyway, we might as well join the fun and laugh at ourselves. We went en masse to the state fair, boldly marched into the Planned Parenthood tent and picked up huge ZPG buttons.

We then strolled leisurely through the fairgrounds, a very pregnant Mama with a ZPG button pinned under my chin (that's where my stomach was by then), Papa wearing his ZPG button pinned to the front of his "Meaner than a junkyard dog" hat, and seven kids all sporting Planned Parenthood buttons. To those bold enough to ask, we had a great reply: "We practiced the rhythm method, and now we have seven musical children!"

Rhythm-maker Number 8 made her arrival on the Ides of September. True to her predestined role as the great equalizer, Becky evened the score sex-wise, bringing the grand total of Harvey-Farleys to four boys and four girls.

While each half of our brood had lost a parent to death, we taught them that death is only a temporary parting. They still have a mother or father very much alive in Heaven. The kids spoke as freely and naturally about "my dad or mom in Heaven," as they did about Jack and me.

As she was growing up, Becky felt cheated. She often asked, "How come I don't have a mommy or daddy up in Heaven like all the other kids do?"

Now, 27 years after the merger, we often forget whose is who. When Rhonda gave birth to our first grandchild, her husband was at work and couldn't be reached in time. So Grandpa and Grandma coached the Lamaze birth. We were both overcome with emotion when we held newborn Jacquelyn in our arms. It was a spiritual moment.

Jack stroked the baby's long, slender fingers, then picked up my hand and kissed my fingertips. Tears in his eyes, his voice breaking, he murmured, "She inherited your beautiful hands."

Which would be fine, except, unfortunately there's not one smidgen of my genes running around in that gorgeous little girl!

—Adell Harvey

Average is Okay

Throughout time, dolls have been a reflection of changing fashions, trends, and ideals of our society. Dolls have accurately mirrored the changes that have occurred in today's world. However, while some of these changes in dolls are for the good, others are not. Take *Barbie*, for example.

Barbie dolls and other teenage high-fashion dolls pose a particular threat to younger children. These dolls cause children to develop different attitudes than dolls with which they can practice parenting. These dolls encourage children to focus on self and to strive to meet the ideal perfection that Barbie sets forth, such as perfect hair, body, boyfriend, clothes, car and house.

During the 30 years that Barbie dolls have been manufactured by Mattel, she has not added a wrinkle to her face nor an ounce to her hourglass figure. In an interview with *Newsweek* magazine, Bill Barton, co-designer of the doll, admitted, "Barbie has become an obsession with little girls." He said that he believes that the bosomy, small-waisted doll can promote unrealistic beauty expectations in youngsters. "If a child is less attractive, she can develop a psychosis about this," he said. Barton attributes the current plague of anorexia in young woman in part to Barbie's idealized slimness. "Girls say they want to be as skinny as Barbie."

So, what is wrong with Barbie? Children become accustomed to these "perfect" ideals that Barbie sets forth. When pre-teens play with the doll, they have a firm understanding of fantasy and reality; younger girls do not. Their image of what is "real" is formed from toys and television. This often causes a reality distortion for them. They grow up believing that to get a "good-looking boyfriend" like Ken, a girl has to be beautiful like Barbie. They also believe that they will own a Corvette and a "dream house." When this fantasy does not come true, they become disillusioned with life.

Parents must realize that Barbie emphasizes physical perfections in an unrealistic manner. Children should not grow up expecting to be beautiful. Instead they should be taught that, nationally, very beautiful women make up a very small percentage of the population. They need to know that most women are *average* but equally accepted in the eyes of God. It needs to be stressed that *average is okay*. It is more important that they focus on their spiritual lives rather than on their physical appearance.

—Joan Hake Robie

D.A.D. Day

Last Fall was bleak for us. We seemed to go from disappointment to crisis to tragedy. It wasn't one thing, it was a gathering storm of difficulty. It hit its zenith when our daughter died a month before she would have been born. A knot in her cord had become totally compressed. Within another week we were trying to comfort my father-in-law as he was dying at home from cancer.

It was a truly terrible time. I prayed, read my Bible and meditated on the goodness of God. I gratefully accepted the meals, the hugs, the cards and the flowers.

My husband was spending his days going from home to his parents, to work, to home, to his parents, to bed; trying to take care of everyone. Then, in our sad house inspiration hit. I gathered the kids together and told them we were going to surprise daddy. There is nothing like working on a secret to bring joy into a house. In two weeks we would have a four day celebration of esteeming daddy. We called it "Daddy Appreciation Days" which made for a nice acrostic—D.A.D.

All the preparations—the writings, drawings, menu-planning, and shopping were great fun. Before daddy came home we hid our work and purchases. It made us greet him more enthusiastically and more tenderly. In creating ways to show our appreciation our appreciation grew. In comforting daddy we made ourselves happy. And as we worked we talked out our grief.

The children painted a colorful banner that said:

D.addy **A.**ppreciation **D.**ays
Oct. 30–Nov. 2
Because Daddy is the BEST

We taped it to the front of the house for all to see, then we cleaned the house with genuine enthusiasm. When my husband arrived home, his favorite dinner was ready to be served. Candles were lit, the house sparkled and we all rushed at him with joy and expectation.

For four days the kids packed special lunches with wonderful, rare treats. They put love notes in his coat pockets, briefcase, and lunchbox. When he came home his favorite foods greeted him on an elegant table along with a gift and candy. We gave him a special sweatshirt that had the kids' hand prints on it and in the middle of the hand prints I cross-stitched "D.A.D."

We also made a "book," a dozen plastic page covers tied together with ribbon. Into the covers we slipped the drawings, writings and Bible verses about fathers that the kids had worked on for two weeks. On opposite pages we put in family photographs of daddy with the children. His homecoming was the day's highlight for us all.

We dealt with our losses by appreciating our blessings. We made daddy (my husband) smile in the midst of his sorrow and that lifted all of our spirits.

—Carol Wolff

My Dad Is An Oak Tree

I grew up in a home with an oak tree right in the middle of the house. It wasn't a red oak, black oak, or even white oak. It's the kind of oak described in Isaiah 61:3 and it's called an *oak of righteousness*. I'm referring to my dad.

I've watched my dad now for forty years. He has never been in full-time ministry. He was and is a businessman. I've seen my dad weather some tough storms. Those of you in real estate know that it tends to be feast or famine.

When my dad was in his early forties, he lost everything. Wiped out financially, he had to start all over—with three boys ready to enter college. It's one thing to be at square one when you're twenty-one; it's quite another when you're forty-three.

I watched him as he saw everything he had collapse. He went from having assets to having nothing but liabilities. He went from a new, spacious home to a small apartment. He literally went from a Cadillac to a Volkswagen. He went from being near the top of the ladder to the bottom.

That's hard on a man. Every day when my dad got up, misery and disappointment were waiting for him. Most of us deal with fear of failure, but my dad actually experienced business failure. I'm sure he was embarrassed and humiliated. That's how I would have felt.

But you should know something about this catastrophe. My dad never stopped being an oak. Because of their root system, oaks can withstand storms that uproot other trees. That perfectly describes my dad.

For as long as I've known my dad, he has gotten up early. He gets up around 5:45 to meet with the Lord. That's a standing appointment he's kept every day for more than forty years. The very first thing my dad does each morning is to pick up his Bible, worn and used, its margins full of notes and its pages frayed.

As a little boy, I can remember several times when I woke up early and went into the living room where my dad was kneeling in front of the couch with his Bible open. While it was still dark, he was taking in his fifty gallons of nutrients from the soil of God's Word.

That's why my dad is an oak. He's been a spiritual self-starter for a long time. He is a man who has meditated and digested the Word of God every day of his adult life. His root system goes deep into the Scriptures. And that's what enabled him to withstand his storm of twenty-some years ago. He stood tall and survived because he has a mighty root system.

—Steve Farrar

Gerhard Frost tells this story in his book, *The Color of Night:* "As a very young child, my greatest fear was of darkness. At times it even kept me awake. My father's study was just across the hall where often he would be at work at my bedtime. In a moment of panic I would cry out, frantic for a response. And the response always came: 'Go to sleep, I'm right here!' With this assurance I would rest. My father didn't bring a light—I would have liked that—but he gave me something better, the assurance of his loving presence. A light would have left me alone. In real need, it couldn't satisfy. Presence, loving presence, is what I craved."

—Alvin N. Rogness

Getting Back on the Team

When Greg was twelve, a problem surfaced between us that I couldn't ignore. It dealt with his reaction whenever I flew out of town for a speaking engagement.

On the day I was to leave everyone in the family would help me pack. Then, at the door they would always send me off with a "Go get 'em, Dad!" or "We'll miss you!"

However, when Greg entered the sixth grade, I noticed that he no longer was a vital part of the going-away party. Instead of lingering at the door with the rest of the family, he would walk away. Soon, his behavior wasn't limited to avoiding me on my outbound trip. For several hours after I returned, he would often keep his distance.

As time passed, he went to great, creative lengths to give me the cold shoulder. Even when I tried to catch him for a moment of conversation, his words were frigid. "Later, Dad," he would cut me off. "I've got to go over to one of my friend's now."

As a counselor, I realized his actions largely reflected his feelings about my traveling. But I also realized I couldn't abandon my monthly trips and still feed my family. Plus, allowing him to ignore me at home and letting his anger build up when I left wasn't doing either one of us any good.

So I decided I would practice what I teach. On the next flight home, I came up with a word picture for him.

It had been two days since I had returned home from my latest business trip. Sure enough, Greg was playing emotional hide-and-seek, but didn't want me to find him.

As was my custom, I would often wake up one of the children early Saturday morning, and then we would go out together for breakfast. This morning, it was Greg's turn.

When I first woke him, I could tell by the look in his eyes and the way he shrank back from my touch, that he was still upset. But when I mentioned going to his favorite breakfast spot, I put a choke hold on any ideas he might have had to avoid me.

Later, as we sat at the table enjoying stacks of pancakes and syrup, I began sharing my word picture.

"Greg," I said, looking him in the eye, "I need to explain something to you, and I'd like to start by telling you a short story. Are you up for it?"

"Sure, Dad, fire away," he replied, swallowing a mouthful of pancakes.

"Let's say you were a star basketball player on the junior high squad."

It was the time of year for the college basketball championship. Like me, Greg was a rabid fan and remained glued to the television from the opening tip-off of the "final four." With popcorn bowl in hand, he watched nearly every game of the NCAA tournament.

"For half the season, you've been the high-point man on your team and the leader in assists as well. Your fellow players and the fans love you so much that every time you go out on the court, they yell, 'Greg-O!' 'Greg-O!' 'Greg-O!'"

My chanting his name in the restaurant brought a quick smile to his face as he devoured another pancake.

"Then one game, you twist your neck pulling down a rebound, and it's really sore the next day. It fact, it gets so stiff that Mom takes you out of school and into the doctor's office.

"After looking you over, the doc says you must wear a plastic neck brace and can't play or practice for the next three weeks. Sitting out of the games is the hardest thing you've ever done. You can only watch your teammates from the stands and dream about playing alongside them.

"Twenty-one long days and nights later, you're finally ready to throw away the neck brace and get back on the team again. But something happens your first day back at practice.

"Instead of the players crowding around, cheering and telling you how glad they are you're back, they ignore you. The guy who took your place is especially cool. Even the coach acts like you never were that important to the team and doesn't put you into games like he did before your injury."

From the moment I mentioned basketball, I could see in his eyes that I had picked the one subject that captured his interest more than what he was eating. I had done the impossible. He had actually put down his fork to listen to my story.

"If something like that happened to you, Big Guy, how would it make you feel?"

"I'd feel terrible, Dad. I'd want to get back on the team."

Returning his look, I paused before saying, "Greg, do you realize that at least once a month you're treating me like this coach treated you in my story?"

"No! I'm not doing anything like that," he said emphatically, "I love you, Dad. I'd never try to make you feel terrible."

"Greg, I know you don't realize it, but every time I leave on a trip, you act just like those guys on the team. For several hours after I'm back home, you reject me and don't want to let me back on the family team.

"If my boss tells me I have to go out of town and miss three days at home, you often keep me out of the game when I get back. Like the guy in the story, it hurts to be sitting on the bench—especially when I don't understand why you won't let me back in the game.

"Greg, I want to be a part of your life. I want to get back on your team when I come home. It hurts being rejected by you, and it's not doing you any good to build up anger against me."

That morning at the table, I saw the light of conviction and understanding dawn on my son's face. He was so caught up in the emotions my story generated that he said he was sorry for ignoring me. Even more spectacular, he assured me things would be different from that moment on. He still wasn't crazy about me traveling, but he said he would never again purposely ignore me.

When I got back from my next trip, he didn't ignore me. And he never has since. As the result of one shared breakfast and a word picture used to sweeten the conversation, we dealt with a problem that could have mushroomed into an angry, distant relationship between father and son. Once again, I saw the personal value of using word pictures with children.

—Gary Smalley

A small boy filled with all kinds of playful ideas anxiously awaited his father's return from work. An extra long day at the office, however, had taken its toll and his father longed desperately for just a few minutes of relaxation. Over and over again, the boy tugged at his dad's leg with yet another suggestion of something they might do together. Finally in total frustration, the father ripped from a magazine a picture of the world and tore it into a hundred pieces. "Here!" he said, handing the child a roll of scotch tape, "Go put the world back together!!" "Ah . . . peace at last!" (Or so he thought). But in just a few minutes he was interrupted again. There before him stood his son and in his hands was a crudely fashioned picture of the world. "Son, that's incredible! How did you ever do it?" "It was easy," said the boy. "You see, on the other side of the picture of the world was a picture of a man and as soon as I got the man straightened out, the world was OK, too!"

One day our Heavenly Father looked down from heaven and saw a broken world—a world that had been shattered into a million pieces by the deadly hammer of sin. But, God loved the world and He loved it in the form of a tiny baby who could make it all new again.

Parenting On My Knees

Face pressed against the glass, I stared through the wall of windows surrounding the nursery. Hot tears stung my cheeks as I swallowed hard to get rid of the giant lump in my throat. Still it remained, as my eyes anxiously swept the room for Seth. The lump grew as my eyes steadied on the bundle in the back isolette. Although tangled amongst a web of tubes and cords, my five-pound baby boy looked rather peaceful. He had no sense of the storm swirling about him, no clue that the tubes protruding from his arms and legs were sustaining him.

A nurse approached his isolette and carefully reaching an arm through one of the portholes, inserted still another tube down his throat. Feeding time, I realized. Although I had wobbled down to the nursery to participate in this very event I was suddenly unable to move, standing frozen at the sight before me, my insides twisting at the thought of being fed through a tube. It seemed so unnatural. Yet, I knew that this method of feeding was effortless on his part and was helping him to store up strength; watching it seemed to drain me of mine. "Doesn't it hurt him?" I silently wondered.

As if she read my thoughts, the nurse turned toward the windows and seeing my glazed expression, motioned for me to come in. Fighting back the tears, I inched my way toward the nursery door. "I must stay strong for Seth," I reminded myself. I forced a smile in the nurse's direction and stared down at Seth's miniature body. He looked like a doll collector's item. "May I hold him when you are done feeding him?" I whispered hoarsely, blinking back the tears now pooling in my eyes.

As she handed me my tiny baby, bundled tightly for warmth, I stared in unbelief at his beautiful face. Holding my son in my arms, I pressed his cheek against mine. I gazed at his angelic face and wondered if he even knew who I was. He was sleeping soundly, which he did most of the time. The doctor said it wasn't unusual for a premature infant to sleep 20 hours a day, but it still worried me. I worried that he wasn't gaining enough weight . . . that the lights weren't curing the jaundice quickly enough . . . about infection taking over . . . that he wouldn't know how much I already loved him . . . that he wouldn't even know who I was because he never seemed to stay awake long enough to notice. Mostly, I worried that he wouldn't wake up at all. Although seemingly weightless in my arms, the weight of Seth's condition, forced me to sit. My heart felt like it weighed 500 pounds.

I sat for what seemed like hours just holding Seth while he slept. I would have held him all night if the nurse would have allowed it. As she glanced at her watch and began her approach, a panic swept over me. I couldn't bear for someone else to take care of my baby any longer. I wanted to care for him, to feed him, to rock him, to love him. And yet, I could do so only in 30-minute segments. Mothering was supposed to be a round-the-clock responsibility, and after only minutes of being awarded the job, they were already replacing me. Yet, I could not compete with the medical prowess surrounding me. I was being denied and it hurt. In my anguish I fell to my knees and cried out to God.

"Oh, Lord," I whispered through my tears, "I need You to sustain me right now. I feel so helpless, watching Seth fight for his life. I cannot help him, but You can. And these doctors can if You give them the wisdom. You gave Seth to me to nurture and train up according to Your ways, but I know You've really only loaned him to me for a time. He truly belongs to You. I know it's not Your desire for me to worry. Your Word says not to worry about anything, but to pray about everything, so here I am Lord. I will not worry anymore. Seth is in Your hands. I trust You with his life. Do with it what You must."

I wiped away my tears and handed Seth to the nurse now standing over me, waiting patiently. She whispered some words of encouragement as she whisked him away for more photo-therapy treatments.

I found myself again at the wall of windows surrounding the

nursery, but this time the view was different. God was working in my heart and my perspective was changing. I no longer saw the tangle of tubes surrounding Seth. Instead I saw my Heavenly Father's hands wrapped around his little body, holding him close. God had heard my prayer and broken through my fear. He must have because Seth's condition no longer seemed hopeless. Rather, it seemed an opportunity to trust God. Although this was my first experience with parenting, somehow I sensed that this was only the beginning of a lifetime of opportunities to trust God with my child's life. He was simply giving me an early start.

Now, more than two years later, I stand peering through another wall of windows at my son. This time I am in my kitchen watching him laugh and leap and play in the backyard with his puppy. He is healthy and strong and the memory of his rocky entry into this life seems to fade with each squeal of glee he produces. Yet I will not soon forget the way my Heavenly Father sustained him, even when his earthly father and I could not.

There have already been countless other moments since Seth's birth that have tested our faith—those moments between worrying and trusting that bring every parent to their knees. But I have learned that as a parent, that is where I stand the tallest—on my knees.

—Laura Sabin Riley

With A Child's Help

Karyn from Missouri was intent on helping her sons develop positive self-esteem. When she would hear them belittling themselves ("I'm so stupid," "I'm ugly," "I can't do anything right") she would give them a special hand signal, and they begrudgingly changed their tune to "I'm very smart, I'm talented, I can do anything I put my mind to, and I love myself." One morning when she was getting ready for a community conference that she was in charge of, she was mentally reviewing the day's activities.

"A thought began to gnaw at me: 'Does the meeting start at 9:30 or 8:30?' Surely, I would have remembered. Still, the doubts hung on. I climbed from the shower and phoned my co-coordinator. Her husband answered, 'Cyndi's long gone. The conference started an hour ago.' My worst fears snapped to reality. How could I have committed such an oversight? I screamed at my children, 'Throw on your clothes—quick! We gotta go, *now!*'

"Splashing on my make-up, I was muttering aloud, 'I'm such an idiot. I don't deserve to be in charge. What a dumb thing to do . . .' While I rambled on, verbally kicking myself, my youngest son walked up, put his hands gently around my face, locked his gaze with mine and said, 'You're beautiful, you're smart, you're talented, you can do anything you put your mind to, and *we love you!*

—**Liz Curtis Higgs**

Asking for Time Together

My granddaughter Christine and I are kindred spirits. We bonded when she was an infant—my first grandbaby. Our relationship has been special ever since, and tea parties have been part of that special relationship.

One Saturday afternoon as we were walking to the mailbox together, ten-year-old Christine said, "Grammy, let's make some scones and have tea."

The next thing I knew, we were in the kitchen whipping up our basic scone recipe. In just a matter of minutes we had popped them in the oven and were setting the table for a simple tea party—just Christine and me.

When the scones were done, we sat down. She poured the tea with practiced ease—we've done this before! We smeared the hot, tasty scones with our favorite jam and whipped topping.

But it's what happened next that made the afternoon so special. Once the tea was poured, we began to talk about friendships, parents, brothers (she has two), and what she could expect as a preadolescent. I was amazed at her knowledge and maturity. We ended up talking about spiritual matters—about God and the meaning of life.

It was only afterward, as I was carefully washing the china cups and returning them to their home in my oak armoire, that I realized what had happened that afternoon: Christine had asked for a tea party.

But what she was really asking for was *time with me*. Asking for tea was her way of saying "I need to talk to you."

—**Emilie Barnes**

They Want Me For One Reason

Ever since that backyard game of catch with my dad, baseball had become my life. It's what I watched on TV when I was indoors. It's what I played when I went outdoors. It's what I read about when I sprawled on the living room floor and spread out the Sunday paper.

My life, was wrapped up in baseball. And my life as a ballplayer was wrapped up in my arm. It wasn't long before that arm gained the attention of the neighborhood. When they chose up sides for sandlot ball, I was the one they all wanted on their team.

They wanted me for one reason—my arm.

It wasn't long before that arm caught the attention of the entire school, when, as a teenager, I pitched my first no-hitter. My name started showing up on the sports page. Before long it made the headlines.

All because of my arm.

That arm attracted the attention of major league scouts, and the part of me that was my boyhood became my livelihood. My ability to provide for my family was not based on how good of a personality I had, how smart I was, or how hard I worked. It was based solely on what my arm could do on game day. The more strikes that arm could throw, the more I was worth. The more games that arm won, the more people wanted me on their team.

When people talked with me, it was the center of conversation. "How's the arm today, Dave?" "Is your arm ready for tonight?" "Better get some ice on that arm; don't want it to swell."

My arm was to me what hands are to a concert pianist, what legs are to a ballerina, what feet are to a marathon runner. It's what people cheered me for, what they paid their hard-earned money to see. It's what made me valuable, what gave me worth, at least in the eyes of the world.

Then suddenly my arm was gone.

How much of me went with it? How much of what people thought of me went with it?

I felt apprehensive. I wondered how my son would react when he saw me. Would he be afraid? Would he feel sorry for me? Would he keep his distance? And what about my daughter? Would she be embarrassed when we went out to eat? How would she feel when people stared? How would my wife feel? What would she think about a man who couldn't tie his own shoes? Would she still find me attractive, or would she be repulsed to see me in my nakedness with my carved-up body?

When I came home from the hospital, I realized that all Jonathan wanted was to wrestle with me and play football on the lawn. All Tiffany wanted was to hug me. All Jan wanted was to have her husband back.

They didn't care whether I had an arm or not.

As important as it had been to my boyhood, as important as it had been to my livelihood, my arm meant nothing to the people in my life who mattered the most. It was enough that I was alive and that I was home.

—**Dave Dravecky**

Be a "Student of Your Children"

Nestled away in a modest condominium in southern Arizona lives a sixty-four-year-old woman. Seven major operations due to rheumatoid arthritis have slowed her down a bit: but she is still busy, active, and lots of fun to visit.

If you were to drop in on her some day, you would see something in her home that pictures what it means to be a "student of your children." While it might not catch your eye right off, whenever I walk into my mother's home, it flashes at me like a neon light. What is it? It is a nondescript-looking bookshelf, but it carries special meaning for my two brothers and me.

One rack of the bookshelf is filled with theology and psychology books, and a second is filled with medical journals and books on genetics. The third shelf seems even more out of place for a sixty-four-year-old, arthritic woman. Lining this shelf are past issues of *Heavy Equipment Digest* and "How-to" books on driving heavy equipment.

These seemingly unrelated books and magazines might lead a person to think this woman is an "eccentric" who reads anything, or perhaps even has a touch of schizophrenia that causes her to jump from one topic to the next. Neither of these explanations would be close to the truth. This collection is actually a beautiful picture of the active commitment our mother has made in giving us the blessing.

Over the years, in my studies in seminary and in my doctoral program, my mother has asked for and read numerous popular books and textbooks on theology and psychology. They are in her bookcase because she has taken an interest in my interests.

My twin brother, Jeff, is a medical doctor who specializes in genetic research in the battle against cancer. To try to understand his field of interest and to be able to converse with him about it, she has read (or tried to read) medical and genetics books. At the age of sixty, she even enrolled in a beginning genetics class at a local university!

To be truthful, she ended up dropping the course after failing the first two major exams. However, sitting proudly on the shelf with other highly technical books is the slightly worn textbook she struggled to understand. Each book is a trophy of her willingness to learn and her desire to communicate with my brother in his areas of interest.

What about the magazines and books on operating road construction equipment? My older brother, Joe, is now Director for Dealer Support for a national company; but for several years he excelled as a heavy equipment operator. Because my mother was also interested in what this son was involved in, she subscribed to *Heavy Equipment Digest* just so she would know about the latest bulldozer or earth mover.

This magazine does not get many subscription requests from sixty-four-year-old, gray-haired, arthritic women— but they did from this one. All because she made a commitment to become a student of each son and of his individual interests.

—John Trent

Take Time To Communicate

Your daughter's timing for being together may not always coincide with your timing. When my daughter, Sheryl, was 12 years old, she came home from a piano lesson with a new piece of music: "Sunrise, Sunset" from *Fiddler on the Roof*. "Daddy, will you play this for me?" she asked. I set aside the book I was reading, rose from my comfortable recliner, sat down at the piano and played the piece several times, much to Sheryl's delight.

After dinner I again settled into my chair to relax and read. "Daddy, will you play it again?" Sheryl begged. My first response, which I did not verbalize aloud, was, "Sheryl, I've already played 'Sunrise, Sunset' enough for one day. I want to read. Play it yourself this time." But I think I heard the Lord saying to me, "You're not too busy. Take time for Sheryl." So I left my chair again and began playing for her. Soon Joyce and Sheryl were standing behind me singing the words to the beautiful tune.

Then it hit me: The lyrics describe a father's feelings about *his* little girl becoming a young woman. I suddenly realized that the words expressed some of my feelings about seeing Sheryl grow up. I played the song several times as Joyce and Sheryl sang. It became a very important and special time in my relationship with Sheryl—and it cost me less than 15 minutes. But I came so close to missing it by saying, "I'm too busy."

—**H. Norman Wright**

Grandmas Make A Difference

The photo studio was packed with mommies in line and kids everywhere. As my daughter waited her turn to see the proofs of the photos taken the week before, I was playing and laughing with Elizabeth, my 18-month-old granddaughter. I soon noticed a little black-haired girl standing alone across the room. Her huge dark eyes never left Elizabeth and I. No one was paying any attention to her and my grandmother's heart reached out.

"Hi!" I said, "What's your name?"

The child dropped her head, shuffled her feet and mumbled something softly.

"What?" I asked. "I didn't hear you."

The reaction was the same. I wondered if perhaps she didn't speak English and didn't understand me. I smiled and started to turn my attention back to Elizabeth when the little girl's demeanor suddenly changed.

Holding her head high, standing tall and looking me directly in the eyes, she spoke loud and clear: "But Grandma calls me Precious!"

—Betty Southard

A Boy Becomes a Man

"I can't see him! I can't see him!" I moaned as I struggled with the binoculars held tightly to my eyes. My heart skipped a beat.

"Over there—to the left. That's his company," my husband replied.

"Do you see him now?"

"No! No!" I cried as the company marched on the parade field, others following it. There were 1,400 of them—1,400 new cadets, plebes—who were marching across the field. It was July 6, 1977. They had just been sworn into the United States Military Academy at West Point, New York. White gloves, white shirts, grey trousers, black shoes, and freshly cut hair made them almost unrecognizable to parents who were straining to see their sons and daughters.

With disappointment, I took the binoculars from my eyes. Tears began to come as I glanced around at the other mothers who were wiping their eyes and blowing their noses. Fathers, for the most part, were maintaining their "cool."

There had been indecision as to where to hold the swearing-in ceremony that day—on the parade field, as scheduled, or in Eisenhower Hall, which was to be the "rain site." Some parents and friends remained at Eisenhower Hall while other brave souls climbed the bleachers, hoping the dark skies would not release the rain. The almost downpour which did come was no match for the love we held for the cadets, our sons and daughters, who would soon be appearing.

It had been morning in the field house, after some announcements and orientation, parents were instructed to leave the building by one exit while future cadets were instructed to leave by another.

So subtly it was done—without fanfare—no emotional "good-byes." Just taking different exits made all the difference in the world. It was all over. Or just beginning!

Hair was cut short. There was the fitting for clothes, final medical check-ups, learning how to salute, learning how to march. All between 10 a.m. and 5:10 p.m., or in cadet terms, 1000 hours and 1710 hours.

Parents were kept busy all day with films about cadet life, basic training, parent orientation by the commandant, tours to key points on the Post, and much more. It seemed that we were running in circles.

I became so weary. My feet began to cry out with discomfort. I was mentally and physically exhausted.

Of course we were proud—all of us. Our sons had excelled in many aspects of their lives. They had proven their leadership ability. This was a great honor. 11,000 boys had applied for 1,400 appointments.

Honor or not, experiences like these tug at a mother's heartstrings. Her little boy is suddenly a man. But to a mother he will always be her little boy.

The companies marched on down the plain, never coming close to the bleachers. I wondered why. Were they afraid that parents would be shocked at how different their sons looked with their short haircuts and white, unsuntanned necks? Or were they really saying, "These are no longer boys. They are men! OUR MEN! THEY BELONG TO UNCLE SAM!"

—**Joan Hake Robie**

Max Jukes lived in New York. He did not believe in Christ or in Christian training. He refused to take his children to church even when they asked to go. He has had 1,026 descendants; 300 were sent to prison for an average term of 13 years; 190 were public prostitutes; 680 were admitted alcoholics. His family thus far has cost the state in excess of $420,000. They have made no contribution to society that is of any benefit.

Jonathan Edwards lived in the same state, at the same time as Jukes. He loved the Lord and saw that his children were in church every Sunday and he served the Lord to the best of his ability. He had 929 descendants; of these, 430 were ministers; 86 became university presidents; 75 authored good books; five were elected to the United States Congress and two to the Senate. One was vice-President of this nation. His family never cost the state one cent but has contributed immeasurably to the life of plenty in this land today.

How is your influence and what legacy will you leave with your children, grandchildren and great-grandchildren?

4

God's Guidance

*He restoreth my soul: he leadeth me in the paths of right-
eousness for his name's sake.*

Psalm 23:3

Just Enough Light

A week in the mountains sounded like the perfect solution. I needed to get away, to think, to pray, to receive God's direction for my life. I have always found His voice to be especially clear when I walked in the woods, so I arrived at our campsite with an expectant heart.

"Lord," I asked in prayer while walking that first afternoon, "please speak to me. Shed Your light on my path, on my writing ministry, on my home and family, on my church work. I feel in the dark about what to do next."

I did not receive an answer that day or the next or the next. I became more anxious as the time went on. I feared that I would return home as confused and upset as the day I had arrived.

Then one evening later in the week, after a time of fellowship, I excused myself early and started down the path to my cabin. A sudden chill came over me as I realized how dark it was on the road and how inadequate my small flashlight was. I had only enough light to cover one footstep at a time.

"Lord, I'm scared," I cried, my voice shaking as I walked between two groves of towering pine without even a sliver of moonlight to guide me. "Please, I can't see but a step at a time. I need more light."

I no sooner had finished my prayer than the answer came. Suddenly I saw that indeed I had enough light—enough for the moment—one footstep at a time. And in that moment I also received the assurance of His guidance that I had been seeking all week.

I believe the Lord was impressing upon me His word from Isaiah 42:16: *I will lead them in paths they have not known: I will make darkness light before them and crooked things straight.*

I took a deep breath, strode forward with confidence and

relaxed for the first time all week. It was all so clear. I did not need a bright flashlight nor a full moon to guide me. I had all the light needed—in Christ Jesus. I knew then the answers, like the light, would come as I needed them—one step at a time.

—Karen O'Connor

Martin Niemoeller, a German pastor imprisoned for opposing the Nazis, illustrated the gravity of remaining silent:

"In Germany, they first came for the Communists, and I didn't speak up because I wasn't a Communist. Then They came for the Jews, and I didn't speak up because I wasn't a Jew. Then they came for the trade unionists, and I didn't speak up because I wasn't a trade unionist. Then they came for the Catholics, and I didn't speak up because I was a Protestant. Then they came for me, and by that time no one was left to speak up."

The lesson is clear: either we speak and stand with the truth, or we lose cherished liberties.

—John Whitehead

Closer Than I Thought

An elderly woman sat to my right in church one Sunday. Her weathered face looked serene, as if she had walked with Jesus for many years. She smiled hello at my greeting.

During the service, our Pastor asked us to share a time when we sensed, without a doubt, Gods presence.

The answers varied: "I can feel Him when I'm in my prayer closet." "When I feel convicted of doing something wrong." "I know He is close when I worship Him in church."

Our Pastor then asked us to share our answer with the person next to us. I mentally scrambled to think of something spiritual sounding.

Turning to her, I blurted out some impressive answer, so awe-inspiring that I have since forgot. However, I will always remember what she told me.

She said, "I know God is here whenever I see a sunset."

That was it. Nothing earth shattering nor grandiose. Maybe she had once been like me—spending so much energy searching for a dramatic glimpse of God, that she missed His touch upon an unfurling pink petal or His kiss in the dew. I determined to learn as she had. I knew He was very near.

—Julie Carobine

A Meal To Last A Lifetime

We had just completed the grueling marathon every mother and daughter participate in toward the end of summer—shopping for school clothes. My trophies were sore feet and an empty wallet. My thirteen-year-old daughter fared much better; she had acquired several new outfits and accessories.

"I can't wait to get home to try on my blue skirt with my shoes; I hope they match," she chattered excitedly as we headed across the parking lot. I marveled at her stamina. The day's ordeal hadn't dampened her enthusiasm. I tried to recall what my energy level had been at thirteen, but at the moment I couldn't even recall having been that age.

She continued to comment on her purchases while I wondered how to impress her with the knowledge that there are more important things in life than clothes.

Part of my uncertainty on how to approach my daughter lay in recent feelings of emptiness in my Christian walk. The Bible passages I read and the sermons I listened to seemed to have lost their meaning. I had begun to pray earnestly for a renewed sense of purpose.

We were halfway to the car when our attention was diverted by a man calling and waving as he approached us. His request was simple—he wanted money to buy food. As I looked at his face I noticed sweat running down his forehead and onto his cheek, which was crusted with blood. He had a chipped tooth and foul breath. His hair was cut short, and he wore a cap with an upturned beak. What held my attention, however, was the appeal in his eyes. They spoke of a need greater than food.

As I looked in my wallet for whatever meager cash I had left, I wondered how to tell someone whose greatest concern is his next meal that God loves him. I found a dollar and my daughter contributed some change. As I handed it to him I asked if we could pray together. He agreed readily.

We were still standing in the middle of the parking lot, so we moved to the sidewalk. He put the money on the ground and sat on the curb with his knees jutting out, resting his elbows on them. I crouched on one knee beside him, put my hand on his shoulder, and asked if he had ever accepted Jesus Christ as his Savior. I could hear my daughter fidgeting in the background and knew she was embarrassed by what she would term, "mother's blunt-ness." Occasionally a pedestrian would walk by and glance at us suspiciously. I began to feel uncertain, wondering if perhaps I had been presumptuous. As we began to pray, however, my feelings of uncertainty were replaced by feelings of elation as he asked Jesus to come into his life.

When our prayer ended, he talked briefly about the hardships he'd encountered while growing up: neglect, rejection, abuse, poverty. His eyes filled with tears when he told me that no one had ever spoken to him with as much caring concern as I had—"Not even my grandmother who raised me."

As he spoke I looked down and noticed that his knee was visible through a large tear in his baggy, gray pants. His shoes turned up at the toes where they were separating from the soles. I struggled to recall the words I had spoken, wondering which ones had conveyed my empathy. Then it occurred to me that it wasn't the words at all, but the simple act of responding to him as a person—the eye contact, my hand on his shoulder, sitting beside him as I listened and prayed. When he came to the end of his reminiscences, he picked up the money and placed it in the pocket of his checkered flannel shirt. I glanced at my daugh-ter, who was still sitting on the curb clutching her packages tightly on her lap and staring at the tips of her shoes.

As we prepared to go our separate ways, I noticed that the desperate appeal on his face had been replaced with a more gentle, peaceful expression.

His parting gesture was as unexpected as it was audacious —a paradoxical mixture of pride and humility. He took my hand in his, bowed over it, and kissed it. The gesture was imparted with all the dignity and grace of a courtier. Then he released my hand, and without a word he turned and walked away. As I watched him leave, the words recorded in Matthew 25:40 came to mind: *Inasmuch as ye have done it unto one of the least of these my brethren, ye have done it unto me.*

—Pauline Jaramillo

Middle Man

Because of a delay in taking off, my homebound flight was late, leaving me at risk of missing my second plane. When we landed at the connecting airport, I rushed through the terminal, arriving at my gate just as they were closing the doors. Relieved I'd made it, I headed down the aisle in search of my seat. I stopped at my assigned row and, to my dismay, found I had the middle seat.

There are some things I don't do. Middle seats head my "no way, I ain't gonna!" list. My mood swing went from "I'm so grateful I caught my plane" to "I don't care what this ticket says, I'm not sitting in that center seat!"

I glanced around and realized, however, that this was the last available seat on the flight, and I would sit there or on the wing. I prayed for an attitude adjustment. I remembered that God will operate on our attitudes but that He requires us to cooperate.

To do my part, I tried to think of a way to make this irritating situation fun. Then it came to me that I could pretend I was Oprah Winfrey and my seat partners were my guests. I would interview them. Now, this had possibilities!

I turned my interview efforts toward the man sitting next to me. I had already observed something about this young man when I was being seated. He called me "Ma'am." At the time I thought, *he must be in the service*, so I asked, "You in the service?"

"Yes, Ma'am, I am. The Marines."

"Hey, Marine, where are you coming from?"

"The Desert Storm, Ma'am."

"No kidding? How long were you there?" I continued.

"A year and a half. I'm on my way home. My family will be at the airport. I'm so scared." As he said this last, he took in a short, nervous breath.

"Scared? Of what?" I asked.

"Oh, all this hero stuff. I'm not a hero, I'm just me, and I don't want my family to be disappointed."

"Take it from me, Marine, your parents just want you to come home safe."

Then Michael told me that when he lived at home, he and his mother were friends. When he joined the service and was stationed in Hawaii, they had written to each other and had become good friends. But when he went to Desert Storm, they became best friends.

"She will never know how she affected my life while I was away," he continued. "I've never thought of myself as a religious person, but while I was in the Storm, I learned to pray. The example I followed was the one my mom set for me when I was growing up."

"What was the most difficult time for you?" I inquired in Oprah fashion.

"There was a four-month space when we had not seen a woman or a child. The day we drove into Kuwait was very emotional for us. The women stood in the doorways, waving, but even more moving was when the children ran to greet us. Since I've been stateside waiting to go home, I've been thinking about my nephews, and I can hardly wait to hear them call me Uncle Michael. The title *uncle* means even more to me than being called *sergeant*."

About that time, the flight attendant was passing by, and I tugged at her skirt. She looked down, and I said, "Know what? He is returning from Desert Storm."

The attendant asked him several questions and then requested that he write his name on a piece of paper. Taking his signature, she headed toward the front of the plane.

Moments later, the pilot came on the intercom and said, "It has been brought to my attention that we have a VIP aboard. He is a returning GI from Desert Storm and is in seat 12F. As a representative of this airline and citizen of the United States of America, I salute you, Michael, and thank you for a job well done."

At that point, the entire plane burst into applause.

The pilot came back on and said, "We are making our final approach into the Detroit Metro Airport."

Michael's breath caught.

I looked up and saw his eyes had filled with tears. He peeked through a tear to see if I had noticed, and of course there I was, goggling at him.

He said softly, "I just don't want to cry."

"It's okay," I told him. "I checked a Marine manual on this one, and it's all right to cry. Some of the most admirable men I've ever known have shed tears at appropriate times, and Michael, this is a right time."

"Then you don't think I need to blame this on my contacts," he responded, grinning.

"I don't think so," I said with a giggle.

As our plane taxied in, I told him the best gift my son brought me when he returned from 18 months in Guam was that after he made his way through the waiting crowd, he scooped me up in his arms and held me for a very long time.

It was time to deplane, and when Michael stood, the men all around us slapped him on the back and pumped his arm, thanking him for his contribution.

Michael's homecoming included a lineup of relatives armed with video equipment, flags, cameras, and banners. When we were close enough for eyes to focus in and distinguish which one was Michael, his family began to chant, "Michael, Michael, Michael."

Even from a distance, I could identify his mom. She was the one leaping the highest in the air. A guard leaned against the wall, watching to make sure no one stepped over the security line. But every time Michael's mom jumped into the air, she came down with her toe just over the line to let that guard know who was really in charge.

As we got closer, she stopped jumping, and her hands went over her mouth to muffle the building sobs. Tears poured down her arms and dropped off her elbows . . . just over the line.

I gave him a final nudge toward his family, and they engulfed him, everyone in tears. I saw Michael find his mom in the crowd and pull her into his arms and hold her for a very long time.

When we got to the baggage claim area, I prayed for the first time ever that my luggage would be delayed. Before long, the whole Desert Storm entourage came down to claim Michael's duffel bags.

Michael was still surrounded by family when I saw a youngster toddle over and pull on his pant leg. I realized this must be one of the nephews he was so eager to see again. When I noticed how young the boy was and remembered that Michael had been gone for a year and a half, I held my breath to watch how the boy would react to his uncle.

Michael's face lit up as he reached down and picked up the young boy. His nephew wrapped his chubby legs around the sergeant's waist, and his arms encircled Michael's neck. Then the boy's mom came over, and I heard her ask, "Honey, who's got you?"

He looked up, his young eyes reflecting his hero, and said, "Uncle Michael."

I could breathe again.

A few minutes later, the thought hit me that I almost missed being a part of this tender event because I hadn't wanted to sit in the middle. I wonder how many divine appointments I've missed because I found my circumstances not to be what I expected and my defiance robbed me of His greater plan?

—Patsy Clairmont

In His Hands

Dense fog hung heavily over the endless highway. It was almost eleven PM on the second day of my first big adventure—driving to a new job in Florida from my home in Kansas.

The previous month I had accepted Jesus Christ as my Savior. Although I didn't know what my new life with Christ would mean, I believed God loved me. But I was *scared.* I prayed for protection. I imagined God smiling down on me, just as my earthly father did when I was a small child. I would trustingly put my tiny fingers in his big, calloused hand as I crossed a busy street.

Suddenly, my senses were jarred and adrenalin surged through my fatigued body as I saw two tractor-trailers jackknife on the road ahead. Too late to apply my brakes, my hands frantically clutched the steering wheel. "God, take me through," I uttered.

Clods of dirt and metal debris shook the car. Time seemed suspended as I passed through a shroud of eerie murkiness. The pounding of my heart deafened my ears. Shaking, I pulled the car over to the grassy, narrow shoulder of the road. In the rearview mirror I could see the collided semitrailers sitting in the middle of the highway. How did I get past them?

Tears began to run down my face as I laid my forehead against my arms which rested on top of the steering wheel. As I thanked God for His protection, a scripture came to my mind. *For He orders his angels to protect you wherever you go. They will steady you with their hands to keep you from stumbling against the rocks on the trail.* (Psalms 91:11, TLB)

My heavenly Father was reassuring his newly-adopted daughter of His everlasting love.

Thank you, Lord!

—Helen Hertha Kesinger

The Paper Chase

One exquisite day in May, I had a luncheon program in Ocean City, New Jersey. After my presentation was over, the morning fog lifted and the oceanside resort was bathed in late spring sunshine . . . glorious! A wise and balanced woman would have given herself permission to take a stroll on the beach, but not this woman. No, I had work to do, a book to write, and no lollygagging allowed. My only concession to the beautiful day was to open the windows and invite the ocean breezes to gently fill the room.

Dutifully, I sat down with a huge file folder of papers and began to divide them carefully into ten neat piles: this goes in this chapter, that goes in that chapter. After four hours, my hard work neatly spread out before me on the bed, I got up to stretch and head out for an early dinner. Not a leisurely trip to a nice food restaurant—that would require time!—just a quick zip through the nearest drive-thru, then back to work.

Twenty minutes later, heading into the hotel with my paper sack dinner, I noticed the wind had picked up. Had I left those windows open? Hm-m-m. As I turned the key in the door and began to push it open, I noticed a strange "whooshing" sound and had a sense of the door opening on its own power. When the bed full of papers came into view, still in neat piles, I breathed a sigh of relief . . . until the door was fully open and a big gust of wind found a way of escape.

In seconds, nearly two hundred pages of notes were blowing everywhere, including through the door and down the hall. "W-a-a-aaa!" came from my lips as I dropped my dinner sack and began chasing and stomping on runaway slips of paper.

A few minutes later, papers clutched willy-nilly in my hands, I made my way back to my room to survey the damage. The sea breeze had created a sea of papers, and all my afternoon labors had been in vain (the perfect word for it, since the word means "a breath, a vapor").

I should've cried. I could've stamped my foot. I would've been justified in letting out one good scream. None of the above happened. I started to chuckle. Then a whole laugh sneaked out. Soon I was doubled over with laughter. I almost missed the bellman clearing his throat behind me as he held out a piece of paper with a bewildered expression on his face. "Ma'am? Did you lose something?"

Yes, I did. Thank goodness.

And I found something too. Annie Chapman, in *Smart Women Keep It Simple*, reminds us that in the Greek games, "The winner of the race was the one who came in first—with his torch still lit."

—Liz Curtis Higgs

© 1992, Bil Keane, Inc.
Dist. by Cowles Synd., Inc.

"Know what we learned in bible class? The Lord is my chauffer, I shall not walk."

Reprinted from *COUNT YOUR BLESSINGS* by Bil Keane.

Missing Teeth

I sat in the dentist's chair emotionally numb from the accident earlier in the day. Falling face down on the asphalt playground of the school where I was a third grader, I had shattered my top two front permanent teeth to jagged points. Dr. Butler stood over me gently shaking his head, compassion radiating from his blue eyes. Looking first at my mother who sat nearby, worry etched on her face, and then at me, he said, "Kathy, you need caps to cover your teeth but since your jaw hasn't finished forming yet, we can't give you permanent caps. We'll have to put on temporary caps." He turned and rustled in a drawer, pulling out a tray of various sizes of caps—they were all silver! I tried not to gasp as I envisioned my formerly beautiful smile now destroyed.

Over the next three years as I wore those two silver caps, I tried to make sure no one saw them. I learned not to smile! Before I fell, I'd loved my teeth, but now I hated how I looked. If I forgot about my teeth and smiled, invariably some child nearby would point and laugh at the girl with two silver teeth. Each time, I shriveled in embarrassment and self-hatred. *Why did that happen to me? Doesn't God love me?* I concluded He must not, otherwise He wouldn't have allowed such a horrible thing to happen to me. I couldn't trust Him.

Eventually, I was able to have two white permanent caps replace the silver ones, but shortly after that, my teeth abscessed from the accident years before and three teeth had to be pulled. *This is another sign God doesn't love me*, I decided. Until my early twenties, I wore a partial plate and then for over twenty years I had a permanent bridge.

In the midst of that, I became a Christian at age 18, and began to dislodge those wrong ideas from my mind that God didn't love me and couldn't be trusted.

Then in 1991, I noticed that one side of the bridge was loose. My dentist, Dr. Winter, examined it and cleared his throat. "Kathy, you are right that the bridge is loose but it's not as simple as recementing it back into place. One of the anchor teeth for the bridge has broken."

I gulped in fear, wondering what it would take to fix the problem.

He continued, "Since the tooth has broken, we'll have to grind down two more teeth, one on each side, to attach the bridge." He paused, looking thoughtful. "But you do have another option. You could consider dental implants."

The thought of grinding down two more teeth seemed horrible to me, so my husband, Larry, and I decided I would get dental implants. Several months later I was scheduled for implant surgery. Through talking with my periodontist, Dr. Gaffaney, I'd learned more about the procedure. The initial surgery would install the titanium implants into my jaw. Then during the four to six months it took for my bone to grow around the implant, I would wear a temporary partial plate. Later the permanent teeth would be attached to the implants.

I'd already explained to Dr. Gaffaney that I was a professional speaker and that my next speaking engagement was just 10 days after my initial surgery. He assured me that would be no problem since by then my gums would be healed enough for me to wear the partial plate. And indeed, it wouldn't have been a problem except that during surgery, Dr. Gaffaney discovered one side of my jaw was too thin and had to put in a bone graft. That made wearing the plate dangerous because it could bump against the graft and dislodge it.

During one of my visits shortly after surgery, Dr. Gaffaney told me I should let the meeting planner for my speaking engagement know I may not be able to speak because I can't wear the partial plate. The meeting planner understood and said she would be praying that I would be able to come.

The meeting was scheduled for Monday evening and the previous Friday I prepared my material. Suddenly, I sensed the

Lord whisper in my heart, "You're going to go without your teeth." I shook my head, disbelieving such a message. "Oh, Father, I don't think they want to have a speaker without her three front teeth." But almost simultaneously, I felt a peace envelop my body and spirit. I looked down at the plans for my talk and realized that my missing front teeth could be the visual aid for the point of my speech. An excitement and anticipation of God's working through me made me hope I had to go without my teeth! For sure, they would never forget the speaker without her top three front teeth. I was thrilled!

Not only did I go to that speaking engagement without my teeth, but to many others over the following month as my mouth healed. One committee for one of those speaking engagements introduced me by singing, "All I want for Christmas are my three front teeth."

During that time, I was awed to recognize the changes in my thinking about God's love for me. As a child, I'd concluded God didn't love me because of my teeth-shattering accident. Now I was speaking before hundreds of people without my top three front teeth and believing, without a doubt, that God loved me and was trustworthy. I had become convinced of this truth: *There is no fear in love; but perfect love casts out fear. . .* (1 John 4:18). I could trust God's love because it was perfect: He wanted only the best for me, with or without teeth.

—Kathy Collard Miller

Seared Consciences

It had been a long week. I was the administrator in charge of organizing Nature Camp for 120 sixth graders. The whole week had been successful except for one major disaster—me. No matter what I did, I could not connect emotionally or spiritually with the girls assigned to my cabin. They were rebellious from the start. The ringleader, Shawna, wreaked havoc and negatively influenced the other girls in our cabin.

It all started with the scavenger hunt. They aggressively leapt into the creek ahead of the others to catch the little green frog that gave them a 20-point lead.

The win was exciting because it was the *only* thing that had gone well. The star rebels—Shawna, Barb, and Carrie, were the shining heroines of the scavenger hunt and had retreated to the cabin to change their wet clothes. I took the rest of the girls down to the chapel to begin Spiritual Emphasis Night. Suddenly, Barb came dashing into the chapel and said, "Mrs. H., we hung our jeans and socks on the ceiling heater. Is that okay?"

"No," I quickly replied. "Get those clothes off the heating element right now—it'll start a fire." A little voice inside me said, *Follow Barb up the hill and be sure those clothes are taken off the heater.* I didn't heed the voice—big mistake!

When the girls appeared they continued creating trouble as usual. I couldn't wait for this week to end!

I left the Spiritual Emphasis Night a few minutes early to go to the cabin and get a book for another counselor. As I walked to the cabin, I realized it was on fire! I rushed down the hill, my heart racing.

"The cabin's on fire!" I screamed. "Call 911!" One of the men rushed to the nearest phone. Help was on its way.

After the ashes settled, Shawna, Barb, Carrie, and the other girls and I huddled near the door of the incinerated cabin. We peered in. All that was left of the girls' jeans and socks that previously hung on the ceiling heater was one inch of denim.

"Barb, why didn't you obey me? I told you not to leave the clothes on the heating element."

Tears filled her eyes. "Shawna said you didn't know what you were talking about."

I looked at Shawna. She hung her head. A tear streaked across her moonlit cheek.

"Shawna . . ." I didn't need to say anymore. Hearts had softened. Those rebellious girls were crying in my arms. "We're sorry. We should have obeyed you . . . we . . . we could have been killed."

That night the Spirit of God moved. Those rebellious girls repented and committed their lives to Jesus. Who would have thought that a week of rebellion and a burned cabin would result in seared consciences and spiritual obedience to God's calling? Maybe Nature Camp wasn't so bad after all.

—June Hetzel

We May Not Understand

When I was a boy, I heard a mystery program on the radio that captured my imagination. It told the story of a man who was condemned to solitary confinement in a pitch-black cell. The only thing he had to occupy his mind was a marble. Which he threw repeatedly against the walls. He spent his hours listening to the marble as it bounced and rolled around the room. Then he would grope in the darkness until he found his precious toy.

One day, the prisoner threw his marble upward—but it failed to come down. Only silence echoed through the darkness. He was deeply disturbed by the "evaporation" of the marble and his inability to explain its disappearance. Finally he went berserk, pulled out all his hair, and died.

When the prison officials came to remove his body, a guard noticed something caught in a huge spider's web in the upper corner of the room.

"That's strange," he thought. "I wonder how a marble got up there."

As the story of the frantic prisoner illustrates, human perception sometimes poses questions the mind is incapable of answering. But valid answers always exist. For those of us who are followers of Jesus Christ, it just makes good sense not to depend too heavily on our ability to make the pieces fit—especially when we're trying to figure out the Almighty!

—James Dobson

Mohawk Mommy

I've been amazed at how my sister, Terri, has handled her bout with cancer with God's help. Even though her life is hanging by a thread, she has kept her humor and trust in God.

When she faced chemotherapy, she told her young children, ages 2, 6 & 8, "Mommy's got a disease called cancer and it could make me die. The doctors have to give me strong drugs to help but it's going to make mommy's hair fallout."

"I don't want you to loose your hair Mommy," cried six-year-old Jillian.

"Well, it's going to happen honey."

"No, mommy, no."

Terri's love and concern for her children put her on her knees in prayer. "Oh, Lord, what can I do to help my children through this?" She sensed God would guide her.

To help with the transition to no hair, Terri had her hair cut to shoulder length. Three or four days later she cut it again to just below her chin. Within another few days it was done in a tapered cut. Then in a day or two she went in and had her head shaved except for a short strip down the middle of her head, a mohawk cut.

"It's so cool!" proclaimed 8-year-old Joseph, "All my friends think it's cool, too."

The contrast between her short dark hair and her pristine white scalp prompted her to decide to color her remaining hair blonde. Because of the chemotherapy in her system, Terri's hair turned a light shade of orange. Only some industrial strength stripper solution turned her back into beautiful bleached blonde.

As Terri's hair started getting loose she'd lay back in a recliner letting the kids come up behind her and pull it out. It became a game. When she wasn't suspecting it, the children would sneak up behind her, snatch a handful of hair and run. When asked, "Why do you let them do that?" she answered with a twinkle in her eye, "How many kids can actually say they snatched their mom bald?"

Terri's children are coping well with the trauma. Her prayers had been answered.

—**Tamera Easterday**

Making the Flight . . .
Missing the Blessing

I was a little late, but not at the panic stage, as I entered the terminal at Atlanta's Hartsfield Airport. The departure monitor informed me that my gate was located in concourse D. That is quite a way from the main terminal, but Hartsfield's airline concourses are conveniently linked by an underground train. No problem, I just needed to keep moving.

As I descended the escalator I saw an aged and frail man standing absolutely motionless with a large 3' x 2' placard around his neck. As he and his cane leaned against the wall, he wore thick glasses, a stubble of gray beard and a 1950's vintage hat. He seemed a bit dour.

Then I noticed the message on the placard: *For whosoever shall call upon the name of the Lord shall be saved.* Romans 10:13. A very fitting invitation from a seemingly ill-fitted source.

As I waited for the train access doors to open I studied the faces of the people who read his message. Some showed visible annoyance, others nervous smiles.

"I am committed to evangelism, but this is not quite my style," I thought. Still, as I considered the rejection and isolation he must feel, I thought about affirming him in his faithful efforts. But my feet didn't move. "What would I say? How would I look?" Suddenly the train was there and I was swept on board by the press of eager travelers, no longer confronted by this unwanted harbinger of hope.

As the train whisked us farther from the main terminal the Spirit of God quietly began to speak. "Why were you in Atlanta, Fred?"

"I came to meet with the leaders of 30 mission agencies regarding reaching Russia with the gospel," I mentally responded.

"You do pretty well in meetings. How about putting the

message into practice?" was the quiet, but firm reproof of the Spirit. Ouch!

Not one to give up easily, I reminded the Lord how ineffective I felt this style of evangelism was in our culture. "In fact," I added, "this fellow serves to reinforce so many of the negative stereotypes that many unbelievers have of Christians. He probably does more harm than good."

I was glad for the cyborg voice of the train computer announcing the stop at concourse A, quenching the heat of the spiritual dialogue. Three more stops and I would be at my terminal. As the doors closed the Spirit began again. "What are your spiritual gifts, Fred?"

"I am an exhorter, an encourager."

"Who gave you those gifts and for whose purposes?"

"You did, Lord, and I am your servant."

"Do you think that old man, also my servant, gets much encouragement?" Silence . . .

The first real pangs of regret rumbled in my soul as the train arrived at and then left concourse B.

The Spirit of God began again: *Therefore, to one who knows the right thing to do, and does not do it, to him it is sin.* (James 4:17 NASB) "If He just wouldn't call it sin," I lamented. Now I was faced with the choice of sin or obedience.

My last plan of resistance was to move from the spiritual to the practical. "If I go back now I'll probably miss my plane. I have a special fare and it would cost big-time if I have to arrange another flight," I said in my good steward voice.

"Isn't the cost of a hardened and unresponsive heart even greater?" was the gentle, but firm response.

I knew what I needed to do, but still I sat welded to my seat as the train left concourse C headed for the last stop. "What should I say?" was my last ignoble peep, not sounding half as convincing as Moses did millennia before. Silence.

The inbound train seemed like it traveled at half-speed. Though I knew they were announcing the early boarding of flight 1229, anxiety and regret over missing the flight was steadily giving way to the joyful anticipation of the fruit of obedience.

In my pocket I could feel the crisp bills that I intended to offer this new friend whom I longed to rendezvous with. I marveled at how rapidly God had given me an eagerness for obedience.

Back at the main terminal I raced back to my starting point. *I'll keep it simple. I'll just affirm him for his faithful service. I'll press the money into his hand, not as a gift from me, but from the Lord.* I felt such freedom and joy.

But his previously occupied alcove was empty. Crushed, I had missed my window of opportunity. Minutes later, I walked onto my flight just before they closed the door.

The following week I used this story to illustrate a point I was making while teaching a Sunday School class. When I finished the story, one of the businessmen in the class spoke up and said, "The man's name is Ron." He had been through Atlanta that very week and encountered the same "Gospel mannequin." Mike had graciously given him more than enough of a love gift for the two of us. Incredible. Thank God that we are a part of a world-wide Body that makes up for the weaknesses of one another.

—Fred H. Wevodau

Forty Years in Forty Seconds

Whoever heard of such a thing—A Flying Evangelist? Believe it or not, it is true. But to fall a hundred feet, landing in a tree, living to tell the story; is miraculous.

Across the country, high by a couple of thousand feet, the Lord and I (Sky-Pilot L. C. Robie) sailed in the Gospel Ship, made possible by Christian friends, to the home port—Union Springs, NY. God always has lots of friends. On the plane's side was lettered: "The Robie Gospel Ship," with the message, "Higher'n he Flies—Jesus Saves." What a profound impression it made wherever it went! Soon several pilots began to bend the knee to Jesus. That was worth a million times the ship! I had found a new avenue for God's message, for I could give it to them in their own language. But one day the words "Jesus Saves" would have a special meaning to me.

It was a lovely afternoon—August 15, 1936. My boys helped me roll out the Gospel Ship. The crowd waited as the powerful one hundred and twenty-five horses were warmed up. God's presence seemed so wonderful to me that afternoon. Meantime, the wind shifted to the East, so that it became necessary to take off over the shorter and more difficult runway—high boundary poles, and tall trees rising on a slight grade. But I had done it before, and the faithful Waco-F, built for the hardest work, and for the private flyer, was equal to the task.

When I gave it the gun, the plane darted down the runway. I sensed that there was not the lift common—something vital was lacking in the air. Too late, then, to stop! We left the ground, hung over it closely, then up went the plane's nose and the ship zoomed over the high electric wires and tall trees, some one hundred and fifty yards. I had nicely cleared the trees, yet the rising grade seemed to be pushing them higher and perilously close. I couldn't level off to hold flying speed, which was fast decreasing. Indeed, at that very moment the wings were very unsteady. Yes, forty years in forty seconds really happened! Then two monstrous trees loomed before me by twenty-five or more feet. To try and force the ship over would mean a half-spin, and almost certain horrible death. I could hear that "Still, Small Voice." I knew what to do and what would happen. Frightened? Not in God's care— perfect calm! His arm was underneath. Then the jolting crash—left mid-wing on the monster limb. Around and down went the nose one hundred and ninety-five degrees. Falling, crashing—had read about it. Through six-inch limbs, settling nearly to the ground, the crash was heard a mile away.

Gas was pouring out. A fire and explosion might follow. No, God was there! The switch had been cut.

Still hanging in the tree, in the Gospel Ship. Then someone called out to me, "Blood!" Out it flowed from my badly cut eye. I climbed down from the tree and looked up at the Gospel Ship—how could I leave it! But kind folks came to its protection, and loving hands to take me to the hospital. One look, and no one doubted that "Jesus Saves."

—L. C. (Sky-Pilot) Robie

The Rev. Henry Howard of Australia tells a story of a ship wrecked on a coral reef in the southern seas. The crew got ashore as they could, some on floating timbers, some on hencoops, some on nutmeg graters! Ashore, they hugged the coast, fearful to go inland lest it might prove to be a cannibal island. They had no special desire to be clubbed and eaten. Presently one of them, more adventurous than the rest, climbed a nearby hillock. After reaching the summit, his colleagues saw him waving his arms excitedly and invitingly and heard him shout, "Come along, boys, we're all right. Here's a church." There wasn't one of that crew who didn't feel safer because the good news had been proclaimed there. Against such a background we see more clearly the significance of the church. It is the light against the darkness, and men in need thank God for the mercy of that light.

5

Grief

*Why art thou cast down, O my soul? and why art thou
disquieted within me? hope thou in God: for I shall yet
praise him, who is the health of my countenance, and my
God.*

Psalm 42:11

Just Like Going to Sleep

On December 7, 1941, Peter Marshall, the famed chaplain of the U.S. Senate, was speaking to the cadets at Annapolis, unaware that as he spoke Pearl Harbor was in flames. Many in his audience would be called upon to give their lives in the days ahead. He told them this story.

"A young boy dying from an incurable disease asked his mother, 'What is it like to die? Does it hurt?'

"His mother answered: 'Remember when you were a very little boy and played very hard and fell asleep on mommy's bed? When you woke in the morning you were in your own bed because your daddy came with his big strong arms and lifted you, undressed you, and put on your pajamas. Death is like that—you wake up in your own room.' "

—Jeanne Hendricks

God Never Loses His Angels

"Where are those angels, anyway?" I, "Mother Teresa," muttered in frustration after searching through all the moving boxes that might contain Christmas items. No, I'm not the Mother Teresa from India but from Fresno, California: mother of 4, ages 10 months to 17 years. No, mother of three, now.

The miniature wooden angels just weren't there. A baby's first Christmas should be just right. I wanted little Ben's to be full of wonder and discovery, all the treasured family traditions and ornaments properly in place. Angels weren't supposed to let themselves get lost. They *had* to be here somewhere!

This last move should have been a snap. It was a snap all right: it made something in my head snap. I had, with reasonable cheer, kept on top of a phenomenally challenging series of events over the last two years. Although never out of diapers, my 15-year-old, handicapped daughter, Lisa, had regressed to a neonatal development level. I learned CPR & nasal gastric tube feeding among other special care skills. I also supported my husband as he navigated the treacherous waters of changing careers three times just before turning 40. I handled two cross-country moves in nine months; the second, six months along in a surprise pregnancy in which there was a 1 in 4 chance of the baby having Lisa's genetic defect. I survived a year in a cramped, leased home, and then ended up right back where I started in the same house I had left two years before. Bills piled up.

The challenge might have been too much if my husband, 17-year-old son, and 11-year-old daughter hadn't been so much help. We all worked together, making the extraordinary care a gracefully accepted norm. My faith that the Lord was leading us, my commitment to a positive attitude, and a generous dose of humor kept us all going.

Still, one thing seemed to heap on top of another. I had coped with the trivial and the important, challenges large and small, babies large and small . . . no, not anymore. We lost Lisa when Ben was 10 weeks old.

Maybe losing someone is a little like moving: you can prepare all you want, but you can't get around the fact that it's hard. I sat in the middle of the "re-re-used" moving boxes where the wooden angels were supposed to be and decided I and the angels had all had one move too many.

No longer focused on Ben's first Christmas, I began thinking about Lisa's last one instead. I picked up a little silver angel with Lisa's name engraved on it. It had been so appropriate for her. Lisa had such a sweet, angelic nature before she had regressed to the point that it seemed she was just a house with no one home.

"Ah, my little lost angel," I whispered, as the tears started. "I'll bet God never loses His angels."

It's odd how grief sneaks up on you when you're not looking. It doesn't really matter that there was nothing more that could have been done. Guilt nibbles at the corners of your conscience like a desperate, starving mouse. Could Lisa have been pulled through pneumonia one more time? Maybe. But there really wouldn't have been any point to the pain it would have caused her. None of the systems in her little, contorted body worked anymore. The silent pain in her unfocused eyes had forced our aching hearts to cross the bridge of letting her go.

Oddly, I had rarely been sad while Lisa was still here. The Lord had sustained me through the 12 years we had dealt with the disability. I had never felt I had to face it alone; sometimes it was *almost* too hard, but never quite. I always believed God could heal Lisa, that He would. I didn't hold it against Him; it just hurt so when the grief drenched me. Like now. Angel. Angels. "Oh, no, I've lost them."

The tiny bell on the silver angel rang softly as I set it sadly back down in its coffin-shaped box. "At least this angel isn't lost," I mused.

Suddenly, I was aware of a thought coming into my mind forcefully enough as it were the Lord speaking out loud. "Lost? Lost? How can someone be lost when you know where she is? You do believe Lisa is with me, don't you?"

"Of course, Lord."

"You know that means she is free of that sad little body?"

"Oh, yes, Lord, I'm so grateful for that."

"You've forgotten that I only lent her to you for a while. She was always mine. The love, experiences, memories, lessons . . . those are the things that are yours. They are treasures that will last forever. And remember, time for you just seems long; you'll see her again, well and whole."

A flash memory of Lisa's pained expression during her final hours tore at my heart. Then, just as quickly I remembered the sense of awe I'd felt as a peace settled on Lisa's face when the struggle ended. Peace on earth . . . that's what we wish each other at Christmas, but we don't give it; God does. God's peaceful presence gently clothed me like a soft, white sari.

The wooden angels turned up in the spring, near the time I'd said good-bye to Lisa the year before. I could almost picture my "little lost angel" surrounded by angels. No, God never loses His angels.

—Teresa Daniels

Mommy Cried This Morning

Mommy cried this morning,
I did not know what to say;
But her tears dried up so quickly,
That we went on with our day.

Then the phone started ringing,
She'd answer with a smile.
It seemed each person told her,
That they'd be by in a while.

So people started coming,
With lots of things to eat.
They'd all hug Mom and Grandma,
I thought it all was neat.

Then Mommy called us to her,
And she sat us on her bed.
My brother sat down at the foot,
And I sat near the head.

"I have something to tell you,"
She said in quiet tones.
"Poppa died this morning,
And he won't be coming home."

"He's gone to live with Jesus,
Do you guys understand?"
She looked at us, we saw her tears,
So I reached for her hand.

"Did Poppa go to Heaven?"
She nodded this was so;
To us, it seemed real obvious,
"Well then, we want to go!"

"You've told us about Heaven,
How great it's s'posed to be.
So tell us please, why Mommy,
Do you cry so easily?"

"Well, Grandma will miss her husband,
And I will miss my dad.
Since Poppa's never coming back,
This is what makes us sad."

"But you will go see him one day
Since he can't come back to you.
But it might take a little time,
God has things for us to do."

Mommy finished talking,
And things seemed quite okay.
'Til she took us to a strange new place,
Evening, the following day.

"I thought he was in Heaven,
This is something new.
Poppa looks asleep to me,
So he's not one, but two?"

Mommy smiled a little,
How could she explain?
I could tell she wasn't sure at first,
But then she made it plain.

"Since our bodies weren't created
To fly away through space;
He had to leave his body here,
To see God face-to-face.

"The part of him that loved us,
Lives on in memory.
He now no longer lives in pain,
He's happy as can be."

I finally understood it,
Almost from his time of birth;
Poppa loved others right up close,
And loved God from the earth.

Now Poppa loves God right up close,
I think he's having fun.
He's hanging out around the Throne,
Just talking with the Son.

Mommy cried again this morning,
But church was a celebration;
The funeral was not an end,
It was Poppa's graduation!

—Sharon Jones

But It's OK

He was but a wisp of a boy, probably no more than five years old. He was sitting on the stairs outside the pediatric unit of the research hospital. A group of us, working as student nurses in pediatrics, encountered him that day as we were leaving.

I had seen him once before with his mother, father, and older sister. I knew that he had an eight-year-old brother in the pediatric unit who had leukemia.

He sat silently that day, dressed in a jet-black suit with a white, button-down collar shirt and a thin, black tie. This was 1973. Button-down collars were out: wide ties were in.

"Are you OK?" one in our group asked.

"Yes'm, I'm OK," he replied slowly in a quiet voice. "I'm waitin' on my daddy." He nodded toward the pediatric unit. "He's in there, gettin' my brother's things. My brother died, you know."

"Yes, we know and we're very sorry," my friend said. Actually I hadn't known about his brother's death. Now my heart ached for this boy and his family.

"But it's OK!" he suddenly exclaimed. His eyes grew brighter. "I'll see him again someday. Right now he's in heaven. He's got wings and all that, and he's flying around with the angels."

I smiled at the thought of "wings and all that," but I also marveled at the faith of that young lad. And I wondered about my own faith. From my youth, I had sought a close walk with God. But would my faith hold up if a tragedy such as this occurred in my own life?

The answer would come on another spring day five years later.

Again I found myself in a metropolitan hospital, but not in the role of nurse. This time I was about to embark on an exciting new role, that of mother. In the opening minutes of a new day,

I gave birth to our first-born child, a son. Overwhelming joy flooded through me.

Then the joy abruptly plummeted as I realized our baby had a bluish tint to his skin. He was limp and unresponsive. I didn't need my nursing experience to know that something was terribly wrong.

The doctor took the baby to one side. I knew that he and the nurses were working with our son. My husband, Chuck, tried to sound reassuring as I asked repeatedly, "Is the baby all right?"

After seemingly endless moments, our son revived and became stable enough to be moved to the newborn intensive care unit. A nurse brought him close so I could see him for a few seconds before she whisked him away.

Much of the rest of the night is a blur in my memory. Excitement, concern, and confusion wrestled in my mind as I lay alone in the darkened room.

Morning finally dawned. Dr. Pfanstiel, our pediatrician, came in.

"I think your baby will be all right," he announced.

The word "think" stuck in my mind. That meant a possibility our son would not be all right. He might die.

Later that morning, Chuck and I visited our baby, but we could not hold him. I wanted to at least touch our son, to reassure him. But as I reached out and gently stroked his tiny foot, he cried and became jittery. I quickly withdrew my hand. We learned that this irritability was the result of an infection.

Day slowly evaporated into night, and Dr. Pfanstiel returned, this time with a definite prognosis. Our son could not live more than a few hours. The infection had been too much for his tiny body.

Chuck held me and asked, "Can't I still hope just a little?"

Something inside me seemed to say the time for hope was past; it was time to accept our son's impending death. Yet this was an acceptance born not out of despair but out of peace.

A few hours later, our son died. I was finally allowed to hold our baby, or at least to hold his body. The nurse wrapped him snugly in a baby blanket and laid his little form gently in my arms.

Now the tears came. I had never felt this kind of love before, the love a mother has for her child. Nor had I ever felt such sorrow. A piercing ache throbbed deep inside me. I now understood what was meant by "a broken heart."

Yet, through the tears and the pain, God gave me peace and strength.

At some point during that day, the memory of a small boy in a hospital stairwell had slipped into my mind. Now as I held my son, that little boy's words echoed in my mind. I silently whispered as I looked at our infant son, "It's OK . . . he's with Jesus now . . . and I'll see him again some day."

And it really was OK. Through days to come the sorrow remained real but so did the peace and the strength.

Did this mean then that my faith had been strong enough? I didn't feel it was strong. Instead I felt weak and tired, like a child longing to be held in protective arms. And God did hold me just as, I now believe, He held a little boy years ago. I came to marvel not at the greatness of my faith, but at the greatness of God's love.

There are still times when I begin to fear what the future may hold and to question my ability to face the difficulties that may come my way. Then I remind myself of the valuable lesson I learned from two boys, a little fellow in a hospital stairway, and the life and death of our infant son. I remember that victorious Christian living is based, not on the question of how strong my faith is, but on the statement of how strong my Father is.

—Cora Lee Pless

The Healing of a Heart

Not all gifts arrive wrapped in colorful paper and tied up with a fluffy bow. Some gifts, especially those from God, can come so carefully disguised that they are easy to miss. Dan received just such a gift.

The first time I met Dan he was sitting across the table from me at a grief support group meeting where I was the leader. An attractive man in his early thirties, he sat hunched over the table, leaning on his hands which covered his face. A circle of sadness seemed to surround him as he avoided eye contact and sighed deeply.

We began with introductions like we always did, with each member stating their first name and their loss. We went around the table until it was Dan's turn. He lifted his head and with eyes misted over with pain said, "I'm Dan. My wife was murdered three months ago." The tightness in his voice revealed the lump in his throat that made it difficult for him to speak. The woman next to me let out a little gasp and then a hush filled the room.

I had been leading grief support groups for almost six years and thought I had heard everything. I was wrong. The story Dan told was one where greed turned to violence; the details were grue-some. In the months ahead I sent many a quick prayer heaven-ward, knowing I was helpless to ease Dan's pain without Divine intervention.

Each week when it was Dan's turn to share, he would open his heart and pour out his pain. He and Barbara had been married for less than a year. They were still honeymooners, looking for-ward to a long, happy life together. But their time together had come to an abrupt halt. In a swift second, all their hopes and dreams were ripped apart, not by accident, but purposely by another human being.

Whenever Dan mentioned his wife's murderer, Robert (name changed), his entire demeanor would change to one of anger and contempt. With fists clenched tightly and eyes flashing with rage, Dan would talk about the details of the day he found his wife's mutilated body. As Dan spoke about the murder, I noticed that he never called Robert by name, but rather referred to him in one word obscenities, as the venom spewed forth from his very soul.

My sessions always include at least one meeting when we discuss anger and one when we cover the importance of forgiveness. However, with this particular group, I knew it was senseless to ask Dan to forgive Barbara's murderer. The tried and true solutions I had been using successfully for six years sounded trite in comparison to the anguish Dan was suffering as a result of the brutal way his wife's life had ended. There were no little exercises or human answers that could heal such a deep, gaping wound.

The months went by. I took a summer break, still keeping in contact with Dan on a daily basis. He lived life one day at a time and made as much progress in his grief work as could be expected. Then it was September and I began to plan for a new session. For the first time I would be leading the group under the umbrella of my church, giving me the added opportunity of incorporating prayer into our sessions.

Dan asked if he could assist with the group and because I knew he still needed the support for himself, I eagerly accepted his offer. Dan quickly became an active part of the new group. He began to make some strides in his personal grief work as he reached out to other members. But, still, he wasn't able to set aside the disturbing image of his wife when he had found her, and he continued to seethe with rage toward the person who had so savagely taken her life.

Several weeks into the sessions, Dan announced that the trial was finally beginning. He had been waiting anxiously for vindication. Dan's exact words were, "I hope he fries!" Knowing the coming week would be especially difficult for Dan, we gathered around him and prayed. We prayed for justice to prevail and we prayed for Dan to be strong during the trial. Then, much to my surprise, one member of the group prayed that Dan would find it in his heart to forgive the murderer and receive peace about the entire situation. *Impossible*, I thought.

Nevertheless, all during the following week I felt led to pray that same prayer. One night as I was preparing dinner my telephone rang and it was Dan. I almost didn't recognize his voice.

"I've just had the strangest experience," he said cheerfully. "I was praying, when all of a sudden I heard myself forgiving Robert. I had no intention of doing it; the words just slipped out. And I knew I really meant them. All at once an incredibly calm feeling settled over me as I found myself praying for Robert's salvation!"

I had to smile. What a generous gift Dan had just received from God—a heart filled with peace. *Ask and ye shall receive*, Scripture tells us. To think I had almost forgotten to ask!

Dan has continued to heal, as pleasant memories of Barbara replace the hurtful ones. He still misses her, but the horrible images that were engraved in his mind are slowly fading as he looks toward to the future with hope. Now he smiles at our meetings as he shares his miraculous story of emotional healing and tells others to pray for the impossible.

"If God could do that for me, who knows what else He might do?" he tells everybody in a voice filled with awe.

Watching Dan's metamorphosis and continual progress has made me aware that with God all things *are* truly possible.

—June Cerza Kolf

Balloons of Life

Steve and Peggy Cantrell from St. Louis, Missouri, shared with me this beautiful story of God's grace.

Ryan Christopher Cantrell entered this world two weeks late on October 4, 1985. He did not cry. His hands were clenched into fists and he had problems breathing. Doctors suspected a genetic problem called Trisomy 18. He was not expected to live. However, God had other plans. Ryan did live for eight months and eleven days.

He was a special little boy, teaching his parents so much about life. When he died on Father's Day, 1986, his parents chose to make his funeral a real celebration of his life. In the service they used children's songs they had sung with Ryan, and one hundred balloons surrounded his body. At the grave site, everyone held a balloon. The pastor ended the service with Jesus' words for Lazarus: *Unbind him, and let him go* (John 11:44 NASB). At that moment all the balloons were released.

Peggy said later, "It was the most beautiful June day, and the rush of the winds swept the balloons into the air. Our eyes were transfixed as we watched them travel toward the west and disappear high into the blue sky."

Steve said, "On Labor Day that year, Peggy and I were jogging in the woods next to our home. We discovered a blue balloon caught in a tree near our driveway. We had been feeling especially low that weekend, and felt this balloon was meant for us. We pulled it down and found a card attached. 'God Loves You,' it read and was signed, Jonathan Meier. We were overwhelmed and will never forget this gift of grace."

Steve and Peggy wrote to Jonathan and told him they found his balloon and message. His mother informed them this was the only one found from a special balloon release at their church. As an infant Jonathan was not expected to live either, but was then seven years old.

—Anne S. Grace

He wrote some of the most beautiful music in the history of humanity. Yet his life could not be called beautiful; it was full of tragedy. By the age of ten, both parents had died. He was raised begrudgingly by an older brother who resented another mouth to feed. Even as an adult, his life was difficult. His first wife died after thirteen years of marriage. Of twenty children from two marriages, ten died in infancy, one died in his twenties, and one was mentally retarded. Eventually he went blind and then was paralyzed from a stroke. Yet he wrote music, great music—music of profound praise, thunderous thanksgiving, and awe-filling adoration.

Who is this victim of so much tragedy? Johann Sebastian Bach—a Lutheran and perhaps the world's greatest composer of church music. Perhaps it was because of the depths of tragedy that he also knew the heights of faith and praise.

So when we seem to be in the deepest depths of despair, look up for the Lord is going to bless us and others.

Let Go of the Loss

About six months after my husband Harold died, a spiritual counselor said to me, "You've been through a long, dark tunnel. You're coming out into the light now, and you're going to find yourself on the edge of a cliff. You need to throw yourself off the cliff and trust that God will catch you."

While I believed him at a profound level, I didn't know how I was to throw myself off this metaphorical cliff. Soon after, I was traveling in Vancouver and somehow lost my journal—the record of my deepest struggles and emotions during the preceding six months. I felt as if I had lost part of myself. Then I realized that God was saying, "This is one way you can abandon yourself to Me. You can let go of your journal and say, 'I give it to you.'" It wasn't easy, but I said "Yes" to God right at that moment. I knew I had no alternative. I had to be willing to let my journal go.

Later that afternoon, a friend was driving along the same busy street in Vancouver when she noticed a notebook lying in a puddle. She stopped to pick it up and saw my name and address on the cover. She returned the journal to me that same afternoon.

In this process of relinquishment, God gave me back what He knew was important to me. But the critical lesson I learned was not to cling so tightly to my losses. Almost every loss is balanced by a corresponding gain in another area. If we are willing to let go of a loss, God will give back to us what we have let go, with an additional sense of himself being personally involved in our lives.

—Luci Shaw

My Miracle Tape

In the afternoon of August 1, 1973, my son, Tim called me from Whitehorse, in the Yukon Territory of northwestern Canada. He was on the way home after spending the summer with his friend, Ron, in Alaska. To my surprise, he began telling me about the wonderful things God was doing in his life. I could hardly believe my ears because, while Tim had always gone along with his Christian upbringing, there had been no light, no fire, no excitement. Now he was on the phone telling me he had a spring in his step and a sparkle in his eye, and he'd be home in five days to tell me what happened that summer in a church he attended in Anchorage.

That night at dinner, while I was telling the rest of the family about Tim's call, the phone rang. It was the Royal Canadian Mounted Police with the news that Tim and Ron had been killed instantly when a three-ton truck driven by a drunk teenager crossed the center line just outside of Whitehorse and crumpled Tim's little Volkswagen like papier-mache.

I went through the identical emotions that I experienced when my son, Steven, died in Viet Nam. I was plunged again into shock and denial. At first I churned with what felt like a knife in my chest. Later, I burned with anger, railing at God for allowing the unthinkable to happen. ANOTHER son taken . . . ANOTHER deposit in heaven . . . wasn't ONE enough?

Again, tears were a blessed relief for me. I didn't deny Tim's death as much as I had Steven's, but I did burn more vehemently because Tim had died so needlessly, so pointlessly, so carelessly.

We buried Tim on August 12, 1973, five years to the day after we buried Steven. Among the speakers at the memorial service, which was attended by several hundred people, was one of the pastors from the Anchorage church Tim and Ron had attended that summer. He told about the dynamic change in the boys' lives and how they gave public testimony of that change at a baptism he officiated. As I listened, I thought, *How I wish I could have been there to hear Tim share his faith and then see him baptized.*

Two months later, around the middle of October, my husband, Bill, and I journeyed to Whitehorse to pick up some of Tim's personal belongings that were salvaged from his car. We also went to the very spot on the highway where he and Ron were ushered into God's presence. Then we flew to Anchorage to visit the church they attended all summer.

Everyone treated us graciously, and a woman on the church staff gave us a tour of the building that included a tape library with *thousands* of tapes. She explained that the church makes a tape of every service and when there's not much to do during long Alaskan winters, folks watch the tapes for entertainment. Some folks can't get to church regularly, but when they do come in from the hinter lands, they often take several tapes back home with them. Not only does the church make tapes of all the services, but many folks bring their own recorders to tape the music or the preaching. In Alaska they like to say that folks aren't bookworms; they're *tapeworms!*

After seeing all these tapes, I asked what any mother would: "Do you have the tape of the night Tim was baptized and gave his testimony?" Sadly, she said she was sorry but the service that night had not been taped. She explained that the man who operated the tape-recording equipment was baptized that night, and no one else knew how to push the buttons!

Coming home from Alaska I felt dejected and that God had surely negated me. Of the thousands of tapes this church recorded, they missed the night Tim gave his testimony. How unfair and cruel could God be?

On December 14, my birthday, a small package came in the mail. It had no return address, but the postmark said Nome, Alaska. I opened the package and found no letter or note, only a well-worn cassette tape that looked as if it had been watched a hundred times. Curious, I put the unlabeled cassette into a videocassette recorder, and in a few seconds I heard Tim's excited voice.

"My name is Tim Johnson, and I'm third in the group that came up from California. Funny, we were headed for South America. I don't know how we got here but . . . uh . . . the Lord works in miraculous ways. Praise the Lord! I'm glad He did.

"I was brought up in a Christian home and Christian schools, but after graduation I departed and went my own way. It wasn't until last December that a friend sat down with me and showed me the real way to the Lord—*the true way.* I was 'on fire' for a couple of months, and then I just fell by the wayside.

"It wasn't until I came to Alaska that things really started happening in my life. Since then, I have a smile on my face, and everyone looks at me like I must have been a sour lemon before. But now it's different, and I'm thankful that I'm here today. Thanks be to God."

The next sound I heard were splashes as Tim was plunged beneath the waters of baptism. As he came up out of the water, I could hear his triumphant words, "Praise the Lord!"

I sat there, stunned. This was the kid who would get embarrassed if we took him to Knott's Berry Farm for his birthday and sang to him. This was the kid whose idea of fun was bringing home funeral bows from the mortuary where he worked and tying them on our pets. This was the kid we had to bribe with a new set of tires to get him to go to Bible conferences.

This was definitely a MIRACLE!

How the tape found its way into our home was a miracle too, and it proves God does work in wonderful ways through His people. Later, I learned from the church in Anchorage that one of their members, a bush pilot, heard about my request for a tape of Tim's baptism service. I'm not sure what bush pilots do (I guess they fly around the bushes a lot), but as this pilot made his many trips into the back country, he began asking folks if anyone taped the service the night the boys were baptized.

Finally, he found a fisherman from Nome who visited the church that night and taped the service. Now I know Nome isn't the end of the world, but I am sure you can see the end of the world from there! The bush pilot asked the fisherman to send the tape to me at my home, which he did. It was the best birthday present I could have asked for. It was, indeed, my MIRACLE TAPE.

That tape was played many times during that Christmas season. The tears would roll down my face, but they were tears of joy. In some strange way, listening to Tim's voice helped me accept what had happened. I saw again that God specialized in bringing triumph out of tragedy and joy out of pain. Problems won't disappear because you pretend they don't exist. Your utter helplessness will not magically vanish. Accepting what happens is a vital step to grabbing that rope in the dark that becomes your lifeline.

—Barbara Johnson

The Death of a Saint

The last statements of dying men provide an excellent study for those who are looking for realism in the face of death.

Matthew Henry—"Sin is bitter. I bless God I have inward supports."

Martin Luther—"Our God is the God from whom cometh salvation: God is the Lord by whom we escape death."

John Knox—"Live in Christ, live in Christ, and the flesh need not fear death."

John Wesley—"The best of all is, God is with us. Farewell! Farewell!"

Richard Baxter—"I have pain; but I have peace. I have peace."

William Carey, the missionary—"When I am gone, speak less of Dr. Carey and more of Dr. Carey's Savior."

Adoniram Judson—"I am not tired of my work, neither am I tired of the world; yet when Christ calls me home, I shall go with the gladness of a boy bounding away from school."

How different is the story of the Christian who has confessed his sin and by faith received Jesus Christ as his personal Savior! For many years Dr. Effie Jane Wheeler taught English literature where I attended college. Dr. Wheeler was noted for her piety as well as for her knowledge of the subjects she taught. In May of 1949, on Memorial Day, Dr. Wheeler wrote the following letter to Dr. Edman, then president of the college, her colleagues, and former students:

"I greatly appreciate the moment in chapel that may be given to reading this, for before you leave for the summer I should like to have you know the truth about me as I learned it myself only last Friday. My doctor at last has given what has been his real diagnosis of my illness for weeks—an inoperable case of cancer. Now if he had been a Christian he wouldn't have been so dilatory or shaken, for he would have known, as you and I do, that life or death is equally welcome when we live in the will and presence of the Lord. If the Lord has chosen me to go to Him soon, I go gladly. Please do not give a moment's grief for me. I do not say a cold goodbye but rather a warm Auf Wiedersehen till I see you again—in the blessed land where I may be allowed to draw aside a curtain when you enter. With a heart full of love for every individual of you. (Signed) Effie Jane Wheeler."

Just two weeks after writing this letter, Dr. Wheeler entered the presence of her Savior, who had kept His promise to take the sting out of death.

In one mail we received four letters. One was from a ninety-four-year-old saint, eager to be with her Lord; one from a woman on Death Row who, since becoming a Christian six years ago, can now look beyond her approaching execution to the glory that lies ahead; and two letters from women whose husbands had just died after many years of marriage (one just short of their forty-ninth wedding anniversary). Each is looking beyond death to the glory that lies ahead.

The great Dwight L. Moody on his deathbed said: "This is my triumph; this is my coronation day! It is glorious!"

—**Billy Graham**

The Source Of All Comfort

The traditional vows we exchanged forty-eight years ago resounded in my mind. We promised to love, honor and cherish one another until death do us part; the two of us had long ago become one. "For better or worse" became more intense than the rhythms of the respirator, or the bell bonging on the monitor in the Intensive Care Unit when Rick's blood pressure spiked to dangerous heights.

When one is suffering, two feel the pain. He'd been in ICU for a month—seven weeks in the hospital over all—with ARDS (Adult Respiratory Distress Syndrome), a devastating lung disease. The respirator tube pulsated oxygen through his mouth into his lungs but he couldn't talk or verbalize emotions.

By 7 p.m., when I'd planned to leave, Rick had grown anxious and restless, although his vital signs were fairly stable. Suddenly, those dull brown eyes shot wide open with a look of terror, darting about as one trapped with no means of escape!

This terror in his eyes ripped at my heart! What more could I do or say? Rick loved the Lord. He knew where he'd spend eternity, and I never felt he feared death, but it's the dying that's terrible.

I ached to hold my lifetime sweetheart close, but the hospital bed and an array of tubes cruelly held us apart. My mind raced to connect his emotions with meaningful times. I played a victorious tape from Promise Keepers, asking him to envision a year ago, when he and his sons and 52,000 other men stood up for God in Anaheim Stadium.

Looking directly into Rick's wild eyes, I assured him, "Jesus knows your heart. Whatever it is; pain in your body, heart or soul, anger, fear—Jesus understands. He is our rock. And Jesus Christ, as He endured the agony of the cross, became our great high priest, He knows what your physical pain and anguish feels like."

The terror he couldn't verbalize and I couldn't comprehend, God understood. The Lord drew my eyes to a picture of Jesus I'd taped to the wall. Our Savior stood smiling with outstretched arms, inviting us to *Come to me, all who are weary and heavy laden, and I will give you rest.* (Matthew 11:28 NASB)

I urged, "Whatever you're feeling—cry out to Him. Tell Him where you hurt. Scream it out from the depths of your heart. Release it . . . you have somewhere to go with your emotions. Jesus understands them all . . . take it all to Him."

Fear, pain, whatever troubled him melted into peacefulness before my eyes. Within a few minutes, Rick slept peacefully. Exhausted, I slipped out of the room, my heart overflowing with bittersweet joy.

From that night until Rick's graduation day into eternal life three weeks later, that terrible expression of terror never returned. In the meantime, although he was unable to speak, I believe he shared the most intimate conversations he'd ever known with the Savior.

—Lila Peiffer

A Message from Our Son

It was July 4, 1986, three months after our baby, Jared, joined Jesus. My husband, Chris, and I were thankful for the ten-and-a-half months we had shared with our precious son.

We decided to go to Laguna Beach, California, for the Independence Day celebrations. After watching the sparkles and rainbow of colors from the fireworks display, we walked arm in arm down Pacific Coast Highway. We looked into a gift shop window and decided to go in. Strolling the aisles I noticed a little T-shirt about the size of a man's wallet, and imprinted on it was "World's Greatest Son." It looked like it would fit Jared's little teddy bear that rests on our headboard. Jared would hold his tiny teddy bear for hours in the crook of his arm. Sometimes he'd grab at the pink nose, almost pulling it off.

After buying the T-shirt, we walked out onto the busy sidewalk and clung to each other, trying to fill the void of where our son used to be. I was feeling heavy-hearted like someone had attached a steel anchor to my chest. As we turned toward the street, I saw a silver heart-shaped helium balloon floating in front of us. Chris grabbed for the ribbon dangling beneath the balloon but it twisted away just out of his reach as if it were teasing him. I grabbed Chris' arm, pulling him back from the street, as he continued to reach for the balloon. The balloon seemed to hang for minutes just outside of his grasp, in the flow of traffic.

Then the balloon slowly turned its face towards us, and as it did so, we were able to read the message. Still holding onto each other, we stared incredulously as we read the message out loud, "I Love Mom." As soon as the words were out of our mouths, the balloon began to rise silently into the heavens.

—**Dr. Lorrie Boyd**

The Day the Blue Star Turned to Gold

It was the time of World War II, and my Papa and Mama were getting ready to leave for church. The red, white and blue service flag with four blue stars hung proudly in the window of the front door. The stars represented two sons-in-law and two sons serving in the U.S. Army and Navy. Vernley would soon be sent to the North Africa Campaign and Wesley was somewhere on the high seas serving in the Navy.

Papa turned slowly in his chair. Was that a timid knock at the door? He opened the door to see a uniformed young fellow quickly shove a yellow envelope into Papa's trembling hand and run away. Mama was now at his side as they read together the heart rending words, "From the United States War Department. We regret to inform you that your son, Wesley Jens Illum, is reported missing in action."

The same love that had cradled them close in conception, bearing, training and letting their children go their separate ways now held Hans and Lilly Illum tightly, molding them together in their agonizing sorrow. After a time of tears, they dropped together on their knees there by the door to worship and give thanks to the Lord for being so good to them to have allowed them the privilege of enjoying this beloved son for twenty-six years. They sent telegrams to the other children and went on to church.

Teenager as I was and "baby" of the seven children, my response to this traumatic experience proved to be dramatically different. Wesley was my friend, my pal, my confidante, my advisor and to say the least, my ideal of manhood.

When the dreadful message reached me, I was visiting relatives deep in the mountains of West Virginia. My sister-in-law and I were returning from a visit with my brother Vernley, who was stationed at Camp Lee, Virginia. It was breakfast time at Uncle Sofus and Aunt Emmas' in their cozy home nestled in this quaint little village.

We walked in the door and I thought, "Why is everyone so serious?"

Struggling for the right words, Uncle Sofus spoke compassionately, "Vonnie, Wesley is reported missing in action." His words had not escaped his lips until I was on my feet with an anguished cry. Suddenly the most terrifying feeling enveloped me. It was like an iron mesh cage was trying to hold me in it's clutches. I ran out of the house and found myself running up the road, the only available exit. When all my energy had been expended, I slumped gasping and sobbing convulsively by the side of the road.

And there He was! God was there! He spoke so gently. Words I had read many times but had never committed to memory. *I will lift up my eyes to the hills. From whence comes my help?* (Psalm 121;1 NKJV) My help comes from the Lord!"

He was holding me. Through foggy vision, I looked up at the mountains which had seemed so strange to this Iowa farm girl during my visit. Yet, now they brought peace.

Satisfaction surrounded me, not like a captors' cage, but as a warm, compassionate, loving Heavenly Father. The One who made the mountains. A Man of Sorrows, was acquainted with grief—even my grief.

Some time after learning of Wesley's death, I received his last letter to me. He referred to Psalm 121, the same passage that God had brought to my mind in that moment of comfort. He wrote, "It is my comfort in my blue moments."

Some months later we received word from two of Wesley's Christian buddies who had survived. They related dreadful details of that disastrous night. He also told of the last prayer he heard Wesley pray the night before: "How I praise God that I know Thee and am ready."

A second telegram was delivered a year later from the U.S. War Department which declared Wesley officially dead. We all knew he was eternally alive.

Regretfully, Papa was convinced that a public memorial service would not be a good thing for the family and friends after a year of not knowing. My first visit to the Pacific ocean several years later was my personal memorial service. I stood there alone on the beach, bitter tears streaming from my eyes, a repulsion toward the ocean overwhelming me. It seemed to represent to me only a watery grave.

Then suddenly God was there and spoke to my heart, "The ocean did not steal Wesley from you. I knew Wesley needed heaven so I took him home." What blessed, clean resignation and peace came over me as He continued to whisper in my heart above the roar of the ocean: "And the millions who sleep in the mighty silent deep soon will reign on this earth once more."

—Lavon Illum Swink

The only survivor of a shipwreck washed up on a small uninhabited island. He cried out to God to save him, and every day he scanned the horizon for help, but none seemed forthcoming.

Exhausted, he eventually managed to build a rough hut and put his few possessions in it. But then one day, after hunting for food, he arrived home to find his little hut in flames, the smoke rolling up to the sky. The worst had happened; he was stung with grief.

Early the next day, though, a ship drew near the island and rescued him.

"How did you know I was here?" he asked the crew.

"We saw your smoke signal," they replied.

Though it may not seem so now, your present difficulty may be instrumental to your future happiness.

—John Yates

Love

*And now these three remain: faith, hope and love. But the
greatest of these is love.*

1 Corinthians 13:13 NIV

My Father's Example

Every household has unwritten rules. Our family was no exception. Our biggest unwritten rule was, "Dad doesn't do dishes." Dad would mow the lawn until sweat soaked his clothes. He would wade in the disgusting filth of a basement filled with stopped-up sewage. He would build us a treehouse so sturdy that it remained intact when the tree toppled. He would cultivate a large garden from plowing to picking. He would cheerfully chauffeur us around town and wake up an hour early to take us to before-school activities . . . and he'd wait on us after school. He continually sacrificed for us . . . doing nearly anything we asked. But as if the rule was engraved in stone, we knew never to expect dad to do the dishes.

Mom and dad have continued to love and support us as we have grown up. And since I bought a "fix-up" house, dad has put on many different hats to help me. A new door, no problem. Helping build a garage? Sure. Fixing the fence so the dog can't climb it, taking my cats to get spayed while I was at work, wrapping water pipes, designing and building utility shelves, painting, sanding? He's taken it all in stride.

I've truly appreciated all that and have been thankful for dad's wisdom and help. Instead of feeling guilty for "putting him out," I'm learning to accept his help as what it is—a gift of love.

However, one night a special gift surpassed anything I could have ever expected. I hadn't been at home much for several weeks. And when I was in the house, I spent every waking moment on writing assignments. As a result, my house had hit the tornado stage—complete with a mammoth pile of unwashed dishes. I promised myself I'd get to them soon . . . and I tried. But I didn't.

After a particularly tough day at the office, I dragged into my house, automatically turned on my computer, and went to the kitchen for a cup of coffee to perk me up. Suddenly, something caught my eye. My dishrack was full . . . of clean, shining dishes.

I figured mom had been there. I called her to thank her for being an angel. "I didn't do them," she revealed. "Your father did."

When I put down the phone, my eyes started watering. That mental stone engraved, "Dad doesn't do dishes" crumbled before my eyes. A small sacrifice on dad's part? Most people would think so. But I felt, for my dad, it was a real expression of love.

Each time I think of this non-verbal "I love you" I say a quick prayer, asking God to help me show that same ultimate selflessness someday when I have kids. And I'm encouraged to sacrifice just a bit more for the people around me.

—Jeanette D. Gardner

Believe What God Believes About You

Overcoming negative feelings, whether they stem from child-hood or a current situation, will take time and effort, but change is possible. The main step you must take in this process is to accept what your heavenly Father believes about you. Christian psychologist, Dr. Dick Dickerson, has written a paraphrase of 1 Corinthians 13 which beautifully summarizes how God looks at you. Read this passage aloud to yourself every morning and evening for the next month, then evaluate how your feelings about yourself have changed:

Because God Loves me, He is slow to lose patience with me.

Because God loves me, He takes the circumstances of my life and uses them in a constructive way for my growth.

Because God loves me, He does not treat me as an object to be possessed and manipulated.

Because God loves me, He has no need to impress me with how great and powerful He is because He is God. Nor does He belittle me as His child in order to show me how important He is.

Because God loves me, He is for me. He wants to see me mature and develop in His love.

Because God loves me, He does not send down His wrath on every little mistake I make of which there are many.

Because God loves me, He does not keep score of all my sins and then beat me over the head with them whenever He gets a chance.

Because God loves me, He is deeply grieved when I do not walk in the ways that please Him, because He sees this as evidence that I don't trust Him and love Him as I should.

Because God loves me, He rejoices when I experience His power and strength and stand up under the pressure of life for His Name's sake.

Because God loves me, He keeps working patiently with me even when I feel like giving up and can't see why He doesn't give up with me, too.

Because God loves me, He keeps on trusting me when at times I don't even trust myself.

Because God loves me, He never says there is no hope for me, rather, He patiently works with me, loves me and disciplines me in such a way that it is hard for me to understand the depth of His concern for me.

Because God loves me, He never forsakes me even though many of my friends might.

—H. Norman Wright

Seeds of Hope

I have been a sales representative in the gift industry for over thirteen years. My job provides me with many opportunities to witness to others. I absolutely "love" seeing the way the Lord changes lives from the inside out. However, sometimes we do not see the results of the seeds we plant.

One day I was on my way to a sales call to a store which is close to my home. (This particular call is one I look forward to because the owner, Pat, and I have become close friends over the years. We usually set our appointments before the shop opens so we can catch up on each others' lives.) After arriving at the store we began our usual visit, but were interrupted when two men stood at the door motioning they wanted to talk to us.

Pat opened the door and politely asked them to come in. The older man explained that they were searching for a special item for a funeral that was to take place in two hours. He held in his hand a carved and painted wooden watermelon slice which was a reproduction of a piece of Americana Folk Art. He told us that he desperately needed to purchase a duplicate. He had given this particular watermelon slice to his fiancee while she was in the hospital. She took great comfort in seeing it on her bedside table because it reminded her of him and his devotion to her. His voice began to crack and he began to cry, explaining further that she had died two days previous. He wanted to put one watermelon slice in her coffin and keep one for himself to continually remind him of their love. He became so distraught that Pat and I found ourselves wiping tears from our eyes.

Pat had sold out of that item the week before. When she told him, he began crying all the more.

"I have a Folk Art collection of watermelons at home," I exclaimed, "and I will be more than happy to drive home and get one of them for you."

The man's countenance completely changed as though I had offered him the cure for all of his pain. He slowly walked over, hugged and thanked me over and over again.

During my short drive home, I became overwhelmed with pity at this man's plight and his apparent hopelessness. (I couldn't help but feel grateful for the endless hope we have as Christians, not a hopeless end.)

I suddenly remembered the "booklet!" Ironically, just two days before, I was in one of my "let's get organized" moods, and decided to clean out a big drawer in our den. I came across a great booklet Charles Swindoll had written entitled, *Destiny*, which explains the Gospel. Had I not had my "let's get organized" mood, I would never have thought of the booklet, much less known where to find it. I immediately knew what a coveted opportunity I had to share this booklet that could provide hope to this grief-stricken man.

A short time later I arrived back at the store. The older gentleman was sitting in a chair with his head in his hands. The younger man was at the back of the store talking quietly to Pat. I walked over to the seated man and softly touched his shoulder. As he looked up I said, "Here's the watermelon slice. I would like to give you this because it will bring you comfort." He got up, took both items from me and once again thanked me enthusiastically. He motioned to the young man and the two of them walked slowly out of the store, got into the car, and drove away.

For several seconds Pat and I stood there in silence, numb with compassion for this man. Pat then shared how the younger man had explained that his friend's fiancee had recently been diagnosed with terminal cancer. Rather than facing the gruesome treatments, she ended her life by hanging herself. Her fiancee had found her!

As Pat and I talked about the opportunity the Lord had given us that morning, I said, "The Lord asks us to simply sow the seed, and today it was watermelon seeds."

—**Judy Hampton**

Caught Speeding

My spirits were soaring as I propelled my '72 Vega south along the interstate. I had just completed my junior year at college and was heading home for the summer. My thoughts were racing as I anticipated the summer break, which would be followed by my senior year and then—graduation! Everything seemed right with my world—until I turned off the interstate and was pulled over by a policeman.

"Did you realize you were speeding back there?"

"No, sir," I answered honestly as I fumbled for my driver's license. Moments later, I drove away with a ticket on the seat beside me. I inched my way out of the city and along the county roads that wound toward home. My speed had dropped and so had my spirits. Suddenly life didn't seem so promising. Neither did going home.

The thing I dreaded most was having to tell my dad. He had warned me that if I didn't drive more carefully I'd get a speeding ticket one day. I could already hear his lengthy lecture, complete with "I told you so."

Then an idea exploded. I was 21 years old. An adult with my own car. Why should I tell my parents about the speeding ticket? I could sneak into town one day and pay the fine. No one would ever have to know.

That's what I decided to do. But strangely, I didn't feel better.

When I finally arrived home, Mom's greeting turned into a question, "What's the matter?"

"Nothing," I shrugged. Her look told me she didn't believe me.

My parents decided to visit my aunt that day, and I went along on the ride that took us into the next county. I don't remember anything that happened at my aunt's that afternoon. The speeding ticket had become all-pervasive, weighing on my mind with greater and greater force.

Eventually, we started home. Dad was driving with Mom sitting beside him. I sat in the back seat, alone with my ticket. Finally, I gathered my courage and blurted out, "I got a speeding ticket today!"

Mom wheeled around and, with a sigh of relief, exclaimed, "So that's what's been bothering you."

Now it was Dad's turn.

"Why, everyone gets a speeding ticket once in a while," he said.

That was it? That was the lecture I had dreaded? Yes, that was it. With those words, Dad assured me of his forgiveness. The great weight I had been carrying lifted.

No one mentioned the ticket again until the next morning. I was getting ready to go with our church youth on an outing when Dad asked, "What did you do with your speeding ticket?"

"It's in my billfold."

"Don't you think you ought to leave it here? You might lose it," he advised.

"Oh, Daddy!" I exclaimed. He was treating me like a child. Even if I lost the ticket, I was sure the officer had filed a copy.

Later, Mom explained why Dad wanted me to leave the ticket. He had planned to take it and pay the fine for me!

I had dreaded a reprimand from Dad and instead received understanding. Now, not only had he forgiven me, he was also willing to take it on himself to pay the fine I owed. I had always known Daddy loved me, but now I saw his love in a tangible way.

—Cora Lee Pless

Serving More Than Sandwiches

On April 19th, 1995, the bomb blast at the Alfred P. Murrah building changed Oklahoma City forever. And on that day Chris Whitney's life was forever altered. Not because of what she lost, but because of what she gave.

The sixty-seven-year-old widow was on her way to a ladies brunch when her car radio announced the tragedy taking place in the heart of Oklahoma City. Her city. "I knew I had to do something," Chris says.

As food service director at the First Christian Church since 1981, Chris knew the value of ministering from the kitchen. She called her minister. With the help of the church staff she delivered 200 sandwiches, and fruit and drinks to the rescue workers. Within an hour of that delivery, the church, about three miles from the sight, opened its doors as headquarters for the Red Cross.

"The families began coming in to bring in their forms of identification for the victims of the blast," Chris says. The First Christian Church dining room became the center of activity. "The families were notified there of any findings," Chris adds, her voice cracking. "It was a common occurrence to walk through the dining room and have someone reach out and say they needed a hug or ask you if you needed one. We came to be an extended family." Chris paused to wipe tears.

Within a few short hours, Chris had found herself at the heart of the crisis. She was no longer just handing out sandwiches and coffee, but hugs and tissues to go with them. "I was there in case the families reached out to me, otherwise I gave them their privacy," she says. "My main job was to encourage them to eat and drink." It was much more than a job to Chris, it was her way of fulfilling the commitment of her church—"Church of tomorrow with the Gospel of Love."

More than anything, Chris wanted to show God's love and extend His comfort. And she did. Along with volunteers, Chris served from 300–500 people—breakfast, lunch, dinner, snacks, cold drinks, and coffee. "We not only fed the families, we served workers from the Red Cross, the National Guard, the Salvation Army, and others," she says.

"I discovered that my biscuits and sausage and gravy was a favorite, especially among the workers, so I fixed it every morning," she adds, remembering a poignant experience.

"The first full day after the bombing a man came in and wanted to help me with breakfast. He made the coffee, poured milk and such," Chris says and pauses. "I worked with him all day and into the night before I realized that he was waiting for word of his son." Fighting back the tears again, she adds, "He didn't make it."

Chris was so much more than the cook—she was a friend to all who needed one. Many of those serving on the medical teams were young students who enjoyed her generous doses of hugs and words of encouragement.

"I didn't do any more than anyone else would have done," she insists. "It was just an extension of what I do." An extension indeed! Chris accompanied the families on their trip to view the lifeless sight of the bombed-out shell. She shared so much more than sandwiches and biscuits and gravy, for seventeen days she lived and shared the gospel of love.

—Mona Gansberg Hodgson

Believing God for the Impossible

Perhaps the most dramatic example of proper thinking, speaking, and doing came to my attention through "The 700 Club." It involved Leslie, May, and Joe Lemke and an extraordinary true-life story of love.

The story began in 1952 when May, a nurse-governess with a reputation for unusual ability with children, was asked to take care of a six-month-old baby named Leslie, who was retarded, had cerebral palsy, and whose eyes had been removed because they were diseased. Leslie was not expected to live long.

The Lord gave May a great love for Leslie, and she began to treat him like a normal baby. She taught him to feed from a nursing bottle by making loud sucking noises against his cheek. Soon she gave up everything else to take care of the child. "I have a job to do for Jesus now," she said, "and I'm going to do it."

By the time he was ten, Leslie could move only a hand and friends advised May that she was wasting her time. But she refused to concede. "I'm doing something for an innocent boy who will be something some day," she said. "I believe in God, and He will do it."

She carried the boy around and spoke her love into his ear, holding him and squeezing him, continuing to treat him like a normal child. Eventually he learned to stand by holding onto a fence and then to walk by following it.

Throughout it all, May prayed constantly for Leslie. Before long, she added a thought to her petitions, repeating it to the Lord several times a day: "Dear Lord, the Bible says you gave each of us a talent. Please help me find the talent in this poor boy who lies there most of the day and does nothing."

May noticed that the boy seemed to respond to musical sounds like the plucking of a string or a cord. So she and her husband,

Joe, bought a piano, and she played him all kinds of music, using the radio and records. Leslie listened for hours, seemingly in deep concentration.

After four years of praying for the boy's "talent" to be revealed, May and Joe were awakened at 3:00 AM one night by the sound of piano music. They found Leslie sitting at the piano playing beautifully, like a trained musician. He was sixteen-years-old.

Over the next ten years, the boy learned dozens of songs—classical, popular, jazz—and has even learned to sing with his playing. His talent was fully manifested through May's constant love and confession that nothing is impossible with God. She discerned God's purpose and spoke it into being, thoroughly rejecting negativism.

—**Pat Robertson**

Come Home

The practice of using earthly happenings to clarify heavenly truths is no easy task. Yet, occasionally one comes across a story, legend, or fable that conveys a message as accurately as a hundred sermons and with 10 times the creativity. Such is the case with the following reading. I heard it told first by a Brazilian preacher in Sao Paulo. And though I've shared it countless times, with each telling I am newly warmed and reassured by its message.

The small house was simple but adequate. It consisted of one large room on a dusty street. Its red-tiled roof was one of many in this poor neighborhood on the skirts of the Brazilian village. It was a comfortable home. Maria and her daughter, Christina, had done what they could to add color to the gray walls and warmth to the hard dirt floor: an old calendar, a faded photograph of a relative, a wooden crucifix. The furnishings were modest: a pallet on either side of the room, a washbasin, and a wood-burning stove.

Maria's husband had died when Christina was an infant. The young mother, stubbornly refusing opportunities to remarry, got a job and set out to raise her young daughter. And now, fifteen years later, the worst years were over. Though Maria's salary as a maid afforded few luxuries, it was reliable and it did provide food and clothing. Now Christina was old enough to get a job to help out.

Some said Christina got her independence from her mother. She recoiled at the traditional idea of marrying young and raising a family. Not that she couldn't have had her pick of husbands. Her olive skin and brown eyes kept a steady stream of prospects at her door. She had an infectious way of throwing her head back and filling the room with laughter. She also had that rare magic some women have that makes every man feel like a king just being near them. But it was her spirited curiosity that made her keep all the men at arm's length.

She spoke often of going to the city. She dreamed of trading her dusty neighborhood for exciting avenues and city life. Just the thought of this horrified her mother. Maria was always quick to remind Christina of the harshness of the streets. "People don't know you there. Jobs are scarce and the life is cruel. And besides, if you went there, what would you do for a living?"

Maria knew exactly what Christina would do, or would *have* to do for a living. That's why her heart broke when she awoke one morning to find her daughter's bed empty. Maria knew immediately where her daughter had gone. She also knew immediately what she must do to find her. She quickly threw some clothes in a bag, gathered up all her money, and ran out of the house.

On her way to the bus stop she entered a drugstore to get one last thing. Pictures. She sat in the photograph booth, closed the curtain, and spent all she could on pictures of herself. With her purse full of small black-and-white photos, she boarded the next bus to Rio de Janeiro.

She knew Christina had no way of earning money. She also knew that her daughter was too stubborn to give up. When pride meets hunger, a human will do things that before were unthinkable. Knowing this, Maria began her search. Bars, hotels, nightclubs, any place with the reputation for streetwalkers or prostitutes. She went to them all. And at each place she left her picture—taped on a bathroom mirror, tacked to a hotel bulletin board, fastened to a corner phone booth. And on the back of each photo she wrote a note.

It wasn't too long before both the money and the pictures ran out, and Maria had to go home. The weary mother wept as the bus began its long journey back to her small village.

It was a few weeks later that young Christina descended the hotel stairs. Her young face was tired. Her brown eyes no longer danced with youth but spoke of pain and fear. Her laughter was broken. Her dream had become a nightmare. A thousand times over she had longed to trade these countless beds for her secure pallet. Yet the little village was too far away.

As Christina reached the bottom of the stairs, her eyes noticed a familiar face. She looked again, and there on the lobby mirror was a small picture of her mother. Christina's eyes burned and her throat tightened as she walked across the room and removed the small photo. Written on the back was this compelling invitation. "Whatever you have done, whatever you have become, it doesn't matter. Please come home."

She did.

—Max Lucado

Hoping for Good News

Rhonda, a 16-year-old high school junior, was the only one of Nancy's three who was a "problem child." She would rebel against her parents' rules, arguing and generally keeping things in an uproar when she was home, though she never got in trouble with the law.

One Friday night, she didn't come home following the football game, and it was way past her curfew. Nancy called the home of the girlfriend who had picked Rhonda up that evening. The girls were not there, causing both sets of parents to spend a sleepless night.

On Saturday morning they called the police to report the girls missing and the car stolen. For three days and nights Nancy and her husband Rick barely slept. In the daytime Rick drove around town searching while Nancy stayed close to the phone hoping for news . . . hoping, praying, and drinking dozens of cups of coffee.

On the fourth day Rhonda called. "Mom, I'm coming home, okay?" she asked.

"Yes, yes, come home," Nancy cried. "Where are you?"

"In Pensacola."

"Are you all right?"

"Oh yeah, we're fine. We've been sleeping in the car."

"Please be careful—I'll be waiting for you," Nancy said.

Several hours later Rhonda came in the front door. Nancy gasped when she saw her: matted hair, wrinkled clothes, and bleary eyes. "Honey, we were so worried about you!" It was all she could manage to say as she grabbed her daughter and hugged her.

Nancy fought anger boiling up within her. "I should be glad she's home, but she doesn't act as if she's done anything wrong," she fumed silently.

That evening they read that a man suspected of murdering several Florida college girls had been arrested just two blocks from where Rhonda and her girlfriend had been sleeping in their car the previous night. Nancy's anger was tempered by that bit of news. And she rejoiced for God's protection over her daughter.

Lord, How Can I Love Her?

But there was still the matter of forgiving Rhonda. In church the following Sunday, Nancy talked to God about her feelings.

"I don't even like Rhonda," she admitted to the Lord. "She's not pleasant to be around. The house is always in turmoil when she's home. She doesn't seem to care that she put us through so much anxiety by running away from home. Lord, how can I love her, let alone forgive her?"

The Holy Spirit's response was almost immediate. In her honest desperation, Nancy opened her heart to God and He turned back the clock in her mind to see Rhonda—apron wrapped about her waist—standing on a chair to dry dishes. Then she saw a flash of her bundled up with coat and mittens on a winter day, standing in the snow beside the laundry basket, handing Mom her brother's diapers to hang. She had been so lovable then! She saw her in the second grade bringing home a valentine with her picture on it that showed her grin with a missing front tooth. As the memories paraded through her mind, her heart softened. She remembered how much she'd loved Rhonda.

"Lord, restore that love to me," she prayed. "In the restoring of that love, I know forgiveness will come."

As she prayed, God sovereignly flooded her heart with love for Rhonda. Instant love—almost more than she could contain.

"Not only did I love her, I even liked her again. I immediately forgave her, and asked God to forgive me, too," Nancy told me.

Rhonda was one prodigal who returned without any significant sign of repentance, though she seemed glad to be back in the shelter of a loving home. But she continued doing dare-devil things that kept her parents anxious all through her senior year. She went away to college, where she changed majors three times.

Eventually she graduated and moved to another city, where she has a well-paying job.

"I look back to that Sunday in church when I asked God to renew my love for her," Nancy said. "From that day, I was able to respond to her with genuine love and forgiveness. Somewhere along the way, that love melted her heart. Now when she comes to visit us she is a loving, caring, appreciative daughter. During one visit she said, 'Mom, I really put you through a lot in my teenage years, didn't I? And I never said I was sorry. Please forgive me.' At last the forgiveness went full circle!"

Love and forgiveness. They make quite a team.

—Quin Sherrer with Ruthanne Garlock

A Special Kind of Love

I had a lot of hatred in my life. It wasn't something outwardly manifested, but there was a kind of inward grinding. I was (disgusted) with people, with things, with issues. Like so many other people, I was insecure. Every time I met someone different from me, he became a threat to me.

But I hated one man more than anyone else in the world. My father. I hated his guts. To me he was the town alcoholic. If you're from a small town and one of your parents is an alcoholic, you know what I'm talking about. Everybody knows. My friends would come to high school and make jokes about my father being downtown. They didn't think it bothered me. I was like other people, laughing on the outside, but let me tell you, I was crying on the inside. I'd go out in the barn and see my mother beaten so badly she couldn't get up, lying in the manure behind the cows. When we had friends over, I would take my father out, tie him up in the barn, and park the car up around the silo. We would tell our friends he'd had to go somewhere. I don't think anyone could have hated anyone more than I hated my father.

After I made my decision for Christ—maybe five months later—a love from God through Jesus Christ entered my life and was so strong it took that hatred and turned it upside down. I was able to look my father squarely in the eyes and say, "Dad, I love you." And I really meant it. After some of the things I'd done, that shook him up.

When I transferred to a private university I was in a serious car accident. My neck in traction, I was taken home. I'll never forget my father coming into my room. He asked me, "Son, how can you love a father like me?" I said, "Dad, six months ago I despised you." Then I shared with him my conclusions about Jesus Christ: "Dad, I let Christ come into my life. I can't explain it completely but as a result of that relationship I've found the capacity to love and accept not only you, but other people just the way they are."

Forty-five minutes later, one of the greatest thrills of my life occurred. Somebody in my own family, someone who knew me so well I couldn't pull the wool over his eyes, said to me, "Son, if God can do in my life what I've seen Him do in yours, then I want to give Him the opportunity." Right there my father prayed with me and trusted Christ.

—Josh McDowell

Unlikely Places

In 1975 our four-year-old Justin was in the hospital recovering from a severe asthma attack. We had planned to spend a traditional family Christmas at home, but as it turned out our young son was one of the few patients in the children's ward who was just too ill to be released. Despite our carefully laid plans, it was clear we would not be home for the holidays.

The whole hospital experience had been painful—for Justin and myself. I felt sorry for him. Instead of sitting on Santa's knee sharing his Christmas wish, or hanging his stocking on the mantelpiece, there he was on Christmas eve day—stuck in a drab hospital, hooked up to an IV and caged by an oxygen tent.

With no friends in town (we were newcomers), the hospital is a lonely place to be at Christmastime. I was disappointed that my own last-minute plans for cookie baking and package-wrapping had been spoiled. And I missed our eighteen-month-old son, Chris, who was at home with Dad in our family room which, when we left for the hospital, had been all aglow with twinkling lights, gaily colored felt stockings all hung in a row, and shining candles.

Justin and I gazed for hours at monotonous gray walls, faded cowboy curtains, and drab construction paper bells left over from Christmases past. I felt angry and frustrated, yet didn't want to show it. I needed to help keep Justin's spirits up until we could get him back home. My husband's family had decided we would all postpone Christmas until the day Justin returned home from the hospital. Until then, they said, we would act as if Christmas hadn't yet arrived.

While we had expected to put Christmas off, God had other plans, and was to use this experience to teach us the true meaning of Christmas.

On Christmas Eve, a man brightly dressed as Santa Claus came bounding down the hall and delivered a cowboy hat to Justin that was just his size. As I watched the man continue down the hall delivering presents, I asked the nurse, "Did some organization send this gift as a yearly project?"

"Oh, no," she replied. "Three years ago a mom and dad's only daughter, three years old, died in this ward on Christmas Eve. Now, each year the parents find out the exact size or need of each child, and have the gifts delivered by Santa so they can remain anonymous. They know what it's like to be here."

While I was pondering this act of kindness, two little Campfire girls brought in a handmade white felt mitten ornament decorated with holly, and presented it to Justin. "Merry Christmas" they chimed as they continued happily down the hall.

Hardly had their words faded away when a family of Mexican-American carolers arrived. Gaily dressed in red and green native costumes, guitars in hand, they sang "Silent Night" to us and concluded their carol-singing with "Joy to the World." (And we were going to "put off Christmas!")

Next a big University of Oklahoma football player in his varsity jersey strolled in and began to chat with Justin. An avid football fan, Justin couldn't believe that a "real live" gridiron hero had come to see him. Justin was all the more amazed and delighted when the burly athlete produced a surprise gift for him.

"A cowboy rifle and spurs!" he exclaimed. "They go with the hat!" The coincidence took my breath away.

The next day, Christmas morning, a tall, thin, shabbily-dressed man quietly entered the room and sat on the edge of Justin's bed. Like a character from a Dickens' novel, his clothes were tattered and worn. Without a word, he took out an old flute and began to play a lovely Christmas medley. One carol blended into another as the simplicity of each song took on a beauty beyond any I had ever known. Finishing his serenade like the little drummer boy, he handed Justin a small cup full of tiny red candies. Then with a smile, he slipped out the door.

Slowly, but clearly, I began to realize that none of the people who had shared their love and gifts with us knew us or had even told us their names. We had done nothing to earn or deserve their gifts. While my own hurts from the past had created a cold barrier around my heart, these simple acts of kindness had caused the walls of neglected feelings to come tumbling down.

That lonely hospital, with its drab walls lined with construction paper bells, had become a place of God's healing and reconciling love. Away from family, friends, and our baby son, without our tree or traditions, God had delivered to us His special Christmas gift. The loneliest and darkest of places had been filled with the presence of angels and the brightest of lights.

—**Cheri Fuller**

Warring in the War Zone

I'd always thought that the only way to fight the Devil was with fervent prayer and fasting . . . until the day a troubleshooting apartment manager by the name of Bob approached our church asking for help. His life was threatened on an average of ten times a day, as drugs and violence were rampant in his complex.

My extremely evangelistic friend, Barbara, jumped with joy at this opportunity. She mapped out a summer schedule so there was an event every two weeks for the entire summer. By enlisting the help of two other churches and our whole church here in Rialto, California, all the dates were covered.

Enthusiasm was high with the first four crusades, but as the program progressed into the hot summer months, the volunteers dwindled down to just Barb and me. Now, I wasn't the peppy, wide-eyed evangelist Barb was, but I had just read in Isaiah that the chosen fast of the Lord was to loose the bands of wickedness, undo heavy burdens, let the oppressed go free, and break every yoke. These apartment complex people were definitely in that category. The apartments were a war zone.

I put on my army fatigues, an old army hat with a peach rose glue-gunned to it, and lead the children in Christian war songs. "We're not afraid of the enemy!" we'd sing. I also wiped runny noses, washed dirty hands and faces and passed out the food goodies. The kids loved Sergeant Celeste. In the later weeks, I'd bring clothes and shoes to the ones with needs. People who use drugs are usually up all night and sleep all day. They sleep while their children fend for themselves and most often lock the little ones out of the apartment.

Barb had scheduled a clown party with lots of food one weekday afternoon. I arrived before Barb and noticed several police cars at one of the gated entrances. I leaped out of my van and asked a man standing near what happened.

"Jus' had a gun battle," he said slowly, "No one hurt though."

"I should just go home, where it's safe," I muttered to myself. "Barb will understand. We really shouldn't be here right now, anyway."

Right then, I felt a tug on my uniform fatigues. A boy of four stood looking up at me with his dirty face. I knew this one had asked Jesus into his heart the first week of the crusades.

"You're the *Jesus* people, aren't you?" he asked excitedly. I suddenly became aware of the children running all over the crime scene.

"Yes, I am," I tried to sound confident. "What are you doing out here right after a shooting?"

"There's always shootin' here," he offered.

Barbs' truck jerked into the slot next to mine.

"Barb, we've got to get these kids into an apartment, quick!" I called out to her. "They could've just been shot!"

The manager lead us to an apartment so we could begin setting up the food and decorations. I was filling Barb in on the situation while we unpacked, when a woman ran screaming right behind our room with the manager and security close on her heels.

"That's it, we're leaving," Barb blurted out, "It's too crazy around here." I quickly began packing up.

A knock on the door caught our attention. We opened it to find more than twenty-five children outside, lined up, waiting for their party. Barb looked at me and shrugged her shoulders. How could we leave them?

Barb called, "Give us five more minutes to get ready!"

By the time we'd gone through this scenario several times because of increasing danger, I mumbled, "This is the last time I pack without leaving."

The clown party took place as the sun set over the brown rooftops of the apartments. I did my singing routine, Barb's daughter did her clown tricks, and Barb taught about Jesus and the Holy Spirit. While the enemy raged without, we prayed and played within. Three children and one mom gave their hearts to Jesus that day. I'd almost missed it.

Some time later, Bob, the apartment manager, returned to our church to share with the congregation what an impact our presence had in those apartments. The death threats against his life ceased and the drug trafficking had come to a stand-still. He was being transferred to another troubled apartment duplex, but his parting words were, "I'll always remember that you were truly the *Jesus People*."

—**Celeste Duckworth**

It was unseasonably warm that day, even for sunny Los Angeles. Everybody was looking for some kind of relief, so the Ice Cream Store was a natural stop.

A little girl, clutching her money tightly in her hand, came into the store. But before she could say a word, the very sharp featured clerk told her to go back outside and read the sign, and stay out until she put on some shoes. She left, and a big man followed her out of the store.

I watched as she stood in front of the store and read the sign: No Bare Feet. Then tears started to roll down her cheeks as she turned and started to walk away. Just then the big man called to her and she stopped. Sitting down on the curb, he took off his number 12 shoes, and set them in front of the girl saying, "Here, you won't be able to walk in these, but if you sort of slide along you can get your ice cream cone." Then he lifted the little girl up, and set her feet into the shoes. "Take your time," he said, "I get tired moving them around, and it'll feel good to just sit here and rest for awhile."

The shining eyes of the little girl could not be missed as she ordered her ice cream cone.

He was a big man, all right. Big belly, big feet, but most of all, he had a big heart.

A Child Like Me

"Open your eyes," Lynne exclaimed excitedly. I could hardly contain myself. Lynne had been working on this gift for quite some time and everything Lynne did was so breathtakingly beautiful. I loved beautiful things!

I could hardly believe my eyes. There before me was a graceful four-feet high hand-painted ceramic carousel horse, standing tall and stately as if signifying royalty. "She is beautiful, simply beautiful," I groped for words. I had always wanted a carousel horse but never dreamed I would have one as lovely as this: painted with the colors of mauve, dusty rose, and cream.

Lynn had masterfully woven a dusty rose ribbon from the top of the white carousel pole to the bottom, tying off the ribbon with a huge bow. Around the horse's neck was a garland of baby's breath. Her eyes were done in a sky blue almost as if to match mine. I felt a sense of satisfaction every time I looked at her.

Two years later on a Sunday morning, I was busy getting ready for our worship service, when I saw my daughter, Tina, and my eight-year-old nephew Joey coming toward me. Joey is the pride of my life: cute, charming, and witty, and I quickly noticed that he was hanging his head.

"Aunt Pat, I didn't mean to." His eyes were now filled with tears, "I didn't mean to break your horse."

My eyes were now filling with tears with the realization of what he was saying. "You, you what? Joey!"

"Adam and me, we were playing catch and the ball . . . I'm sorry."

"But Joey, don't you know you're not supposed to throw balls in the house?" I said, trying to restrain myself. I wanted to spank him, reprimand him, ask him what kind of parents he had that allowed little boys to throw balls in the house.

But in that moment the Lord spoke to my heart, reminding me gently of when my children were little and how I am a child in my Father's eyes.

I looked at Joey in his humanity and drew him into my lap. Holding him close to me I wiped the tears from his eyes, gave him a big hug and said, "Joey, it's okay, we'll talk about this after church." Giving him a big kiss I scooted him off my lap and sent him on his way with Tina.

As I watched them walk down the aisle there were tears in my eyes—tears of thankfulness. There was a time when that possession would have been more important to me than the person. God allowed me to see that Joey was far more important than a carousel horse.

Now I keep the broken carousal horse as a reminder that every day God picks me up in His arms and holds me on His lap when I have broken something: a relationship, a trust, a promise. It is then my heavenly Father picks me up, holds me close, and lets me know that everything will be okay. Then He scoots me off His lap and sends me on my way—until the next accident.

—Pat Clary

When Love Sneaks In

During the last 15 years I'd only seen my mother twice. I'd purposely stayed away until I healed enough to control the volcanic anger that had boiled and simmered inside for so many years.

But, finally, I visited her. My first evening there we talked well into the night. I told her how she used to mockingly call me "Little Dub," the nickname for my father who had abandoned us when I was a baby. She would shout at me, "You're no good, you're just like your father." Immediately, she began crying and said, "I'm so sorry I did that to you. I knew I shouldn't have."

I could instantly forgive her because of her remorse and genuine shame. Wanting to release other old ghosts from the past, I invited her to a walk on the beach.

The next day we struggled to walk on the freshly churned sand. As I walked along, I silently begged, "Where do I begin, Lord?"

"Not now, child." He said. "Just keep walking."

Ahead I noticed a snake sunbathing in the sand. Any snake has the power to paralyze my mother with fear—even a harmless one like this. I gently told her to stop walking and in that moment it slithered into the nearby underbrush.

I remembered how afraid I was of snakes when I was three years old. Except I couldn't pronounce the word right; I called them "sneaks." When I'd call Mom into my room in the middle of the night, terrified they were crawling under my sheet, she would straighten out the covers and tuck me back in.

After a few more turns in the difficult sand we made it to the top of the Oregon dunes. I hadn't expected it to be so windy and cold, not as conducive to speaking my mind about the past. I suddenly felt like a child again...afraid to express myself for fear of rejection. I remembered how she'd reduced me to a crumpled piece of trash by a cold, cruel remark or by being back-handed unexpectedly off my chair at the dinner table onto the cold floor, and the devastating blow of allowing a new "Daddy" into our lives as he left soiled handprints all over my innocence. I wanted her to take responsibility for her actions and inactions. Yet I also wanted my mommy to kiss the hurts away so I could go on with my life.

Before I knew it we were back where we began. However, neither of us was sure which trail was the correct one. We parted ways to try to find our way out of the sandy labyrinth. I discovered the trail a few yards ahead and backtracked to find my Mom.

On the crest of the dune I could see her making her way down the steep, sandy slope. "Mom!" I cupped my hands like a megaphone to keep the wind from carrying my words to sea. "Mom, it's a dead end. You can't get out that way."

Her face mirrored her fear and I saw her for the first as a child who needed love, help, and mercy.

"Stay right there!" she cried. "I'll lose my way If I can't see you."

I nodded yes, until I could no longer see her frail body laboring up the unforgiving ledge of sand. Then I ran to her. All I could think of was protecting her and removing her fear.

I heard her before I saw her—breathing in heavy gasps, sliding back with each step. I melted with love when I saw the relief on her face to see me. Together we climbed out of the pit and into the light.

As we continued walking, her following me, I prayed silently, "Lord, am I ever going to release these hurts from the past? I don't want to hurt her. I just want the pain to go away."

"Then let it go." He answered.

"How?" I asked, more confused.

"Give me your hurts and I will make them disappear."

"Okay," I whispered, then slowly began letting the pain and bitterness out. I felt lighter as they crawled away like harmless snakes disappearing into the foliage of His arms.

Turning, I saw my mom carefully placing her feet in my

footprints, following my every step. My eyes filled with tears as I realized I'd been following His footsteps. His love in me was now showing her the way out, too.

As soon as I returned home, I wrote Mom a letter telling her it took a very big person to admit her wrongdoing and how much I loved her. When I was signing the card, the Lord showed me my father's nickname, Dub, spelled backwards is, "Bud." For the first time in my life I had actually experienced being friends with my Mom—we were now "buddies." Now whenever she sends me a note it starts with, "My dear little Bud."

Love conquers all and chases the "sneaks" away.

—Lille Diane Greder

A friend of mine used to work in a small neighborhood dress shop named The Fig Leaf. One Saturday afternoon a little girl came in with her piggy bank and announced she wanted to use all her money to buy her mother a Mother's Day gift. My friend helped her pry all the coins out of the bank and told her she had enough for a nice blouse. Would her mother like that?

"Oh, yes! A blouse would be perfect," responded the child eagerly.

"What size is your mother?" the clerk asked.

"She's the perfect size!" declared the little girl. So my friend sold her a size 34 blouse.

The Monday after Mother's Day the child and her mother returned to exchange the blouse for a size 42. The fashion world's idea of a perfect size and the daughter's idea of perfect were worlds apart! The difference was a heart full of love.

—Nancy L. Dorner

7

Marriage

And be ye kind one to another, tenderhearted, forgiving one another, even as God for Christ's sake hath forgiven you.

Ephesians 4:32

Mirror, Mirror

On our honeymoon, I stepped out of the shower, and while putting on my makeup, verbally criticized my physical attributes. From head to toe, I complained about the way I was put together. I was desperately hoping to get my new husband's attention so he could rescue me from my insecurity about myself!

Bill was lying on the bed admiring God's creation when I began my personal evaluation. Inside he was growing angry. After all, I was criticizing his wife! But instead of reacting in anger, he got up and walked toward me. He wrapped his arms around me and gave me a reassuring hug.

Then he stepped back, took my face in his hands and said, "Pam, let me be your mirror. You are gorgeous! Let me reflect back to you the beautiful woman God has created you to be. If we have to throw all the mirrors in the house away, we will! From now on, I will be your mirror!"

—**Pam Farrel**

Romance Is Dead?

My wife and I had a several-month-long disagreement over her desire to spread her wings. She wanted to return to school and begin work on her writing career. My response was to get angry with her. We still had children who were at home full-time. Pam's dreams were an inconvenience to my life and I didn't like it! I fought her for months before I came to my senses. I realized I wasn't fighting Pam, I was fighting God. He had placed this dream in Pam and I was blocking the dream.

I finally could encourage Pam in her pursuits and wanted to find a way to make up for the grief I had given her. One day, she was in a medieval literature class. The professor was leaning against the chalkboard and had just announced that romance was dead. He pointed out that it was an idealistic fallacy in the middle ages and unobtainable today. A chorus of women in the room agreed. "Yeah, all men are jerks," they resounded.

In the middle of this, I broke into the room unannounced. I walked over to Pam's desk in the middle of the room. I set down a dozen red roses, bent down over her left shoulder, whispered "I love you," gave her a kiss and left the room as quickly as I had come in.

"Is it your birthday?" the startled professor asked Pam.

"No."

"Your anniversary?"

"No."

"Then what's the reason."

"I guess he just wanted me to know he loves me!"

I had fought Pam in a big way as she tried to pursue her dream. I wanted her to know in just as big a way that I believed in her dream.

—Bill Farrel

Easter Threads

It was Easter Sunday morning and we were preparing to go to church. My husband, Barry, was getting dressed in his usual attire—a pair of jeans, cowboy boots and plaid shirt. I began to entertain thoughts of telling him that he should dress up more for church. The more I thought about it, the more barbed the retorts that came to mind. I was working up a pretty good steam when suddenly I came upon the perfect snide remark. This one would really get him. I was all set to say, "Couldn't you do better for God." Oooh, I could see the knife going in and twisting.

Suddenly, I was aware of God's presence. In His still small voice he said, "Have I ever let you down when you've kept your mouth shut?" I winced in astonishment, but there was no doubt what I'd heard in my spirit. If God wanted me to keep my mouth shut, I would, and just see what He had planned.

I didn't have time to argue anyway. I had a Sunday school class waiting and following that I would be playing the piano for church. I gave Barry a quick kiss and left. He still had horses to feed and chores to do before he would leave for church.

An hour later, I sat at the piano playing the prelude as members of the congregation entered the sanctuary. The seats were filling up fast with those extras who only visit once or twice a year. Our little chapel held about seventy- five worshippers and it would be filled to capacity.

Then a hush fell over the congregation. As the double doors opened wide, my cowboy entered—dressed in a three piece western suit, lizard skin boots and a silver-belly Stetson hat. My heart skipped a beat and so did my fingers, and I giggled to myself. I could just hear God chuckling and saying, "See, I never let you down when you keep your mouth shut."

—**Karen Robertson**

The Big Things . . . Like Legos

"I'm ready to move on, if you are . . . I love you," my husband whispered in my ear. He slipped his arm around my shoulder as I leaned against the kitchen counter.

How could I honestly return those words? My wounds were still bleeding from last night's conversation. I still felt misunderstood. I didn't feel love for him. I felt nothing but rejection. The "I'm sorry" I had heard was empty. It was like the "I'm sorry's" I make the children say when they've pushed and shoved, or taken away someone else's toy . . . just words.

As I searched his eyes I wanted to see a look of understanding. I wanted to hear words of affirmation. I wanted to be able to say "I love you," but I couldn't do it. I didn't want to "move on." I wanted to continue the discussion, finish making my point and feel as though he had truly heard me. If he wasn't willing to do that, I wasn't willing to "move on."

From experience I knew this would pass. In a week, I would wonder why I made a big deal over such a little thing. Then I would wonder how I ended up with the most wonderful husband on earth. However, at this moment I wondered what good he was to have around.

My thoughts were interrupted by crying in the children's room. "He took my Legos without asking!" Daniel shouted.

"He wasn't using them and I wanted to build a house," four-year-old Philip replied.

"But they are my new toy." Daniel added, "I don't want him to lose any pieces. Besides he never asked, 'Please' to use them."

I hoped this would be one of those easily solved battles. I couldn't deal with more conflict this morning. My own battle was playing over and over in my mind.

"Oh, Daniel, won't you please let him use the Legos?" I pleaded from the doorway.

"I don't feel like sharing. They're mine and I want them!" Daniel began picking up all the Lego pieces on the floor and snatched the pieces in his brother's hands.

I grabbed hold of Daniel and sat him down on his bed. Hugging his stiff, resistant arms in mine I spoke softly. "Remember the book we were reading last night? Do you remember the words we asked, 'What would Jesus do?'"

The words stung as I heard myself reminding my five-year-old what the book said. "There are times Jesus wants us to give, and even forgive when we don't *feel* like it. Jesus must have a big smile when we do what He wants us to do and He knows it's extra hard for us to do. God knows it would be easy for you to forgive Philip if he took Bun Bun without asking. Your stuffed rabbit isn't that important to you. Why, I bet you could easily 'share' it with him for the rest of the day, maybe even the week. But your Legos . . . that's a different story, isn't it?"

"Yea, Mom," Daniel nodded, "that's a *big* different story!"

"Mom, do grown-ups have *big* things too," he hesitated, "like Legos?"

"Oh, Honey, they sure do. Grown-ups have to ask Jesus to help change their hearts when it comes to *big* things . . . like Legos."

"So, Daniel, what do you think Jesus would do?"

Without hesitation he replied, "He'd forgive Philip and let him use the Legos. He'd probably even help him build the house."

Jumping off my lap, he announced, "I'll tell you what Philip . . . tomorrow you can use my Legos all day."

He picked up the case holding his Legos and walked toward the door. "I'll be right back," he announced, "I need to ask Jesus to help me change my heart for today. This one is too hard to do by myself."

His words moved me from my seat unlike any preacher's words at a revival meeting. As I knelt at his bed, the dark bedspread was dotted with tears. If *my* five-year-old could do something he didn't feel like, so could I. It was my turn. What I needed to do this morning was "just move on" to my knees. I needed this little boy to remind me that "this one was just too hard to do by myself."

"Oh, Lord, it's too hard to 'just move on' when I want to get even. It's too hard when I don't think I've received a *proper* apology, or I feel misunderstood or unappreciated. Oh Lord, if you only knew how I felt."

No sooner had I said those words, than I was embarrassed. Of course, He knew how I felt. More than anyone in the world He knew what it was like to feel misunderstood and unappreciated. Did He not want a *proper* apology from Peter, or to get even with Judas? Jesus forgave the thief as He hung on the cross, even though he didn't deserve it. If He could forgive them, if He could forgive me, how could I not forgive my husband?

"Oh, Lord, forgive my selfishness. I need You to help me forgive. Put Your love back in my heart. Amen."

Moments later Daniel ran back into the room spilling Legos in front of his brother. "Philip, you can use my Legos all day if you want."

What truly changed Daniel's heart that morning? Maybe it was the unexpected knock at the door that held an invitation to play with the neighbors. Of course I'd like to believe he had the same kind of conversation that I'd had with the Lord.

Daniel invited the neighbors in and suddenly there was a trail of children walking through my kitchen to the backyard. My husband's sheepish eyes met mine as he reached for my hand and squeezed it gently. "Honey, looks like you're going to have your hands full. It's a good thing I have to go to work today . . . doesn't look like you need 'another' kid around here!"

Did I just hear an apology? Maybe, maybe not; however, my cold, unyielding heart was now warmed.

"I do love you," I said as I reached to give my husband a hug. "Thanks to a little boy who helped move me to my knees, I am ready to just move on."

— **Jan Northington**

Assess Your Expectations

Recently my daughter, Heidi and I, along with her girlfriend, visited my parents over spring break. When we returned from our long drive home, I subconsciously expected Steve to be waiting for us. I also expected the house to be clean. When I arrived, however, Steve was out fishing. He had cleaned fish in the sink and left a smelly mess in the garbage. There was mud on the kitchen table, and the bed was unmade. Then I found his note: "Hi. Glad you're home. I've gone fishing. I'll be back at dark." I was so disappointed he wasn't home that I immediately flew into a rage and got mad at everybody. That's how disappointment works—expectation turns to disappointment, which turns to anger, which turns to hostile/aggressive behavior. And when disappointment leads us to sin in this way, we need to seek forgiveness for our misplaced anger.

When Steve got home that night, the first thing Heidi said was, "Mom's been mad at you all afternoon." He looked at me with surprise and confusion. Rather than rail against him angrily and irrationally, I said, "You had no idea what I expected, but this is what I thought I would come home to: I expected you to be here waiting to greet me with open arms, and I thought the house would be clean. I missed you."

Had I spent all day thinking, "If he really loved me he could read my mind," as I once did as a newlywed, I would have wallowed in pity and Steve never would have known why. By letting Steve understand my disappointment and how it turned to anger, he and I both learned how detrimental disappointment from unmet expectations can be in a relationship and to our sense of joy."

—Annie Chapman

Encouragement

When I was a senior in college, I came home for Christmas vacation and anticipated a fun-filled fortnight with my two brothers. We were so excited to be together we volunteered to watch the store so that my mother and father could take their first day off in years. The day before my parents went to Boston, my father took me quietly aside to the little den behind the store. The room was so small that it held only a piano and a hide-a-bed couch. In fact, when you pulled the bed out it filled the room and you could sit on the foot of it and play the piano. Father reached behind the old upright and pulled out a cigar box. He opened it and showed me a little pile of newspaper articles. I had read so many Nancy Drew detective stories that I was excited and wide-eyed over the hidden box of clippings.

"What are they?" I asked.

Father replied seriously, "These are articles I've written and some letters to the editor that have been published."

As I began to read, I saw at the bottom of each neatly clipped article the name Walter Chapman, Esquire. "Why didn't you tell me you'd done this?" I asked.

"Because I didn't want your mother to know. She's always told me that since I didn't have much education I shouldn't try to write. I wanted to run for some political office also, but she told me I shouldn't try. I guess she was afraid she'd be embarrassed if I lost. I just wanted to try for the fun of it. I figured I could write without her knowing it, and so I did. When each item would be printed, I'd cut it out and hide it in this box. I knew someday I'd show the box to someone, and it's you."

He watched me as I read over a few of the articles and when I looked up, his big blue eyes were moist. "I guess I tried for something too big this last time."

"Did you write something else?"

"Yes, I sent into our denominational magazine to give some suggestions on how the national nominating committee could be selected more fairly. It's been three months since I sent it in. I guess I tried for something too big."

This was such a new side to my fun-loving father that I didn't quite know what to say, so I tried, "Maybe it'll still come."

"Maybe, but don't hold your breath." Father gave me a little smile and a wink and then closed the cigar box and tucked it into the space behind the piano.

The next morning our parents left on the bus to the Haverhill Depot where they took a train to Boston. Jim, Ron, and I ran the store, and I thought about the box. I'd never known my father liked to write. I didn't tell my brothers; it was a secret between Father and me. "The Mystery of the Hidden Box."

Early that evening I looked out the store window and saw my mother get off the bus—alone. She crossed the Square and walked briskly through the store.

"Where's Dad?" we asked together.

"Your father's dead," she said without a tear.

In disbelief we followed her to the kitchen where she told us they had been walking through the Park Street Subway Station in the midst of crowds of people when Father had fallen to the floor. A nurse bent over him, looked up at Mother and said simply, "He's dead."

Mother had stood by him, stunned, not knowing what to do as people tripped over him in their rush in the subway. A priest said, "I'll call the police," and disappeared. Mother straddled Dad's body for about an hour. Finally an ambulance came and took them both to the city morgue where Mother had to go through his pockets and remove his watch. She'd come back on the train alone and then home on the local bus. Mother told us the shocking tale without shedding a tear. Not showing emotion had always been a matter of discipline and pride for her. We didn't cry either and we took turns waiting on the customers.

One steady patron asked, "Where's the old man tonight?"

"He's dead," I replied.

"Oh, too bad," and he left.

I'd not thought of him as the old man, and I was hurt at the question, but he was seventy-three and Mother was only fifty-three. He'd always been healthy and happy and he'd cared for frail mother without complaint, but now he was gone. No more whistling, no more singing hymns while stocking shelves; the Old Man was gone.

On the morning of the funeral, I sat at the table in the store opening sympathy cards and pasting them in a scrapbook when I noticed the church magazine in the pile. Normally I would never have opened what I viewed as a dull religious publication, but just maybe that secret article might be there—and it was.

I took the magazine to the little den, shut the door, and burst into tears. I'd been brave, but seeing Dad's bold recommendations to the national convention in print was more than I could bear. I read and cried and then I read again. I pulled out the box from behind the piano and under the clippings I found a two-page letter to my father from Henry Cabot Lodge, Sr., thanking him for his campaign suggestions.

I didn't tell anyone about my box; it remained a secret until we closed the store two years later and moved in with Grandma, leaving the piano behind. I gave my last look to the empty kitchen with the old black stove standing staunchly alone while the bottle of kerosene gurgled loudly in the corner. I went quietly to the den, and as if in some religious rite, I reached behind the old piano where I'd practiced lessons and played hymns on Sunday evenings and pulled out the box.

Father left me no money, but he left me the box. He had little education and no degrees, but he gave me and my brothers a love for the English language, a thirst for politics, and an ability to write. Who knows what Father could have done with just a little encouragement?

—**Florence Littauer**

The Broken Christmas Present

I remember the first Christmas present I ever received from my new husband. We were newlyweds in love and didn't have two pennies to rub together. We did all of our shopping at a well-known establishment in Somerset, Kentucky, called BIG K. They were so gracious to give us a line of credit with only 18% interest so we could do our Christmas shopping.

We took turns gift hunting so we wouldn't ruin the element of surprise when we opened our gifts on that magical morning. My turn was first, so after I finished I waited for my husband in the car.

The sun set and the temperature dropped. I could see my breath in the air and I was getting cold. So I kept a close eye on the door. Finally, I spotted him coming out of the store with a shopping cart as full as Santa's sleigh. He even looked a bit like jolly old Saint Nick with a twinkle in his eye and a grin on his face. He maneuvered the cart carefully through the parking lot. His grin turned to disappointment when he hit a speed bump and my present, the glass lamp, went tumbling to the cold hard pavement with a big crash. It broke in two.

We didn't wait until Christmas. That night we glued the lamp back together and it's been in our bedroom ever since. I'm glad we didn't give up and throw it away. For every time I turn the switch on for light it illuminates my memory of a parking lot where two newlyweds shed tears over a little inexpensive lamp and worked side by side in gluing the pieces back together. When all was said and done, we had a wonderful Christmas.

We've hit several speed bumps in our marriage that sent us crashing to our knees. But thank God, He's the glue that mended and held us together over the years, Christmas after Christmas.

—Georgia Curtis Ling

Call It Commitment

For us, the final key to holding on was learning not to panic every time we hit a crisis.

When we are getting along well we say we are *connecting*. When we are connected we love being together, we talk easily and laugh freely, we touch each other naturally and lovingly, we encourage each other, we celebrate each other's uniqueness, we serve each other joyfully, and we tease each other playfully. Connection is the goal of marriage; it is the oneness the Bible talks about. It's wonderful, it's happy, and it's fun.

But we discovered long ago that it takes precious little for us to *disconnect*. Sin, temperament differences, exhaustion, outside pressures, the demands of life—any one or all of these can push us into a way of relating that is anything but wonderful and happy and fun.

Early in our marriage, whenever we disconnected, we panicked. We thought any slip from perfect oneness signaled disaster. We were on the ropes. Divorce was inevitable. We might as well tag the furniture and divvy up the silverware. There was no hope and no turning back. We felt like we were caught in an angry current, destined for a deadly crash on a rocky reef. We always managed to avoid the crash—just in the nick of time—but that didn't lessen our fear of disconnection.

Then one night, during a sensitive discussion of our then current disconnection, we realized that because we both meant our wedding vows, had a spirit of reconciliation, and were willing to plow through the work of conflict resolution, we did not have to panic over disconnection. We did not have to assume we were headed for ruin. We could untag the furniture and put away the silver. We weren't going anywhere. We were *committed* to one another.

That made a tremendous difference to us. We quit thinking of disconnection as a precursor of disaster, and quit predicting gloom and doom. We began to call disconnection the "commitment phase." Instead of focusing on the negative, we reminded one another of the positive: In spite of the difficulty we were facing, we had a rock-solid commitment to one another that would see us through disconnection and back into oneness.

—**Bill and Lynne Hybels**

I'm Learning

Romance was never my strong suit. I proposed to Lynne in her parents' garage; I took my Harley-Davidson on our honeymoon; I thought our best anniversary was the one we spent watching a video of "Rocky III." I had to grow in the gentle art of romance.

So for starters, I figured that meant flowers. Beyond that, I didn't have a clue, but I knew I could get the flower job done. As confirmation from God that I was moving in the right direction, who do you think set up shop out of the trunk of his '58 DeSoto at the corner opposite our church? The flower man!

So, quite regularly, on my way home from work or from meetings, I would pull over to the side of the road, buy a bundle of roses or carnations from the flower man, and take them home to Lynne. What a husband! I thought as I handed over my three bucks.

Yet when I proudly presented these flowers to Lynne, fully expecting her to hire the Marine Corps Band to play "Hail to the Chief," her response was rather lukewarm.

"Gee thanks," she said. "Where'd you get these?"

"Where else? My buddy the flower man—you know, the guy with the '58 DeSoto at Barrington and Algonquin. I'm a volume buyer now. Because I stop there so often he gives me a buck off, and if they're a little wilted, he gives me two bucks off. I figure they'll perk up when you put them in water."

"Of course," she said.

I did that regularly for quite some time—until Lynn's lack of enthusiasm for the gift drained my enthusiasm for the practice.

Some time later, on our regularly scheduled date night, Lynne and I decided to clear the air on anything that might be bothering either of us. We do that now and then. We sit down in a cheap restaurant (not only am I unromantic, I'm also Dutch) and say, "What's going on? Is there anything we need to talk about? Is there anything amiss in our relationship?" On that particular night, Lynne took out her list and started checking off items, and I said, "Ooooh, you're right on that one. Sorry. Eeeh, that one too. Yep. Guilty as charged. Guilty. Guilty. You're right again." She ended her list, and I was in a pile. I said, "I really am sorry. But trust me. I'm going to do better."

She said, "Now, what about you?" I really didn't have any complaints, but after hearing her grocery list, I thought I should say *something*. I scrambled. "Well, I do have one little problem. Have you noticed the absence of flowers lately?"

"No," she said. "I haven't really paid attention." *How could she say that?*

"We have a problem. I can't figure it out. Hundreds of thousands of husbands pass by that corner. Do *they* stop for flowers? No! Do I stop? Yes! Do you play 'Hail to Chief' when I get home? No! What gives? What's your problem?"

Her answer made my head spin. She looked me straight in the eyes and quietly said, "The truth is, Bill, I'm not impressed when you give me half-dead flowers that came out of the trunk of a '58 DeSoto that you were lucky enough to run into on your way home from work. The flowers are cheap and the effort is minimal. The way I see it, you're not investing enough time or energy to warrant a wholehearted response from me. You're not thinking about what would make me happy; you're just doing what's convenient for you."

I said, "Okay, let's get this straight. You would be happier if I got up from my desk in the middle of my busy day, threw my study schedule to the wind, walked all the way across the parking lot, got in my car, and made a special trip to Barrington where I'd have to pay quadruple the price just because it said Barrington on the bag? And you wouldn't mind if the extra time that took would crimp my workout schedule at the Y? (Remember, Lynne, high blood pressure and heart disease run in my family.) And you wouldn't mind if I came home late because of *all* the extra running around I'd have to do to get you *expensive* flowers? Is *that* what you're telling me? *That* would make you happy?"

I was proud of myself. I missed my calling. I should have been a lawyer. The jury would have been spellbound. They would have been thoroughly convinced.

Without batting an eyelash, Lynne said, "Yes, that would make me happy."

I couldn't believe it! "What're you talking about? What you're asking for is neither practical, economical, nor an efficient use of time."

"That's a great definition of romance, Bill. You're learning!"

—Bill Hybels

8

Perseverance

Blessed is the man who perseveres under trial, because when he has stood the test, he will receive the crown of life that God has promised to those who love him.

James 1:12 NIV

The California Supreme Court decided in May that the U.S. Constitution prohibited invocations at commencement exercises. Keeping within the controversial ruling, students at a Riverside County high school in Yuca Valley found a unique way to invoke God's blessing upon their graduation ceremony.

The ceremony proceeded with the typical addresses to the graduation class. Each one was challenging and inspirational but only the one delivered at the end received a standing ovation.

The graduating student walked proudly to the microphone to deliver his address—a sneeze. The entire student body stood to their feet and in unison said, "God bless you." The audience erupted in applause for the blessing that was bestowed upon the 1991 graduating class.

—Tim Wildmon, AFA *Journal*

A little boy was offered the opportunity to select a dog for his birthday present. At the pet store, he was shown a number of puppies. From them he picked one whose tail was wagging furiously. When he was asked why he selected that particular dog, the little boy said, " I wanted the one with the happy ending." If we want to reach out for a life with a happy ending, we have no choice but to accept the living Christ as our Lord and Savior, follow Him daily, and rejoice in the eternal life that awaits us.

—*Sermons Illustrated*

A Friend's Challenge

Weary from the long road of healing from abuse issues in my background, battered by life's unexpectancies which continually robbed our finances from health, stressed by a job that presented little security and continual change, and restless to find some meaning in my life, I found myself wandering in a spiritual desert.

When a friend challenged me to focus on the good things that had happened in my life, I discarded the thought. It's too unrealistic. But her challenge kept creeping into my mind. I found myself searching the past for inspiration. Nothing really spoke to my heart with any kind of "that's it" revelation. "I just want to get through the tenting of the house for termites and the move of my office at work, and get the dog through his deworming from the annual siege of tapeworms. Then I'll have time to think about it."

The following weekend was the Fourth of July, and it came into our lives with a bang. On Saturday my husband's car ran over something that slashed a hole in his tire, causing a blow out. On Sunday our daughter, who had recently acquired her driver's license, was backed into by a person with no insurance or identification, causing damage to the front of the car we had just paid off this year. On Monday our youngest daughter was sitting with some friends when someone on a bike rode by, tossing a fire cracker into the air. It landed on her, burning through her shorts and into her skin, causing a second-degree burn of a substantial size. Also on Monday, my husband spent the day putting two new tires on both cars, denting once again our limping bank accounts. He had decided to wait to replace the muffler and tailpipe which had broken loose on his car, and the catalytic converter that had begun to rust.

On Tuesday I spent an hour-and-a-half past our appointment time with my daughter in the waiting room of our doctor's office, hoping that the on-call doctor would finally poke his head through the door to see her. On Thursday I walked through the process with the auto insurance claims office to see how much it was going to cost to repair the car. In between, I went to work and tried to dig out of the boxes of materials that had been moved from my old office into the area where I would spend this work year—without having any shelves to store anything.

Yet, my friend's challenge kept nipping at the corners of my mind. "Why can't God allow blessings to drop into our lives with the same frequency as He allows trials?" I asked inwardly as I carefully bandaged our daughter's tender leg. "Be grateful it didn't land on her face or in her eyes," an inward voice seemed to be saying, "and that your husband wasn't on the freeway when his tire blew out, and that your daughter wasn't hurt in the car accident . . ."

Focus. I realized that my wandering in the desert had become an experience much like that of the Israelites. I was crying out for the milk and honey of the Promised Land even though God was providing daily manna. I had found myself looking at the fly speck *on* the window, rather than looking *through* the window to the sights outside. "Why, Lord?" seemed to be more frequent in my vocabulary than "Thank you, Lord." I knew I needed an "attitude adjustment."

I also knew that it wouldn't come overnight, but at least the ship had begun to turn into the waves instead of being engulfed by them. I knew that I must begin reassessing my life, the way I spent my time and energy (like playing less Tetris on the Nintendo and reading more of the Scriptures), much like a ship's captain pours over the ship's logs when he realizes that it has been steered off course. I also knew that I had to be more willing to be open to see God's blessings, no matter how small they seemed, rather than dwelling on the trials.

One thing special about God is that He meets us where we are and effectively leads us forward once again.

—**Christi Anne Sheppeard**

Keeping a Promise

One of the most remarkable stories concerns a man called Robertson McQuilken. As a young man, he dreamed of becoming the president of Columbia Bible College in Columbia, South Carolina. He adored his father, who had held this position, and he aspired to someday take his father's place.

Robertson McQuilken's dream came true. One day he did become the president of Columbia Bible College. When he took that position, he sensed an affirmation and a powerful call from God.

Dr. McQuilken served as president of Columbia Bible College for a number of years and did so with distinction.

Then one day this very special man realized he had a tragedy on his hands. His wife began to show the symptoms of Alzheimer's disease. This was no slow-moving case, and in a matter of months there were dramatic consequences. She not only lost her memory of much of their life together, but she was unable to even recognize him. She lost all awareness that he was her husband.

Robertson McQuilken made his decision. He resigned the presidency of Columbia so he could give full-time care to his wife. Without hesitation he walked away from his calling as an act of love for her.

There were realists who told him there was no point to what he was doing. Anybody could take care of his poor wife, they told him, but not anybody could be president of Columbia Bible College. And after all, she didn't even recognize him when he came into the room to help her.

Then there were pious critics who brought up the fact that he was walking away from a calling from God. He was letting his personal concern for his wife interfere with his service to the Lord, they said.

The man's answers were magnificent. To the realists he readily admitted that his wife didn't know who he was. But that wasn't the point, he told them. *The really important thing was that he still knew who she was* and, furthermore, he let them know that he recognized in her now-forgetful self the same lovely woman he had married those many years ago.

Then he turned to the pious critics. His words to them were even more profound: "There is only one thing more important than a calling. And that is a promise. And I promised to be there for her 'until death do us part.'"

—Tony Campolo

This isn't so bad . . . last year I was Mary's donkey.

Let's See What You Can Do

I carried a registration packet stamped "P.E. Exempt" as I hobbled with a locked-knee gait to the field house of Eastern Washington State College. A little over a year earlier, I was an all-star high school athlete. Now I could barely walk.

I fell half a dozen times before I found the physical education department and my adviser, Dr. Richard Hagelin. I sat down, dropped my Canadian crutch and admitted, "I can't run, jump, do pushups or pull-ups, climb or jump rope. But I want to major in physical education."

I thought he'd tell me to forget it.

I'd always dreamed of becoming a physical education teacher. In high school I played on championship basketball and football teams and also lettered in track and baseball. I had other dreams: playing guitar, learning to fly, marrying a great gal and having brilliant children.

But one hot July night, soon after high school graduation, I came home sick. My neck was stiff and I thought I had the flu. My mother had reason to worry, because the brand-new Salk polio vaccine hadn't reached our small town yet.

I became one of the last polio cases in the nation. Within four and a half days, I couldn't move. As the worst passed, I was left with legs 80 per cent paralyzed; my right arm useless, and a left arm only 50 per cent functional. One doctor told me I'd never walk again.

But I had my family—and my faith. My parents had always taken us to church. When I was about ten I went to the altar of that little church and told the Lord I'd put Him first.

Maybe that's why I really never questioned the Lord or got bitter about polio. I knew He'd help me go on from there. After months of excruciating rehabilitation and several surgeries, I left my wheelchair behind and headed for college.

I'll never forget that critical moment in Dr. Hagelin's office as I laid out my fragile hopes. He didn't hesitate a moment.

"Let's see what you can do," he said.

Several years later I graduated as a teacher with a Masters degree, certified for both elementary and secondary physical education, and landed a job over able-bodied candidates.

In college, I fulfilled a few other dreams. I learned to play guitar despite a useless right arm, got some guys together in a band and played to help pay college expenses.

Then one day in the cafeteria line I noticed a pretty girl. I went up and down the line inquiring who knew her, then asked them to introduce us. I couldn't believe my own boldness! Later I called Judy for a date. When she took me home to meet her mother, I was treated to a steak dinner which ended on the floor when I tried to cut it.

But Judy could overlook those things. A football player she'd been dating remarked of me, "That guy's a cripple." She replied, "He's not crippled when you get to know him."

We were married In 1959 and had three children while I pursued a career in education. I started off as an elementary physical education specialist. I couldn't run and jump with the kids, but I was creative. I used an 18-inch wooden art mannequin named "Woody" to show kids how to tumble or stand on their hands. Teachers throughout the state came to watch my classes.

Dr. Hagelin's encouragement—"Let's see what you can do"— shadowed me as I pursued other dreams. I took flying lessons, was granted a license with no restrictions, and even flew my own plane from Chicago to Seattle. I also flew an ultralight. And I taught myself to play golf with my left arm only, scoring regularly in the 80s on 18-hole courses.

Later I became an elementary principal, determined to make my school a happy, secure place where children could pursue their dreams. We emphasized positives, like honored trips to the office to sign the principals "Good Kids Book." I received several state principal awards. But God was in the midst: every morning I drove around that school, praying for it.

I never knew how my faith would affect people. One time a scared third grader sat in my office. She was transferring from a small private school and had developmental problems. I encouraged her to believe she could succeed in our school.

Nine years later that girl graduated with honors from high school. In a senior essay about her life she'd written, "Mr. Miller encouraged me and taught me to smile and believe in myself."

I remembered I had a person like that in my life. So three decades after college graduation, I wrote Dr. Hagelin to tell him what his affirmation had meant to me. Now retired and going blind, my letter encouraged him! Later, I was able to speak at my alma mater and honor him, and then help him toward his dream of getting a seeing-eye dog.

God used his words many years away. A few words can change a life. Let's see what you can do!

—Dan Miller

I heard about a little girl who experienced a major breakthrough in her life when she learned to tie her own shoes. Instead of excitement, she was overcome by tears.

Her father asked, "Why are you crying?"

"I have to tie my shoes," she said.

"You just learned how. It isn't that hard, is it?"

"I know," she wailed, "but I'm going to have to do it for the rest of my life."

—Heidi Husted

In Pursuit Of Excellence

It was my birthday in 1986. To my surprise, there was no package from my parents: only a card. Feeling somewhat disappointed, I ripped open the card and what I found inside brought tears to my eyes: there was a certificate for the purchase of a set of Choirchimes®, a unique kind of handbells. I felt so ashamed for those moments of thinking that my parents didn't care, yet simultaneously was ecstatic about the possibilities that lay ahead. For many years I had lived with a desire to develop a music ministry for nursing homes. Now that dream could become a reality.

I began to practice every evening after work and several hours on weekends for several months, working hard to develop a small repertoire of songs. Wondering if I was ready, I determined there was only one way to find out. I made a call to a nearby nursing home and scheduled a time to provide a musical program.

In the months that followed I arranged to share my music in at least two or three nursing homes every month. I'd be the first to admit that I wasn't very good, but they loved to have me come anyway. As a perfectionist, the programs were devastating to me, however, I just couldn't dishonor this expensive gift from my parents. Reluctantly I continued sharing the music. It was helpful that the residents in the various nursing homes were accepting and grateful. Little by little my skills and confidence improved. Within a year I was asked to play the chimes during a church service. At first, I just couldn't accept. "I'm not good enough, yet," I kept telling myself. But after repeated invitations, I finally agreed.

Wow, was I ever nervous! Here I was set up at the front of a small church planning to play the offertory and a special number. *Surely I could get through just two songs,* I thought. The time came for my music so I began to play. Initially things went amazingly well and I was pleased that the offertory was actually pretty good. Pride swelled within me. Then it happened: a baby cried and I lost my concentration. For several seconds (they seemed like an eternity) I felt panic-stricken. Somehow I was able to reach deep inside and fumble through the remainder of the song.

"Oh, no, I blew it! I'm such a failure," I berated myself. Deeply disappointed, I resolved that this was not where my music belonged; my place was in nursing homes—this would be my first and last time to play in a church.

After the service a dear lady came rushing over to talk with me. She said, "For several months God has been working on my heart about playing this beautiful organ just sitting on the platform. I have been arguing with Him that I wasn't good enough to play for church. It was evident that you were doing your best and you continued in spite of a major mistake. I know how much I appreciated your music in spite of it. I now realize how much a person can be touched by music even if it's not *perfect!* I'm going to start playing the organ next week. "

I was learning that you didn't always have to be perfect to be effective. In time, I faced doing a program where Dad and Mom would attend. I had created the self-imposed pressure of a perfect program in honor of them. After all, they had provided the chimes as a birthday gift. My performance went well except for one wrong note that no one seemed to notice. Suddenly I felt devastated. On the way home I really had to get tough with myself. I thought, *"You fool, why would you evaluate an entire program based on one wrong note?"*

I made myself literally count every note and realized that I had played more than a thousand notes perfectly.

Do I remain committed to excellence? A resounding yes! Never will I accept less than my best! However, I am no longer shackled to excellence based on perfection but rather on a willingness to maintain an emphasis on touching the lives of others.

—Betty J. Price

Checking on the Job I Already Have

A little boy went into a drug store, reached for a soda carton and pulled it over to the telephone. He climbed onto the carton so that he could reach the buttons on the phone, and proceeded to punch in seven digits. I listened to the following conversation.

He said, "Lady, I want to cut your lawn."

The woman replied, "I already have someone to cut my lawn."

"Lady, I'll cut your lawn for half the price of the person who cuts your lawn now."

The woman responded that she was very satisfied with the person who was presently cutting her lawn.

The little boy found yet more perseverance and offered, "Lady, I'll even sweep your curb and your sidewalk, so on Sunday you will have the prettiest lawn in all of North Palm Beach, Florida."

Again, the woman answered in the negative.

With a smile on his face, the little boy replaced the receiver.

The druggist walked over to the boy and said, "Son, I like your attitude, I like that positive spirit. Son, I would like to offer you a job."

The little boy replied, "No thanks. I was just checking on the job I already have."

—Dr. Eric Scott Kaplan

9

Prayer

Devote yourselves to prayer, being watchful and thankful.

Colossians 4:2 NIV

Two children who were walking to school were afraid lest they would arrive late. One of the two children said to the other, "Let us kneel down and ask God to help us not to be late." The other child, however, who seemed to be more practical about it all, counter-suggested: "I'm going to pray while I'm running so I won't be late. God is going to help me run fast enough so that I won't be late."

God will not do for us what we can do for ourselves, but when we have done our best, He will do the rest.

In a religious midwestern farming community a drought had threatened to ruin the entire season's crop. In a last ditch effort, the local pastor asked the entire community to assemble at one of the farms to pray for rain. The crowd gathered and the pastor rose atop a tractor to address the farmers. He said, "Brothers and sisters, I see that you have all come here today to pray for rain."

"Amen!" responded the crowd.

"Well," said the preacher, "do you think you have sufficient faith?"

"Amen!" the crowd shouted again.

"O.K. I believe you. But this one thing is troubling me."

The farmers were silent, waiting for the preacher's words. "Brothers and sisters, where are your umbrellas?"

Snow Angels

Fresh sparkling snow covered the ground. Our Girl Scout troop from La Mirada, California, was ecstatic at the prospect of spending an entire weekend in the dazzling whiteness. Our troop, its four leaders and their husbands were excited to experience our first winter outing.

Many of us had never seen snow up close and personally like this. The snow motivated the youngsters to run outside and play. They busied themselves with throwing snowballs at one another, building snowmen, and making snow angels (lying on their backs and raising their arms up and down to resemble the outlines of angel wings in the snow.)

We as leader-mothers and our husbands surveyed the accommodations at this temporary location. The spacious cabin had been lent to us for our use by a generous parent. There in the beautiful Crestline mountains, it provided enough space for cozy closeness and a warming shelter. Soon, we sorted out the groceries to be eaten into meal-sized portions: lunch today, dinner tonight, and breakfast for tomorrow morning, and of course, multitudinous snacks.

It was evening before I began to feel a sense of foreboding concerning the weather and our isolation. Snow had begun falling and the wind crashed against the cabin walls. Through a large picture window high in the second story of the cabin, we could make out the branches of a tall tree as it creaked about in the constant blowing of the wind.

This was my first snowstorm. Though I had seen snow on infrequent visits to these mountains, I had never seen it falling before. And fall it did, all night long. Finally, we all dozed off. I slept fitfully because the constant bold gusts of wind made me a little nervous.

In the morning, we sensed the gravity of our situation. The cabin sat beyond the region that the snow plow regularly serviced. On our isolated stretch of the road, the heavy snowfall covered all the cars and the roadway in snowy down quilts, beautiful but chilling.

Even we novices knew there was no way to clear the road. The men dug a path to the cars and uncovered them but we were hopelessly cut off far from the road. We all looked at each other apprehensively. What if? We had enough food for one meal, no more. The thought of being snowbound cast a dreary pall over us.

I, being the only Christian in our little group, began silently to pray for God's providence and for Him to send the snow plow up to our desolate stretch of road. Considering our isolation, the answer to my prayer request would be amazing indeed, but I continued until I felt the sense of peace that only God can give.

Soon others around me expressed anxiety, casting nervous glances at the glowering skies and up the impassable road. The snow kept falling steadily and silently. We busied ourselves cleaning up and packing the snow-cleared cars for our prospective trip downhill. A seemingly short time later, we heard a wonderful sound that happily pierced through the stillness of the falling snow. A heavy equipment plow was chugging up our hill.

The operator told us, "I've never come up this far before, but I kept hearing something in my head that said, 'Go up to the top today.' So here I am."

The word angel means a "messenger sent to carry out the will of God." I have never seen an angel, but I felt the man who drove the snowplow on this errand of mercy was our own personal "snow angel." It was our Heavenly Father who was the real inspiration for this hour—our loving, Heavenly Father who sees and speaks to all our needs with patience and deep caring.

The girls, still playing happily in the bountiful snow, never sensed our anxiety. As the leaders were packing the kitchen supplies, one of them asked me, "I wonder what made the plowman come up this far?"

I simply smiled and said, "I prayed."

—Linda Claire Scott

With Wings As Eagles

I glanced up at the clock above my son's hospital bed. I thought sadly of the painful hours and the many hospital beds Rick had occupied over the past six months. I thought how his life and the lives of our entire family had changed since the day Rick was struck and thrown from his motorcycle by a speeding car.

On the bedside table there was a Little League team picture and close-up photo of Rick's eleven-year-old son, Ricky. Rick and Ricky had laughed and played horseshoes together at a family picnic only the day before the accident, but neither of them were laughing any more.

There was a serious problem with Rick's left leg. The injuries to his shoulder and face had healed leaving only a few scars. But a deep area of missing flesh the size of a silver dollar just above his ankle would not heal.

Twice the doctors had attempted the difficult ten-hour "Muscle Flap" operation where a muscle from the patient's stomach, shoulder or back is grafted over the open wound. Twice the procedure had failed, leaving Rick physically exhausted and emotionally despondent. The doctors were considering amputation if the third muscle flap operation did not work.

"I can't take another operation. I know I'll die on the operating table if they try that operation again," Rick told me over and over again.

My reassuring words did nothing to soothe Rick's fears, and I noticed that even my own positive attitude was beginning to waver. Although I'd been praying for Rick's healing since the day of the accident, I began to feel my prayers were inadequate. I called the prayer group from my church and two other prayer lines to ask for help.

In addition to physical healing, I knew Rick needed a healing of his spirit. Witnesses to the accident had told him it was a miracle he hadn't been killed. During the early part of his recuperation, Rick said he was sure God must have had a reason for sparing his life. But when the two operations on his leg failed, and as the days in the hospital turned into weeks and months, he started believing that perhaps he was meant to die after all.

It seemed that nothing could lift Rick out of his mood of hopelessness and despair. Attempting to cheer him up, his three brothers told jokes and read him the comics. I even tried singing to him, but nothing worked.

Then one day I brought in my Bible and began to read aloud. At first he paid no attention. The next day I tried again. This time I read Isaiah 40:31 *They that wait upon the Lord shall renew their strength. They shall mount up with wings like eagles; they shall run and not be weary; they shall walk and not faint.*

For the first time in a long time, I saw a flicker of interest on Rick's face. I immediately thought of the ceramic eagle I had on my desk at home with that same scripture verse engraved on a plaque on the pedestal base beneath the outstretched wings. The next day I brought my eagle to the hospital and placed it close to Rick's bed.

When I came back to see Rick that evening he seemed to be in a better mood than he had been in a long time. Little by little over the next few days I saw his spirits brighten. I asked his nurses about it and they told me that almost every time any of them entered Rick's room he was reading aloud the verse on the bottom of the eagle statue.

A few days later, Rick unexpectedly informed the doctors he was ready to have the third (and last possible) muscle flap operation on his leg. This time they would use the large muscle from Rick's back. They could not use just a portion of the muscle, but had to use it all, wrapping it around his leg. If the operation was successful, there would be a "debulking" operation several months later to remove the excess muscle after the missing flesh on his leg filled in. If the operation was not successful, well, I couldn't bear to think about that.

There was something different about Rick the day they wheeled him into the operating room. Because this was an unusual operation, there were several extra doctors and medical students there to observe the procedure. Rick greeted them all with cheery confidence. Just before they put the anesthesia mask over his face, he grinned and assured the group, "Don't worry. Everything's going to be fine. God's in charge."

Rick was right. God *was* in charge, and everything went just fine. This time the operation worked. This time his leg did not reject the muscle. Oh, there was terrible pain in his back and leg and sometimes there still is, but Rick has a good life, two legs and an unshakable belief in the power of prayer. He sold his motorcycle and now he collects statues and posters of eagles to remind him of his favorite Bible verse.

—Diana L. James

Is Anyone Listening?

The importance of attentiveness to God's guidance is illustrated by this story about the great Methodist Missionary, Dr. E. Stanley Jones.

Jones spent two weeks each year traveling from city to city in India to raise funds for his Mission. He scheduled three talks each day to prominent citizens in an attempt to gain their financial support. He would address one group at breakfast, a second at lunch, and a third at dinner. The next day he would repeat his appeals to three groups in another city.

One night after his third presentation, he rushed to the airport where he had booked the last flight of the day to his next day's destination. As he stood in line to get his seat assignment, they announced that his flight was oversold and requested that passengers give up their seats in return for an additional free round trip ticket to the city of their choice.

When the agent had finished his announcement, Jones thought he heard the Lord whisper to him, "Step out of the line." He hesitated. If he didn't take this flight he would miss at least two of his meetings the next day—and the money he hoped to raise thereby. He stayed in line.

When he was nearly to the podium he again felt God urging him to step out of line and give up his seat. Again he hesitated, not sure if it was God speaking to him, or only his imagination. But when he was just one person away from the airline agent, he again heard God speak, this time in no uncertain terms: "STEP OUT OF THE LINE!" Jones obeyed and someone else took his place.

That airliner crashed and all aboard were killed. When the media learned that Dr. Jones had not been aboard as scheduled, they rushed to interview him. When told why he had not been aboard the ill-fated flight they were incensed.

"Do you mean to tell us that you were the only one God loved enough to warn?" they asked incredulously.

"Oh no!" came Jones' quick reply. "I don't mean that at all! I know God loved every person aboard that plane at LEAST as much as He loves me. But, you see, I was the only one who was listening."

—Nancy L. Dorner

After praying for everybody she knew, every one of her relatives, and all her pets, the young girl added, "And dear God, take care of Yourself, too. If anything happens to You, we're all sunk!"

Let God Be God

Jim: As they wheeled my daughter, Becki, down the hospital hall toward the emergency room, I just knew they'd be back with her soon. After all, hadn't our church been praying around the clock? Even though God hadn't healed the cancer in her leg yet, wasn't it just like Him to wait until the very last moment? What a tremendous testimony it would be when Dr. Kline told Sally, me, and Becki's sisters, along with the huge group of friends around us, that the tumor had suddenly disappeared.

Hours later, Dr. Kline came out to meet us and he didn't say what I wanted. Instead, he told us they had to amputate Becki's leg. The remaining bone didn't seem to be affected by the cancer so her life was saved, but her leg was gone! She'd never run with it again. What would the people of the church where I pastored think of prayer? How could God have let us down? Oh, Lord, she's only sixteen years old!

I turned to Sally and said, "We need to be very strong now. We'll have to get through this time on our own. It's obvious that God isn't going to help us."

Sally: I was surprised at Jim's comment. God hadn't answered our prayers the way we wanted or had asked, but I knew He would prove Himself faithful. Becki healed quickly and since she still had her tremendously positive view of life, I knew they hadn't amputated her spirit.

Becki: I also had hoped God would give me a miracle, but when He didn't, I knew He would strengthen me. God promises to give me everything I need. If I needed two legs, He wouldn't have taken one away. I was determined to not have a pity party even though it took a lot of energy to go through the process of recuperation and eventually learn to work with my prosthesis.

Jim: As I struggled to work through my doubts, several good friends let me unload. I asked them, "Was God so busy answering somebody's prayer to find a parking place that he didn't have time to heal Becki's leg? How can I possibly go back into the pulpit and teach the Bible as true?" In time I realized I had a choice. Would I let God be God? I finally saw that the only thing I had to fear was isolating myself from Him.

In the weeks after Becki's surgery, I had to admit that prayer is not coming to some giant celestial smorgasbord where I can pick up any goodie I would like. Rather, prayer is my agreement with God, an acknowledgment of who He is and consenting to His purpose in my life, whatever that is. He wants me to grant Him the right to be God, telling Him that I am willing to allow growth to come through pain and problems. My struggle dissipated. Eventually I could say, "O.K., God, I don't understand it, but I trust you to care for all of us. I'll let you be God."

Sally: I was relieved to see Jim dealing with his grief. What helped me most was seeing Becki's response to her loss. One day Becki was roller-skating. She had been skating with a partner, so she wasn't using her crutches. As the music ended, she came rolling off the floor on just her one leg.

A little boy caught sight of her for the first time and exclaimed, "You've lost your leg!"

In fake surprise she replied, "I did? Oh, dear. I'm always losing things. My mother is going to kill me for this. Will you help me hunt for my leg?"

The little boy very earnestly started looking for Becki's other leg. Eventually she led him to her crutches and explained about her missing leg.

I hurt deeply for Becki and the pain she went through after the operation and as she adjusted to life without a leg. But Becki's sense of humor helped me more concretely trust God with the realities of her amputation.

Becki: God has used the loss of my leg to give me a deep compassion for people in pain. I have a degree in recreation therapy and have had the privilege of ministering to many people with disabilities. Plus, He's used me in ways that I never expected.

Several years after the surgery, someone said to me, "Your unembarrassed attitude about your body really helped me accept myself. I'm sort of heavy and I've always been embarrassed about the way my legs look. But when I saw you going around in shorts or a bathing suit, not afraid of your stump showing, it made me realize how ridiculous I was about my imperfect body. Since then, I've been able to accept many things about myself and realize they are part of what makes me unique."

Now, many years later, I'm married to a pastor, Craig Sanders, and we have three active daughters. As a pastor's wife, I do a lot of entertaining and developing women's groups. I run three or four days a week on my crutches, bike, ski, and have my own chair-caning business in my home. God has been gracious to me and I thank Him for His hand upon my life.

—Jim and Sally Conway, Becki Conway Sanders

Copyright 1988
Cowles Syndicate, Inc.

"We asked God to bless this LAST night!"

Reprinted from *COUNT YOUR BLESSINGS* by Bil Keane.

God Had Granted Me the Desire of My Heart

After I woke up in recovery from the surgery that amputated my arm, the first thing I felt was how parched my mouth and throat were. The first thing I heard was the sound of moaning from the patients on either side of me. I looked at the foot of my bed and saw two hazy figures standing there. Were they angels? My eyes came into focus. Almost angels. They were Jan and my mom. And when I blinked my eyes a few times, Dad came into focus. Jan came alongside the bed and put her hand on my forehead. I was a little cold after surgery, and her hand felt warm and soothing as it brushed across my brow.

The next day I tried to get out of bed. I started feeling a little queasy so I lay back down. Then I caught my breath and went to the bathroom. That's where I saw myself for the first time since the surgery, in that little bathroom mirror. I stood there pale and rumpled in my hospital gown, staring at the image that stared back at me—the image of a one-armed man.

I was shocked at how radically they had cut the arm back. The incision started at my neck and went in a diagonal to my underarm area. The arm was gone. The shoulder was gone. The shoulder blade was gone. And the left side of my collarbone was gone.

"Okay, God. This is what I've got to live with. Put this behind me; let me go forward."

And when the one-armed man looked back at me, there was peace in his eyes.

I cleaned myself up a little and took a walk down the hall. The nurse who had administered the anesthesia stopped me.

"I really appreciated your prayer," she said.

I took a step back. "What prayer?" I asked.

"You prayed this beautiful prayer for the doctors and the staff. In fact, you prayed twice."

I was totally blown away. It was one of the things I really wanted to do before I went under, but I had no memory of my doing it. None.

Then she went on to say, "I've heard a lot of people praying for loved ones as they go into surgery, but that was the first time anyone has ever prayed for us."

A couple of days later Dr. Brennan was making his rounds, followed by about six interns and fellows. He took the gauze off my wound and checked the incision, the stitches, the drain. It was a brief visit. When he and the others left, one of them stayed behind. A man named Jim. He told me his parents were missionaries in Mexico. He commented on my prayer in the operating room and how peace seemed to permeate the room.

At that point I realized God had granted me the desire of my heart—to pray for the medical team that would perform the amputation. He let me do it in spite of the anesthesia.

—Dave Dravecky

A Helping Hand

As the rain fell softly upon my window today, I enjoyed taking the opportunity to look through my past yearly engagement calendars on which I write all my activities and coming appointments. They are keepsakes, both for their reference and sentimental value.

On this nostalgic foray through my past, I came upon an entry about the King Tut Exhibit held in the Los Angeles area in 1978. Many years have passed and still this memory is as clear and sharp as if it were yesterday. It had been raining that day as well. Our family had looked forward to attending this exhibit and the tickets to see it were in great demand.

I was determined that we would have the opportunity to see this fine collection of Egyptian artifacts on this once-in-a-lifetime tour of America. I left home that morning as soon as I could to join the others standing in line at our local department store, where the tickets were being offered.

The line wound halfway through the store aisles and was starting out the side door into the adjoining covered mall.

I took my place and waited patiently. After over an hour of standing in line, my turn came to purchase the tickets so I handed the clerk the department store's charge plate.

"I'm sorry," the clerk said, "we don't accept charge cards for these tickets . . . only cash."

I was shocked. I had not brought my checkbook and had only a few dollars on hand. The cost was around twenty dollars for our family of five and there were only a few tickets left for the Saturday date: the only one available that we could all attend together. I was crestfallen. I turned dejectedly away to start back home, empty-handed.

As I began to leave, a young woman behind me said, "Here,

let me pay for your tickets." And she handed me the required cash. I told her that I couldn't let her do that, she didn't even know me.

"No, I want to," she continued. "This is my way of being helpful to people. Please use my money. You can send the money to me later."

I took her offering gratefully and purchased my tickets. Then I wrote down her name and address to enable myself to send her a check, which I did the next day. She wrote a note back to me to tell me a little about herself. She was a special education teacher in our school district and enjoyed opportunities to assist people. She even mentioned she considered it a ministry.

That morning I had prayed that my day would go smoothly and that I would be able to purchase the five tickets. This generous young woman was there, standing behind me for over an hour, ready and willing when the need arose to be God's perfect answer to both my plight and my early morning prayer.

—Linda Claire Scott

Some folks are like the little boy who, when asked by his pastor if he prayed everyday, replied, "No, not everyday. Sometimes I don't want anything."

10

Relationships

With all lowliness and meekness, with longsuffering, forbearing one another in love; Endeavouring to keep the unity of the Spirit in the bond of peace.

Ephesians 4:2,3

Sisters

When my friend, Sadie, was taken to the emergency room at a local hospital, I rushed over to be with her as soon as I received the news.

Sadie was both surprised and pleased to see me. "How did you get them to let you in?" she asked, knowing visitors were not usually allowed in the emergency room.

I, too, had been concerned about that on the drive over. However, I knew Sadie needed a friend to comfort her. In desperation, I had decided if worse came to worst, I would be forced to tell a lie and say I was Sadie's sister. I hoped I wouldn't have to resort to that and I asked the Lord for guidance.

After I explained all this to Sadie, she threw back her head in hearty laughter. While I was trying to figure out why Sadie was laughing, I glanced down at our clasped hands—my very white one held gently between her two black ones.

—June Cerza Kolf

Together is Better

We'd been running every day, but this was something else. We'd been sweating from the time we rolled out of the rack before daybreak, but now moisture drained from every pore in our bodies. Sure, this was the physical training stage of U.S. Army Ranger school, and we expected exertion. Even exhaustion. But this was no morning PT rah-rah run in T-shirts.

We ran in full field uniform. As usual, the word was "You go out together, you stick together, you work as a unit, and you come in together. If you don't come in together, don't bother to come in!"

Somewhere along the way, through a fog of pain, thirst, and fatigue, my brain registered something strange about our formation. Two rows ahead of me, I noticed one of the guys out of sync. A big, rawboned redhead named Sanderson. His legs were pumping, but he was out of step with the rest of us. Then his head began to loll from side to side. This guy was struggling. Close to losing it.

Without missing a step, the Ranger on Sanderson's right reached over and took the distressed man's rifle. Now one of the Rangers was packing two weapons. His own and Sanderson's. The big redhead did better for a time. But then, while the platoon kept moving, his jaw became slack, his eyes glazed and his legs pushed like pistons. Soon his head began to sway again.

This time, the ranger on the left reached over, removed Sanderson's helmet, tucked it under his own arm, and continued to run. All systems go. Our boots thudded along the dirt trail in heavy unison. Tromp-tromp-tromp-tromp-tromp-tromp.

Sanderson was hurting. Really hurting. He was buckling, going down. But no. Two soldiers behind him lifted the pack off his back, each taking a shoulder strap in his free hand. Sanderson gathered his remaining strength. Squared his shoulders. And the platoon continued to run. All the way to the finish line.

We left together. We returned together. And all of us were the stronger for it.

Together is better.

—Stu Weber

We are each of us angels with only one wing, and we can only fly by embracing each other.

—Luciano de Crescenzo

Accountability

Back in 1987, our Colorado University football team was preparing to go to Norman, Oklahoma, to play the Sooners. They were the top-ranked team in the country and coming home to play after being on the road. In addition, our C.U. team was extremely young. For as long as anyone could remember, the Sooners had intimidated Colorado not only with their talent, but also with their downright offensive demeanor. Colorado had become a cakewalk for them. They had won 13 of the previous 14 head-to-head matchups and had averaged more than 40 points a game in doing it. Colorado was one of the big reasons Oklahoma was turning out All-Americans and Heisman Trophy winners!

Clearly, we needed to try a new approach. I had to find some way to motivate my players to give the performance of their lives. I finally decided to issue a challenge based on their word as young men. On the Thursday night before the game, I laid this on them: "Men," I said, "no one is getting on that plane for the trip to Norman until he has looked me in the eye and told me what I can expect of him in Saturday's game." The next morning, I set aside three hours and met individually in my office with the 60 players who would be making the trip. Three minutes each; that's all it took.

As I summoned each young man into my office and had him sit down across from me, I'd look at him and say, "Now, son, I want to know what I can expect from you when we go to Norman to play Oklahoma."

Each one looked me squarely in the eye and said something like, "Coach, you can count on me to play every down to the best of my ability. I'll play my heart out against Oklahoma." Then, depending on his position, each player added, "I'll block better than I've ever blocked before. I'll tackle with more author-ity. I'll run with precision and strength."

I'd tell each man, "I'm going to hold you to your word," then add that I wanted him to be positive and excited so his team-mates would pick up on that attitude.

Having set the tone with those meetings, the team that boarded that plane was on a mission. I knew that collectively, those 60 players would spend themselves in a valiant effort. I didn't know if we could win, but I knew we wouldn't lose because of a lack of effort. Those young men would play their hearts out—and they did.

The game was contested at night and nationally televised on ESPN, so I realized that a lot of the high school players we were trying to recruit around the country would be watching. And what they saw, before the night was over, was that we would no longer lay down for O.U.! We did, indeed, spend ourselves, trailing by just four points at half-time, though we eventually lost 24–6. But the good news was that each of us knew he had given himself for the team. Each player kept his promise and extended himself. We had taken a significant step forward as a team.

If that kind of dynamic exists in a man's word to a football coach, how much more is it at work when men gather in Jesus' name, look each other squarely in the eyes, and say what can be expected of them? When that happens, there's an unleashing of God's Spirit, an outpouring of His grace and strength.

—**Bill McCartney**

A Mandate for Mentoring

I was born into a broken home in the city of Philadelphia. My parents separated before I was born. I never saw them together except once—when I was called to testify in divorce court. I'm sure I could have been reared, died and gone to hell, and nobody would particularly have cared, except that a small group of Christian believers got together in my neighborhood to start an evangelical church.

Walt belonged to that church, and he went to the Sunday school superintendent and said, "I want to teach a Sunday school class."

The superintendent said, "Wonderful, Walt, but we don't have any boys. Go out into the community. Anybody you pick up—that's your class."

I'll never forget the day I met him. Walt was six feet, four inches tall. He said to me as a little kid, "Hey, son, how would you like to go to Sunday school?"

To me, anything that had "school" in it had to be bad news.

Then he said, "How would you like to play marbles?"

That was different! Would you believe we got down and played marbles, and he beat me in every single game? I lost my marbles early in life! By the time Walt got through, I didn't care where he was going—that's where I wanted to go.

Walt had picked up 13 of us boys, nine from broken homes. Today, 11 are in full-time vocational Christian work. And Walt never went to school beyond the sixth grade.

I can't tell you a thing Walt ever said. But I can tell you everything about him, because he loved me more than my parents did. He loved me for Christ's sake. And I'm ministering today, not only because of a man who led me to Christ and discipled me, but also because he started that mentoring process.

—**Howard Hendricks**

God's Mysterious Ways

I did not think of her as my stepmother. She was simply "Dad's second wife," someone he had married after being married to my mother for 22 years.

She and my father were also married 22 years before he died of cancer. When he could no longer write in his big, sprawling handwriting, she wrote to us, keeping us informed of his progress.

One day, after he was gone, I sat thinking and I realized she loved him as much as did my mother. They both had shared 22 years of his life, but she had nursed him through that last difficult year, changing dressings and even learning to give shots.

I found that God had now given me the strength to love her as a person, as an individual in her own right, not just as my dad's wife. I decided she needed to know this. Finding a beautiful "Thinking of You" card, I wrote and told her how much I appreciated what she had done for Dad, especially the last year. I told her that I loved her.

A week later I received a response. "Thank you for remembering my birthday," she wrote. "It was the only card I received."

I did not know it was her birthday. I only know God brought to my mind one particular day that I should write and thank her for all she had done. And it had arrived on the one day when she needed the encouragement the most—her first birthday alone without my father!

—**Donna Clark Goodrich**

A Night to Remember

I jumped into my car that chilly September evening and sped away from the curb as fast as I could—relieved to be away from the house, the kids, the dishes, and the endless diapers. All I wanted was some time to shop—alone. "I deserve it," I told myself defensively, as I swung into the crowded parking lot. Little did I know then that God had other plans for me that night—plans that would alter my life for all time.

I pulled into a parking space at the shopping mall and got out. My whole body relaxed as I inhaled the cool night air. Squeezing between the other cars, I hurried down the pavement to the side entrance of a store.

On the landing in front of the door a young woman, about 30, sat in a wheelchair with two little girls beside her. She had a tiny, deformed frame, shiny blond hair, and gnarled hands which seemed lifeless in her lap. I chilled, wondering what it would be like to be so restricted, yet so young.

I continued past them into the store. Lured by all the windows and shops, I browsed for over an hour. It was good having no one to think about but myself.

At 8:30, I walked out into the cool dark night, startled to see the woman and girls in the same spot as before. I looked at them for a moment, feeling uncomfortable, then dashed to the car. But as I reached for the door, something within me stopped me from opening it. I had to go back. My mouth went dry and I could feel my stomach knotting with tension. A tug-of-war waged in my mind. An old warning sprang at me like a ghost, "Don't talk to strangers . . . But another part of me knew that if I drove off I wouldn't be able to forget them or face myself.

Shaking, I rushed back. "Is anything wrong?" I asked, twisting a stubborn strand of brown hair behind my ear.

Nothing could have prepared me for her speech. Each syllable a separate battle, she gulped and searched carefully for the words. "We ordered a cab nearly two hours ago and it hasn't come."

"I'll call for you again," I offered, and turned toward the door, but she insisted I take a coin for the phone. My heart ached as I watched her struggle with her purse.

Like a child I fumbled through the directory searching out the cab company, my heart pounding as I stammered my request into the phone. I replaced the receiver quickly, then raced back out to the curb and said, "I'll stay with you till it comes."

But impatience grew as I watched the shoppers and another 15 minutes go by. People passed—pity, curiosity, embarrassment on their faces. I could see myself in the crowd. Is that how I had first looked at her?

She interrupted my thoughts. "Thank you for stopping. People usually don't."

My face flushed. If she only knew how much thought and concern for *myself* had gone into my decision to even talk to them. Then suddenly, I said, "I'll drive you home. Do you live far?"

The older girl, a pretty blond with bangs and large blue eyes, said, "Over there, pointing toward a large apartment complex about half a mile away.

The girls wheeled their mother to my car and helped her into the front seat. Next, they collapsed the wheelchair and piled it into the trunk of my car, then climbed into the back seat. It was apparent they had much practice taking care of their mother.

I introduced myself, and the woman gave me her name— Kathy. Then she added, "And these are my two daughters, Lisa and Laurie."

We talked as we drove. The conversation relaxed me and I felt warm in the company of these new friends. A few minutes later we pulled up to their apartment building and brown-eyed Laurie said, "We can make it from here. Thanks for the ride."

"I'm divorced and live here alone," Kathy said. "The girls' father is picking them up tonight."

As they wheeled their mother to her door, I called after them, "Maybe we'll see each other again." I felt certain we would.

My eyes and heart filled up as I drove home that night. My difficult day with diapers, a pesky telephone, and scattered toys faded from my mind. Never again would I face a day or watch a sunset in quite the same way. This lovely young woman had shown me how plentiful life is even in its simplest form.

As I got ready for bed, I felt like a new baby discovering its wiggling fingers and toes for the first time. I suddenly became conscious in a new way of my hands, the movement of my feet across the carpet, and the sound of my voice. Things were different that night.

Since then, Kathy and I have become friends. Because of her, I am better person. I look back at that night and thank God that a shopping trip, a tardy taxi, and a conscience that wouldn't let me along brought us together.

—Karen O'Connor

My First Miracle

Becky. As long as I can remember she's been part of my life. She is my oldest sister Sherry's best friend. Our parents were close friends, so our families were always together while growing up.

Sherry and Becky attended elementary and high school together and even went to the same church. They played basketball, softball and were in some of the same academic clubs. They were not inseparable and always had other friends, but they always maintained a close friendship. That friendship was greatly needed when tragedy struck Becky's life.

At the age of 17 she was diagnosed with ovarian cancer. It looked fatal. I witnessed a strong, healthy young woman shrink to a skeleton who constantly knocked on death's door. There was little hope she would survive. God blessed her with a friend like Sherry so she didn't have to face fear and death alone.

I remember my sister taking me with her to visit Becky in the hospital. Sometimes she would be so weak all she could do would give us a little smile and raise her hand in a waving motion an inch off the bed. When other friends couldn't face the "cancer" word and Becky's fate, Sherry was right there holding her hand and praying for healing.

Sherry recruited me to pray for Becky's healing and that was the first miracle I ever witnessed. For the story had a happy ending. Becky miraculously pulled through. She married her high school sweetheart, Dallas, who sat by her bedside day after day, never giving up hope. She went on to college and now has a medical career.

A few years ago while vacationing with my sisters in California, Sherry said Becky and her husband were also there on vacation and she was meeting them for lunch. Once again, she invited her little sister to tag along. As I sat across the table from

Becky, Dallas and Sherry and admired pictures of Becky's adopted baby girl, I just smiled to myself and thanked God for their friendship that has lasted over 30 years. I also thanked Him for a sister who took me on a miraculous prayer journey 22 years ago.

My sister taught me a lot about friendships and prayer that year. I've treasured those lessons.

—Georgia Curtis Ling

What I Learned From A Gazelle

It was a perfect day to be at the zoo, especially in the charming company of my five-year-old grandson. As we strolled along we came to a high place where we looked down at a pleasant grassy park. A herd of gazelles lived there. Their graceful beauty added to the peaceful, relaxed atmosphere. But suddenly we noticed a commotion in a clump of bushes. One of the delicate creatures had been grazing nearby and didn't notice that her hungry mouth had led her head right under the branches. When she raised up, her antlers were securely caught. She thrashed, she jumped, she tugged, she weaved from side to side. But every movement merely tightened the grip of the branches. How we wished that we could help her. I said softly, "If only we could tell her, 'Bow your head down close to the ground and back out gently,' she would be free again."

Finally, after a gigantic wrench, she pulled back, free, but with an enormous clump of branches in her antlers. After a few moments, she gained her equilibrium and walked away, her head held high and proud. She seemed to be saying, "That embarrassing incident didn't really happen. It was just your imagination." But her huge crown of leaves somehow didn't add to her dignity.

All too soon our happy day came to an end. As we later reviewed our memories, the story of that gazelle was our favorite. It became very special to me when I realized that it was quietly reminding me of the best solution for a nagging problem in my life.

I was having trouble relating to someone; yet it was important that I do so. I wanted to lash out and speak my mind. But that would only make matters worse. When the gazelle fought, it tore out part of the bush. It won a battle but it left a scar. I resolved not to do that. Instead, I bowed my head in prayer and then backed off gently.

Years have gone by now. God answered by mellowing both of us. The bridge that might have been destroyed by "having the last word" is now pleasantly growing stronger. I'm glad I bowed my head and backed off gently.

—Ruthie Lindal Swain

The Present

The annual school Christmas concert was to be the one and only highlight of an otherwise bleak winter on the Canadian prairie. Our small farming community had become the passive victims of an economic squeeze.

Unaware of the burden it placed upon our young shoulders, the new teacher suggested we draw names for a gift exchange. The names we had chosen were to remain top secret, but it didn't take long for news to spread on the school grapevine. Long before the night of the concert, I knew who had drawn my name. He was a boy from a large family that had just recently moved into our community onto a farm that rarely produced anything other than a few head of scrawny cattle.

"Don't count too much on a present," my mother cautioned. Caught up in the excitement of the season, I was in no mood for such pessimism.

The day of the concert, the school basement was packed with people. In the corner stood the tree in all its glory, the gifts piled high around it. Bits of wrapping paper had transformed the smallest tokens into bits of magic.

The concert got under way and there were skits, drills, and recitations, with teachers doing the prompting from behind the bed sheet curtains. A hearty round of applause followed every presentation, until at last a doll cradle placed in the center of the bare stage indicated the nativity pageant.

As the curtains closed on the manger scene, the chairman of the school board rose to make closing remarks. It was time for the distribution of gifts. I sat in suspense, my heart pounding with anticipation. On every side of me people were opening gaily wrapped parcels. There were any number of things to delight a small girl—cheap perfume, fancy soap, dime store jewelry. *Surely*, I thought, *my turn will come soon.*

The boy who had drawn my name was opening a cap gun, aiming it at his friends, planning a game of cops and robbers. I edged over closer to the tree. There were only three presents under it now. Then two. Then none.

I tried to be brave as my mother wrapped my coat around my shoulders. I pulled on my mittens and boots. As we stepped outside into the cold prairie winter, the tears froze on my cheeks.

I hated that boy for drawing my name. Hated everything there was about Christmas and celebrating and singing "Joy to the World." On the way home, I sat in silence, until at last the bitterness inside me exploded. "Why did that boy even draw a name?"

"Well," my mother replied gently, "sometimes it's very hard to admit you're poor, even poorer than the rest." I had the feeling she was speaking from experience. "Maybe that boy wanted to give somebody a present just as much as you hoped to get one."

As we rode home on that starry December night, she began to elaborate on some of the harsh realities of life. By the time we reached the warmth of home, I had begun to understand that what we get out of life is not so important.

The real tragedy is in having nothing to give.

—Alma Barkman

An old legend tells of a noisy carpenter's shop in which the tools of the trade were arguing among themselves. Brother Hammer was told by his fellow tools that he would have to leave because he was too noisy. To which he replied, "If I am to leave this carpenter's shop, Brother Drill must go too; he is so insignificant that he makes very little impression."

Little Brother Drill arose and said, "All right, but Brother Bolt must go also; you have to turn him around and around again and again to get him anywhere."

Brother Bolt then said, "If you wish, I will go, but Brother Plane must leave also; all his work is on the surface, there is no depth to it."

To this Brother Plane replied, "Well, Brother Ruler will have to withdraw if I do, for he is always measuring others as though he were the only one who is right."

Brother Ruler then complained against Brother Sandpaper and said, "I just don't care, he is rougher than he ought to be and he is always rubbing people the wrong way."

In the midst of the discussion, the Carpenter of Nazareth walked in. He had come to perform His day's work. He put on his apron, and went to the bench to make a pulpit. He employed the bolt, the drill, the sandpaper, the saw, the hammer and the plane and all the other tools. After the day's work was over and the pulpit was finished, Brother Saw arose and said, "Brethren, I perceive that all of us are laborers together with God."

Isn't it wonderful! God uses all of us and our unique gifts in the building of His pulpit.

—Stanley E. Sayers

11

Spiritual Life

*So then, just as you received Christ Jesus as Lord, continue
to live in him, rooted and built up in him, strengthened in
the faith as you were taught, and overflowing with thankfulness.*

Colossians 2:6,7 NIV

Pebbles

The Lord had brought to my mind the issue of tithing. I had felt a need to give more to God than our family offering alone. I had tithed when I had been working and felt a great satisfaction in it, but the thought had not occurred to me to continue when my outside income ceased. I began giving a tenth of my grocery money, since I had no other source of income at this time. Though it was only a small amount, I could feel God's hand of blessing nonetheless. I also received a sense of peace from following God's instruction.

This was reward enough for me, but I couldn't help but see God's hand at work when shortly afterward, my daughter called me from graduate school. She told me, "Mom, I've got some good news! A friend of mine has received a large amount of money, and she has decided to tithe it. She gave it to me; she knew I was planning a career in the Lord's work and could use it. It's a thousand dollars, Mom!"

Well, I was thrilled—what a tremendous blessing and encouragement for our daughter. Not only was she blessed (and our family vicariously), but she in turn was able to bless others. She tithed her tenth—one hundred dollars—which she sent to a family in the Philippines with whom she had visited when on a short term missionary assignment there. As a result, that family, too, was blessed and inspired by the Lord's commandment of tithing.

So it goes, one by one, like ripples when a pebble is dropped in a pool, ever outward from its source until it reaches the surrounding shores. The tiny stones of tithing bring ripples of blessing far larger and more outreaching than even the original gift when dropped into the deep pool of life.

—Linda Claire Scott

Entrapment

While gazing up and down the counters during my Christmas shopping, my eye was caught by a beautiful golden birdcage containing a tiny jeweled bird perched on a swing. A key protruded from the bottom of the cage. I twisted the key and a music box performed a familiar tune as the enticing bird preened and turned, opening and shutting its tiny beak. It was adorable. But with a glance at the price tag, I knew I couldn't afford this gift for anyone on my list. So I went on perusing the aisles, searching for the perfect gifts for those on my Christmas list.

My arms were loaded down with my purse and packages and my mind was full of gift-giving thoughts. *Did I buy a present for* everyone? Had I missed anyone? With only a few days left till Christmas I had shopped hurriedly but carefully and was feeling relieved that I was on the verge of finishing my shopping.

I was still checking off my tally mentally, when I arrived at the car and gingerly placed all the packages in the passenger seat.

Suddenly, I remembered that this was the night of the church gift exchange for our Sunday school fellowship group. Had I picked up something to bring to it? I looked through the brightly colored sacks. I opened one from my favorite department store and was surprised to find the lovely gilded birdcage with its tiny jeweled occupant. How had this gotten there?

Glancing at the price I recalled why it was that I had only admired this bright amusement and had focused immediately on the other lower-priced enticements. It was a lovely gift indeed and I personally would have loved to have it, but, since the cash register receipt was also in the bag, I knew it belonged to someone else. Someone was probably worrying right now about where they had left the birdcage in their rushed shopping.

I sighed with fatigue and trudged back into the crowded store, trying to remember which counter I had visited, and how the birdcage became mixed in with my menagerie of packages. Finally finding one that appeared suitable, I explained to the sales clerk why I was bringing it back. I asked her to keep her eye out for someone who might have lost this lovely trinket.

She appeared surprised that I would have brought it back at all and said so. After all, she told me, she might never find the owner and no one would have noticed what had really transpired. But I would know and so would God.

The dictionary defines entrapment as "to deceive or to trick into difficulty as to incriminate oneself." The Enemy had set up an ambush, an entrapment as glitteringly attractive as the gilded cage in which the jeweled bird sat. The Enemy never tempts us with something dull or unattractive, but only with things that are desirable to us.

But I knew how my conscience would react. I knew that if I kept it, every time I saw that beautiful music box I would feel encased within my own cage of guilt. I knew that if I accepted the birdcage in this way, it would be tantamount to stealing.

This bauble was indeed more expensive than I could afford, but not in just a monetary way. For keeping it would cost me a piece of my integrity, and that truly was too high a price to pay.

—Linda Claire Scott

Don't Spill It!

As I looked across the front seat of my police unit, I observed the uniform of the 1970's middle-class Southern California teen: tie-dyed T-shirt, bell-bottom pants and a pair of sloppy plain-toed boots with heels worn down a half inch. His long hair flowing past his shoulders was the only evidence that he could grow any, since it was obvious that a razor had never touched his chin.

Jeffrey was what we called a civilian ride-along, a high school boy getting his first look at what it meant to be a policeman. But on that hot Indian summer's night in September, sixteen-year-old Jeffrey would experience the ride of his life. However, the beginning of the watch didn't give us a clue of what would follow.

Though in general I didn't want to endanger such a temporary companion on his night to ride along, I was secretly a bit disappointed that tonight's calls hadn't been very challenging or exciting. I wondered if Jeffrey thought the only thing policemen did was to respond to ordinary calls through dinner time.

However, during a slight lull, we quickly ducked into a hamburger place. But just as we were getting back into the car with our food, my radio crackled to life as the dispatcher gave me a call.

"Unit 31, and any units to assist, a two-eleven in progress. Two suspects armed with sawed-off shotguns at the Circle K Market."

Jeffrey looked over at me, wide-eyed, and said, "Is that an armed robbery call?"

"You bet, and we're going to be first in. When we get there, stay in the car and keep your head down."

Quickly jerking the car into gear, I squealed out of the fast food restaurant's parking lot with a lurch, then flipped on the lights and siren as we flew to the scene. I reached over and handed my drink to Jeffrey, saying, "Don't spill this. I've got to finish this hamburger before we get there." Then I took a big bite out of the hamburger I held in my right hand as I drove with my left. Cars in front of us pulled over to the side to avoid us slamming into them. At one point as I rounded a corner, it felt like the car rode only on two wheels.

I'll never forget the look on this kid's face. His eyes seemed to want to pop out of his head and he had the most incredulous, fearful, and stunned look on his face as he watched me drive at high speed to this call. It was almost comical how he would look down at my Coke, look up and stare at the road, glance over at me again and look back down at the glass in his hand. He was totally bewildered and on sensory overload. Unlike me, he was stressed out.

Looking back now, I think he feared spilling the drink, wondering what I might do to him if he did. Jeffrey couldn't grasp the fact that my training and experience allowed me to function with great calm in an arena of extraordinarily high stress.

Jeffrey appeared visibly relieved when we arrived at the scene and the owner of the store came running out shouting, "They just went southbound around the corner in a blue Ford pickup."

Just then two more units arrived and I directed them to give chase. I remained at the scene and obtained a detailed description of the suspects and took the crime report. Unfortunately, we never did find the suspects.

Jeffrey couldn't quite comprehend it, or totally trust it. But a policeman's training and experience prepares one to function capably and effectively on the street in tense circumstances. Similarly, as Christians, our spiritual training is meant to provide us with the ability to function with Godly reactions under extraordinarily high stress.

—D. Larry Miller

"He's Alive!"

Years ago I was in a Christian theater group that traveled around doing a musical based on C.S. Lewis' *Lion, Witch and the Wardrobe.* I helped repair costumes, sets and props and make the bookings. I had booked a show at a children's hospital. When the kids arrived for the show in wheelchairs and even on gurneys, as well as by foot, it was obvious that we were going to be quite crowded in the room. We decided to remove some of the set pieces but even then, the children were right next to the actors throughout the performance.

I've wondered if that physical closeness added to the performance and its reception or if it was the suffering of the children that made them such a keen audience. At any rate, during the scene where the white witch humiliates and kills the good lion, Aslan, the children were totally caught up in the action.

They didn't stir or speak but more than a few were quietly crying. I was offstage in a hall, waiting to go on, when the activities director came furiously bustling towards me.

"What is this?" she whispered loudly and fiercely. "You didn't tell me this was going to happen! Look at those children! You're breaking their hearts!"

I replied, "Don't you get it? Aslan is like Jesus. He'll live again, just wait."

Just then two actresses, playing sisters, were singing a beautiful song called "Why Did This Have to Happen?" They sang about Aslan taking the punishment for their traitor brother, all while sitting in front of Aslan's body. When they finished their song they cried on each other's shoulders. While in this posture of grief Aslan sat up behind them.

That's when the children came to life. They shouted with joy, clapped and laughed as they wiggled in excitement. The ones closest to the two women were tugging on the women's clothes, shouting and waving their hands—anything to get their attention. "Look! Look! He's alive!" they called.

It was like being at the very resurrection of Jesus: a happy pandemonium that seized every believing heart, as they shouted "He's alive!"

—Carol Wolff

Why God Never Received Tenure at a University

- He had only one major publication.
- It was in Hebrew and Greek.
- It had no references.
- He wasn't published in a journal.
- Some doubt He wrote it Himself.
- He may have created the world, but what has he done since?
- The scientific community can't replicate His results.
- He never got permission from the ethics board to use human subjects.
- When one experiment went awry, He tried to cover it up by drowning the subjects.
- He rarely came to class and often told His students, "Read the book!"
- Some say He had His Son teach the class.
- He expelled His first two students.
- His office hours were irregular and sometimes held on a mountaintop.
- Although there were only 10 requirements, most students failed.

—**Author Unknown**

Giving to God

Ruben and his wife attended a "Sweetheart Meeting" where, at the end of the meeting, I asked couples who desired help in their marriages to come forward for prayer. I didn't know him and his wife, but something about them standing before me caught my attention.

"When was the last time you took your wife on a honeymoon?" I asked Ruben.

Ruben answered truthfully, "I have never taken my wife on a honeymoon."

Ruben remembers that "at this point you graciously blessed us with the money in your pocket so we could go on our first honeymoon." I had spontaneously reached in my pocket and handed them $220, all my travel expense allowance.

What I didn't know until Ruben wrote me weeks later was that they had never gone on a honeymoon because they were never married! Living together for seven years, having become Christians just months before the meeting that night, they stopped having sex two months earlier until they could save enough to be married.

Ruben wrote, "With eight children between us, saving money was hard, especially since I was unemployed and a recovering drug addict. When I was saved and delivered from drugs, I chose to depend upon my Lord for everything we did. We had been praying earnestly for money to get married when we went to the meeting."

They were married three days later, on Valentine's Day. The money he received that night covered the license and three nights at a nice hotel. But Ruben explains the amazing part of the story this way:

"We came to your meeting with enough money to cover our

gas and parking. Well, as you were taking the offering I remembered I had $2.20. The Holy Spirit spoke to me and said, 'Who is your Provider, who do you trust?' Needless to say, I put my $2.20 in the offering . . . and then we were blessed with the miracle. What an awesome move of God!"

The principle Ruben's obedience illustrates is: *You gain by giving what you cannot buy with money.*

—Edwin Louis Cole

Years ago it was the custom for the people to bring their gifts to the front of the building. A well-known preacher was making an appeal to the people to give for a good cause. Many came to present their offerings of love. Among them was a little crippled girl who hobbled along at the end of the line. Pulling a ring from her finger, she placed it on the table and made her way back up the aisle.

After the service an usher was sent to bring her to the preacher's study. The preacher said, "My dear, I saw what you did. It was beautiful. But the response of the people has been so generous that we have enough to take care of the need. We don't feel right about keeping your treasured ring, so we have decided to give it back to you."

To his surprise the little girl vigorously shook her head in refusal. "You don't understand," she said. "I didn't give my ring to you, I gave it to God!"

—Joe R. Barnett

Ups and Downs

God has designed thousands of ways for the animal kingdom to come into existence but, in my estimation, the birth of the baby giraffe is of all births the most impressive. See it once and you'll never forget it.

The zoo health center was called at 9:30 a.m. and we were informed that the female Angola giraffe was giving birth. If the veterinarian and I wanted to watch we could. Neither of us had ever witnessed a giraffe birth before, so we quickly headed for the giraffe barn. We parked and walked quietly to a location where about seven of us were afforded an earthbound view of an elevated event. I sat on a bale of hay next to Jack Badal, a man considered by most of us to be the greatest animal keeper alive. He was a man of few and well-chosen words, and when I sat down, he only nodded and continued to suck the sweetness from the alfalfa stem he had pulled from the hay bale on which we sat.

I noticed the calf's front hooves and head were already visible and dripping with amniotic fluids. I also noticed that the mother was standing up. "When is she going to lie down?" I said to Jack, who still hadn't said anything.

"She won't," he answered.

"But her hindquarters are nearly ten feet off the ground. That calf might get hurt from the fall," I said. Jack gave me that look that told me I had probably said something that revealed my ignorance.

I wondered why no plans were being made to procure a fireman's net to catch the baby, so I asked. "Listen, Gary. You can try to catch the calf if you want, but remember that its mother has enough strength in her hind legs to kick your head off, which is what she'd do if you get anywhere near that calf. They've killed lions that tried to get their calves."

I was able to sit quietly for a while and observe the calf's journey down the birth canal. Its neck and front legs were fully extended and dangling freely, ten feet above the hard ground on which it was soon to fall. It seemed unbelievable to me that in just a few minutes this newborn was going to be introduced to such trauma. Ten feet! To the hard ground! (It had taken me twelve years to get up the nerve to jump off a high dive approximately ten feet high into clear deep water. This giraffe calf was going to top that during its first thirty minutes of visible existence.)

The moment we had anticipated was not a disappointment. The calf, a plucky male, hurled forth, falling ten feet and landing on his back. Within seconds, he rolled to an upright position with his legs tucked under his body. From this position he considered the world for the first time, shaking some of the last vestiges of birthing fluids from his eyes and ears.

The mother giraffe lowered her head long enough to take a quick look. Then she positioned herself so that she was standing directly over her calf. She waited for about a minute and then did the most unreasonable thing. She swung her pendulous leg outward and kicked her baby, so that it was sent sprawling head over heels (or hooves, in this case). I turned to Jack and exclaimed, "Why'd she do that?"

"She wants it to get up, and if it doesn't she'll do it again."

Jack was right—the violent process was repeated again and then again. The struggle to rise was momentous, and as the baby grew tired of trying, the mother would again stimulate its efforts with a hearty kick.

Finally, amidst the cheers of the animal-care staff, the calf stood for the first time. Wobbly, for sure, but it stood. Then we were struck silent when she kicked it off its feet again.

Jack's face was the only face not expressing astonishment. "She wants it to remember how it got up," he offered. "That's why she knocked it down. In the wild it would need to get up as soon as possible to follow the herd. The mother needs the herd, too. Lions, hyenas, leopards, and hunting dogs all would enjoy young giraffes. They'd get it, too, if the mother didn't teach her baby to quickly get up and get with it."

Jack waved good-bye with his alfalfa stem and returned to his section to care for his animals, something he did better than anyone I have ever known.

I've thought about the birth of that giraffe many times since that spring morning. I have seen its parallel in my own life. There have been many times when it seemed that I had just stood after a trial only to be knocked down by the next. It was God helping me to remember how it was that I got up, urging me always to walk with Him in His shadow under His care.

Consider it pure joy, my brothers, whenever you face trials of many kinds, because you know that the testing of your faith develops perseverance. (James 1:2,3 NIV)

—**Gary Richmond**

A View of Heaven

On my television program, "The 700 Club," I did an interview with Dr. Richard E. Eby, a well-known California obstetrician and gynecologist. In 1972, Dr. Eby said he fell from a second-story balcony and split his skull. He told me that he died (whether for minutes or hours, he doesn't know) but miraculously returned to life and at the time of the interview was perfectly healthy and normal. During the experience, Dr. Eby related, his spirit left his body and apparently went to heaven, or paradise. As one would expect, he found it to be a most beautiful place. At one stage he entered a field of flowers and as he walked along, he was overwhelmed by their beauty. "Wouldn't it be wonderful if I had a bunch and could smell them," he thought. But as he started to bend over, he looked at his hand, and it was already full of flowers.

At another point, he was thinking how good it would be to go to a distant valley, and suddenly he was there.

As a scientific man, he naturally analyzed these experiences carefully and concluded that in heaven the mere thought produces the action. As the psalmist declared: *Delight yourself also in the LORD, And He shall give you the desires of your heart. Commit your way to the LORD, Trust also in Him, And He shall bring it to pass.* (Psalm 37:4,5 NKJV)

In his brief visit to heaven, Dr. Eby was delighting himself in the Lord, doing His perfect will, and the yearnings of his heart were immediately fulfilled. He didn't have to speak to them. On earth a translation is required, but not so in the ultimate kingdom. One day we will not need telephones, mass transit, or computers; the speed of thought exceeds the speed of light. But now we need the spoken word.

—Pat Robertson

Pao, Senhor?

He couldn't have been over six years old. Dirty face, bare-footed, torn T-shirt, matted hair. He wasn't too different from the other hundred thousand or so street orphans that roam Rio de Janeiro.

I was walking to get a cup of coffee at a nearby cafe when he came up behind me. With my thoughts somewhere between the task I had just finished and the class I was about to teach, I scarcely felt the tap, tap, tap on my hand. I stopped and turned. Seeing no one, I continued on my way. I'd only taken a few steps, however, when I felt another insistent tap, tap, tap. This time I stopped and looked downward. There he stood. His eyes were whiter because of his grubby cheeks and coal-black hair.

"Pao, senhor?" (Bread, sir?)

Living in Brazil, one has daily opportunities to buy a candy bar or sandwich for these little outcasts. It's the least one can do. I told him to come with me and we entered the sidewalk cafe. "Coffee for me and something tasty for my little friend." The boy ran to the pastry counter and made his choice. Normally, these youngsters take the food and scamper back out into the street without a word. But this little fellow surprised me.

The cafe consisted of a long bar: one end for pastries and the other for coffee. As the boy was making his choice, I went to the other end of the bar and began drinking my coffee. Just as I was getting my derailed train of thought back on track, I saw him again. He was in the cafe entrance, on tiptoe, bread in hand, looking in at the people. "What's he doing?" I thought.

Then he saw me and scurried in my direction. He came and stood in front of me about eye-level with my buckle. The little Brazilian orphan looked up at the big American missionary, smiled a smile that would have stolen your heart and said,

"Obrigado." (Thank you.) Then, nervously scratching the back of his ankle with his big toe, he added, "*Muito* obrigado." (Thank you *very much*.)

All of a sudden, I had a crazy craving to buy him the whole restaurant.

But before I could say anything, he turned and scampered out the door.

As I write this, I'm still standing at the coffee bar, my coffee is cold, and I'm late for my class. But I still feel the sensation that I felt half an hour ago. And I'm pondering this question: If I am so moved by a street orphan who says thank you for a piece of bread, how much more is God moved when I pause to thank him—really thank him—for saving my soul?

—**Max Lucado**

A monk, in his travels, once found a precious stone and kept it. One day he met a traveler, and when the monk opened his bag to share his provisions, the traveler saw the jewel and asked the monk to give it to him. The monk did so readily.

The traveler departed, overjoyed with the unexpected gift of the precious stone that was enough to give him wealth and security for the rest of his life. However, a few days later he came back in search of the monk, found him, gave him back the stone, and entreated him. "Now, please give me something much more precious than this stone, valuable as it is. Give me that which enabled you to give it to me."

How God Views You

When I speak on Godly self esteem, I often use the story I found in the book, *A Marriage Made in Heaven*, to explain how God views us as his beloved children:

"The story is told of a primitive culture where brides were purchased from their parents using cattle as an exchange medium. An average woman might merit the bride-price of two cows, an exceptional woman might bring three; while a less desirable woman's family would receive one.

"Into this society, the story goes, a rich and attractive suitor came, looking for a wife. All the families paraded their eligible daughters before him. Everyone was surprised when he announced his intention to negotiate with the family of a young woman who was unattractive and clumsy.

"*Perhaps it's a bargain he's after*," the townspeople speculated, wondering if perhaps he would offer chickens instead of cows. To everyone's amazement, he offered the girl's family six cows for their daughter and quickly whisked her away for a long honeymoon.

"When they returned, months later, no one recognized the new bride. Gone were the slumping shoulders and dull eyes. It was as if she were a new person, radiating beauty and confidence.

"No, her husband had not bought her beauty treatments or a facelift. He had begun their relationship by showing her in a tangible way that he thought she was important and valuable. She had begun to act the part, to see herself as he saw her, and throughout the rest of her life she was viewed with awe by all her friends—a six-cow woman."

It then goes on to say how God views them (and you), as not just a six-cow woman (or man), but as a thousand-cow valuable child of God. Since He sent His most precious gift, Jesus, the more we focus on Him, the more godly self-esteem we'll have.

—Kathy Collard Miller

The hymnwriter Fanny Crosby gave us more than 6,000 gospel songs. Although blinded by an illness at the age of 6 weeks, she never became bitter. One time a preacher sympathetically remarked, "I think it is a great pity that the Master did not give you sight when He showered so many other gifts upon you." She replied quickly, "Do you know that if at birth I had been able to make one petition, it would have been that I should be born blind!" "Why?" asked the surprised clergyman. "Because when I get to heaven, the first face that shall ever gladden my sight will be that of my Savior!"

One of Miss Crosby's hymns was so personal that for years she kept it to herself. Kenneth Osbeck, author of several books on hymnology, says its revelation to the public came about this way: "One day at a Bible conference in Northfield, Massachusetts, Miss Crosby was asked by D. L. Moody to give a personal testimony. At first she hesitated, then quietly rose and said, 'there is one hymn that I have written which has never been published. I call it my soul's poem. Sometimes when I am troubled, I repeat it to myself, for it brings comfort to my heart.' She then recited while many wept, 'Someday the silver cord will break, and I no more as now shall sing; but oh, the joy when I shall wake within the palace of the King! And I shall see Him face to face, and tell the story—saved by grace!' "

At the age of 95, Fanny Crosby passed into glory and saw the face of Jesus.

That is the sure hope of every child of God!

The Starfish

There was a young man walking down a deserted beach just before dawn. In the distance he saw a frail old man. As he approached the old man, he saw him picking up stranded starfish and throwing them back into the sea. The young man gazed in wonder as the old man again and again threw the small starfish from the sand to the water. He asked him, "Why do you spend so much energy doing what seems to be a waste of time?" The old man explained that the stranded starfish would die if left in the morning sun. "But there must be thousands of beaches and millions of starfish," exclaimed the young man, "How can your effort make any difference?" The old man looked down at the small starfish in his hand and as he threw it to safety in the sea he said, "It makes a difference to this one."

—Irv Furman

A university professor tells of being invited to speak at a military base one December and there meeting an unforgettable soldier named Ralph who had been sent to meet him at the airport. After they had introduced themselves, they headed toward the baggage claim.

As they walked down the concourse, Ralph kept disappearing. Once to help an older woman whose suitcase had fallen open. Once to lift two toddlers up to where they could see Santa Claus. And again to give directions to someone who was lost. Each time he came back with a big smile on his face.

"Where did you learn to do that?" the professor asked.

"Do what?" Ralph said.

"Where did you learn to live like that?"

"Oh," Ralph said, "during the war, I guess." Then he told the professor about his tour of duty in Viet Nam, about how it was his job to clear mine fields, and how he watched his friends, one after another, blown up before his eyes.

"I learned to live between steps," he said. "I never knew whether the next one would be my last, so I learned to get everything I could out of the moment between when I picked up my foot and when I put it down again. Every step I took was a whole new world, and I guess I've just been that way ever since."

The abundance of our lives is not determined by how long we live, but how well we live. Christ makes abundant life possible if we choose to live it now.

—Barbara Brown Taylor

One Step Back

Dave had returned from Viet Nam and when I saw his face in the service that night I could read his thoughts like a book. His guilty face seemed to say: "I've been gone so long. Failed so foolishly while overseas, that I compromised my commitment. I'd love to return to the fullness of the Lord's way, but I don't deserve to do so." It was as though he felt he needed to earn his way back to God.

When my message was concluded, I went down from the platform to where Dave was seated, head buried in his hands. I simply whispered, as I leaned over to his side,

"Dave, it's not a mile or a thousand steps to come back, it's only one—one step from where you are to where Jesus is—right now."

He looked up, his eyes flashed with hope, and he stood and took one step—into my arms, and then both of us went to the altar to pray.

Today, Dave is a gifted Christian counselor, his home a center of vital joy and life in Christ, for that night he came back—and built an altar of permanence.

It can be built *before*, by hearing God's wisdom.

It can be built *after*, even though you've wandered.

And the earnest, humble heart wanting to walk with God will be profited by His abundance of grace and mercy!

—Jack Hayford

Why I Believe in Angels

It's popular these days to believe in angels, but it hasn't always been that way. A few years ago, it was strange for those who were part of the intellectual community to even believe in God. When Billy Graham published his famous book, *Angels,* it was somewhat controversial, even in the Christian community.

I've never even questioned the existence of angels; I was raised by Gram! She had painted the angel picture that was hanging in her bedroom; she had the famous picture of the guardian angel helping children across a bridge hanging in her hallway.

We were poor, and she was a down-to-earth person. But when she told us one story, she became ethereal . . . the story of the time she saw the angel wings. She was ill and dying; her children, pastor, and his wife were praying with her. They had called Daboy (my Grandpa—our family is famous for strange nicknames!) home from work, not expecting her to be alive when he arrived. She continued to grow weaker for a few minutes; then suddenly she sat up in bed saying, "Oh, do you see them? Do you see them?" The death angel was leaving her room.

Moments later, my Grandpa drove up. They ran to tell him of Gram's marvelous recovery. But before they could he replied, "I know." (I was only 4 at the time; my sister 5. My mother was handicapped and divorced; we lived with Gram.) On the way home, Grandpa had asked God to give Gram 15 more years so she could raise us—the "little girls."

When I left for college, Gram started painting again (I could never understand why she didn't have time for hobbies until after I left). One day I said, "Gram, paint the angels for me!" That ethereal glow enveloped her again as she responded, "I can't!"

"Why?" I asked.

"Because they don't make colors like that on earth. They were every color of the rainbow; they were shiny; they had a glow." Unable to communicate what was in her mind's eye, Gram finally shrugged and said, "There just aren't colors like that here!"

Years later, I was privileged to hear Betty Maltz tell of her near-death experience. She especially caught my attention when she said, "I walked through a field with grass and wild flowers of every color imaginable, but they weren't the colors we have here; they were beautiful. The grass was green, but it wasn't our green." She, like Gram, couldn't even find words to describe it.

By the way, God gave Gram more than the 15 years Grandpa prayed for! As I write this, she is about to celebrate her 104th birthday. (I wonder if it has anything to do with the fact I've never grown up).

Yes. I believe in angels. And I can sit in the midst of the intellectually elite without ever having to question the existence of God. Gram didn't just talk about angels; she lived a life that would never cause us to question His goodness, His integrity, or His ability to care for His children.

—Sharon Marshall

Applying Your Makeup Inside and Out

W hy is it that some of us wear makeup and some of us choose not to? Whether you do or don't, there are some interesting comparisons to our outer makeup and what "our makeup" should consist of.

If you look at yourself closely in the mirror you may see more than you bargained for. There's an old saying, "your eyes are the mirror to your heart." What is it that you see? Is your heart empty? Full of bitterness and the like? *If anyone acknowledges that Jesus is the Son of God, God lives in him and he in God.* (l John 4:15 NIV)

After evaluating ourselves we may find we need a good facial scrub to remove the dead skin and clean deep down. Our hearts need that too. *If we confess our sins, he is faithful and just to forgive us our sins, and to cleanse us from all unrighteousness.* (1 John 1:9 NIV)

Next a good toner will help shrink the pores, remove any leftover residue on the skin. We have been thoroughly cleansed, now . . . *rid yourselves of all malice, and all deceit, hypocrisy, envy, and slander of every kind. Like newborn babies, crave pure spiritual milk, so that by it you may grow up in your salvation, now that you have tasted that the Lord is good.* I Peter 2:1–3 NIV)

You'll want to protect your skin with a good moisturizer, one without mineral oil which can clog pores. We also need a protector in this world. *But the Lord is faithful and He will strengthen and protect you from the evil one.* (2 Thessalonians 3:3 NIV)

Next we apply a concealer. The concealer covers blemishes and other imperfections on the skin. *Blessed are they whose transgressions are forgiven, whose sins are covered.* (Romans 4:7 NIV)

The foundation also helps protect our skin from pollutants. We need a foundation ourselves, something that will get us through the rough times in our lives. *The rain came down, the streams rose, and the winds blew and beat against that house, yet it did not fall, because it had its foundation on the rock.* (Matthew 7:25 NIV)

Brushing a little blush on the cheeks gives the impression of a happy, healthy person. What a joy it is to see a beautiful smile on someone's face. *A happy heart makes the face cheerful . . .* (Proverbs 15:13 NIV)

You can now add eye shadow, liner and mascara. This brings attention and definition to your eyes. If others can see Jesus in your eyes, nothing can compare to their beauty. *Looking unto Jesus the author and finisher of our faith . . .* (Hebrews 12:2 NIV)

Last but not least, apply your lipstick carefully. The best way is to use a small brush. We must also be careful what comes through our lips. *But know you must rid yourselves of all such things: anger, rage, malice, slander, and filthy language from your lips.* (Colossians 3:8 NIV)

If you choose to wear makeup or not, that is your choice. It is also our choice as to how we will live our lives. For those who choose to live a godly life, let your beauty . . . *be that of your inner self, the unfading beauty as a gentle and quiet spirit which is of great worth in God's sight. For this is the way the holy women of the past who put their hope in God used to make themselves beautiful.* (I Peter 3:4,5 NIV)

—**Elizabeth Nagy**

Relax!

Not long ago, someone asked me what I did for relaxation. "I jog," I replied. "Oh," said the lady. "That's wonderful. Could I ask what you think about as you jog? Do you memorize the Scriptures, pray for the needs of the world, or wrestle with some deep theological problem?" I have to admit she looked a little startled (and certainly a mite disappointed), when I answered, "Quite frankly, I am thinking, *One more tree! Just one more tree!*" It was not all that long ago that I came to understand I did not *have* to turn everything into a spiritual exercise.

—**Jill Briscoe**

The Ugly Bedspread

The bedspread was ugly. I had bought it in desperation at a garage sale for $5.00. "Yuk," I said, each time I made the bed. I grimaced as I spread the cover.

Then one day I was leafing through my sister's Penney's catalog. There was the same bedspread with a well-known designer name. $85.00!

Suddenly the bedspread took on a new beauty—once I discovered how much it cost.

At one time I didn't think much of myself. I felt ugly. "Yuk," I said each time I looked in the mirror.

Then one day I heard the story of salvation; how Christ had given His life on Calvary—for me. And suddenly my life took on a new beauty—once I discovered how much it cost.

—**Donna Clark Goodrich**

Like Flying A Kite

You have to receive God by faith—by faith in His Son, the Lord Jesus Christ. And when that happens, there isn't any room for doubt. You don't have to question whether or not God is in your heart, you can know it.

Whenever anyone asks me how I can be so certain about who and what God really is, I am reminded of the story of the little boy who was out flying a kite. It was a fine day for kite flying, the wind was brisk and large billowy clouds were blowing across the sky. The kite went up and up until it was entirely hidden by the clouds.

"What are you doing?" a man asked the little boy.

"I'm flying a kite," he replied.

"Flying a kite, are you?" the man said. "How can you be sure? You can't see your kite."

"No," said the boy, "I can't see it, but every little while I feel a tug, so I know for sure that it's there!"

Don't take anyone else's word for God. Find Him for yourself and then you too will know by the wonderful, warm tug on your heartstrings that He is there *for sure.*

—Billy Graham

Do not be afraid of opposition—a kite rises against the wind, not with it.

As you know, we consider blessed those who have persevered. You have heard of Job's perseverance and have seen what the Lord finally brought about. The Lord is full of compassion and mercy. (James 5:11 NIV)

Underground Commitment

Stories from the underground church in Russia never fail to jolt us awake. This past week I came across another one. A house church in a city of the Soviet Union received one copy of the Gospel of Luke, the only scripture most of these Christians had ever seen. They tore it into small sections and distributed them among the body of believers. Their plan was to memorize the portion they had been given, then on the next Lord's Day they would meet and redistribute the scriptural sections.

On Sunday these believers arrived inconspicuously in small groups throughout the day so as not to arouse the suspicion of KGB informers. By dusk they were all safely inside, windows closed and doors locked. They began by singing a hymn quietly but with deep emotion. Suddenly, the door was pushed open and in walked two soldiers with loaded automatic weapons at the ready. One shouted, "All right—everybody line up against the wall. If you wish to renounce your commitment to Jesus Christ, leave now!"

Two or three quickly left, then another. After a few more seconds, two more.

"This is your last chance. Either turn against your faith in Christ," he ordered, "or stay and suffer the consequences."

Another left. Finally, two more in embarrassed silence with their faces covered slipped out into the night. No one else moved. Parents with small children trembling beside them looked down reassuringly. They fully expected to be gunned down or, at best, to be imprisoned.

After a few moments of complete silence, the other soldier closed the door, looked back at those who stood against the wall and said, "Keep your hands up—but this time in praise to our Lord Jesus Christ, brothers and sisters. We, too, are Christians.

We were sent to another house church several weeks ago to arrest a group of believers."

The other soldier interrupted, ". . . but, instead, *we were converted!* We have learned by experience, however, that unless people are willing to die for their faith, they cannot be fully trusted."

—Charles Swindoll

A serviceman wrote about a bit of unintended comedy during a company inspection at the Redstone Arsenal in Huntsville, Alabama, the U.S. Army's guided missile school.

The inspection was being conducted by a full colonel. Everything had gone smoothly, until the officer came to the man standing next to the soldier who recalled the incident.

The colonel stopped, looked the man up and down and snapped, "Button that pocket, trooper!"

The soldier, more than a little rattled, stammered, "Right now, sir?" "Of course, right now!"

Whereupon the soldier very carefully reached out and buttoned the flap on the colonel's shirt pocket.

For some reason, peculiar to our human nature, it is always easier to see the unbuttoned pockets of others than it is to see our own. Splinters in other people's eyes seem to be more obvious than planks in our own eyes. *Why do you look at the speck of sawdust in your brother's eye and pay no attention to the plank in your own eye?* (Matthew 7:3 NIV)

—Hugo McCord

Windshield Wiper Sermon

One rainy afternoon I was driving along one of the main streets of town, taking those extra precautions necessary when the roads are wet and slick. Suddenly, my son Matthew spoke up from his relaxed position in the front seat. "Mom, I'm thinking of something."

This announcement usually meant he had been pondering some fact for awhile and was now ready to expound all that his seven-year-old mind had discovered. I was eager to hear. "What are you thinking?" I asked.

"The rain," he began, "is like sin. And the windshield wipers are like God, wiping our sins away."

After the chill bumps raced up my arms, I was able to respond, "That's really good, Matthew." Then my curiosity broke in. How far would this little boy take this revelation? So I asked, "Do you notice how the rain keeps on coming? What does that tell you?"

Matthew didn't hesitate one moment with his answer. "We keep on sinning and God just keeps on forgiving us."

Amen.

—Sharon Jones

No Control

Rushing out of the house, coffee cup and briefcase in hand, I was stretching the limits of efficient time management. Power and control. I'd become a product of the world; measuring success by titles and possessions. What happened to the young woman who asked Jesus into her heart 18 years before? I'd stuffed Him in a closet and jumped head first into a life of personal achievement and gratification.

By September of 1990, my relationships with my husband and children were at an all-time low. Restlessness and rebellion seemed the internal mood that hung over us all like a dense fog.

Sitting alone one morning at the kitchen table, I slowed down long enough to drink in the beauty of the dream home I'd longed for and finally acquired. I felt as if I were seeing it all for the first time. I'd never slowed down long enough to enjoy all these beautiful things I had desired all my life.

Life under my own power and direction was heading for a defeating dead end. And so that day at the kitchen table, in an effort to find balance and peace in a life spinning *out of control*, I brought Jesus out of the closet. With a broken spirit, I began to dust off the remnants of sin and self which had put Him there in the first place. With new power and passion, I approached each day with renewed hope.

Over the next 10 months my life took several dramatic turns. We moved to San Diego and got involved in a great church. Christian friends and activities seemed to be multiplying like rabbits around us and we became caught up in a flurry of activity and Christian service. My old performance-based nature was hard to kill.

I seemed to be back on remote control. One morning, no sooner had the prayer left my lips, "Lord, teach me your peace and balance," I was off and running; running to a business meeting 70 minutes away—I had 60 minutes to get there on time.

The freeway traffic was flowing fast for a Monday morning. As I returned my cellular phone to its cradle and placed my right hand back on the steering wheel, an unusual heaviness fell into my hands. "Whaaaaat . . . ? Oh, my Lord," I said out loud. The steering wheel had come completely off the column. My first thought was . . . "I'm going to get hurt today."

I tried in vain to replace the steering wheel, but it seemed like time stood still. *No control!* Since I couldn't brake, I kept my foot on the gas to avoid being rear-ended by another driver, wondering exactly where my car was going to end up.

My heart was pounding as I clearly realized, *I had no options.* My life and safety were no longer in my power and my heart cried out silently to the Lord, "God, I can't do anything, it's up to You." A peace came over me immediately and I sensed my car beginning to veer left into the fast lane of traffic.

Miraculously, I cleared the first lane and then the second. I don't know where all the cars were for those split seconds, but they seemed to disappear. I imagined that there must be half a dozen angels guiding me across that treacherous route.

Time seemed to suddenly kick back into itself. Still traveling at about 50 miles per hour, my car smoothly crossed onto the left shoulder, the front tire barely skimming the concrete safety curb. At that moment, I slammed on the brakes and came to a screeching halt, the barrier stabilizing my car and preventing me from spinning into the rush hour traffic.

Suddenly, I became aware of the loud whoosh of cars passing me at 70 miles per hour. Dropping the steering wheel into my lap, I raised my shaking hands and yelled, "Hey, everybody, slow down, don't you know . . . you're really not in control of anything!"

God had captured my attention. Today, when life starts to become a flurry of activity and productivity, I imagine holding a disconnected steering wheel in my hands and asking, "Lord, where do *You* want me to drive today?"

—**Danna Demetre**

Credits

"Make Me Like Joe!" from *Everything You've Heard Is Wrong*, Tony Campolo, Word, Inc., Texas, 1992. Used by permission of publisher.

You Can't Outgive the Lord adapted from *Love For A Lifetime*, James C. Dobson, Multnomah Press, Oregon, 1987. Used by permission of publisher.

Be Alert from *Wild Things Happen When I Pray*, Becky Tirabassi, Zondervan Publishing House, Michigan, 1993. Used by permission of publisher.

Every Talent Counts from *Time Out!*, Dick Hagerman, Evergreen Communications, Inc., 1989. Used by permission of author.

Who'll Cry at Your Funeral? from *The Man In the Mirror*, Patrick Morley, Wolgemuth & Hyatt Publishers, Inc. Tennessee, 1989.

Unguarded Places from *Where Have All the Lovers Gone?*, Pamala Kennedy, Thomas Nelson Publishers, Tennessee, 1994. Used by permission of publisher.

Easy to Grab, Hard to Let Go from *A New View From the Zoo*, Gary Richmond, Harvest House, Oregon, 1995. Used by permission of author.

A Prayer Experiment Brings Astonishing Results &

Do You Want Mountain Moving Faith? from *A Woman's Guide to Spiritual Power Through Scriptural Prayer*, Nancy L. Dorner, Starburst Publishers, Pennsylvania, 1992. Used by permission of publisher.

Pants With No Pockets from *Living Above the Level of Mediocrity*, Charles Swindoll, Word, Inc., Texas, 1987. Used by permission of publisher.

Peace of Mind from *How To Fail Successfully*, Jill Briscoe, Fleming H. Revell, New York, 1982. Used by permission of author.

Truths for Our Families adapted from *Family Shock*, Gary Collins, Ph.D. Tyndale House Publishers, Inc., Illinois, 1995.

Average Is Okay from *Turmoil in the Toy Box II*, Joan Hake Robie, Starburst Publishers, Pennsylvania, 1989. Used by permission of publisher.

My Dad is an Oak Tree from *Point Man*, Steve Farrar, Questar Publishers, Oregon, 1990. Used by permission of publisher.

Getting Back on the Team from *The Language of Love*, Gary Smalley & John Trent, Focus on the Family, Colorado, 1988. Used by permission of publisher.

With A Child's Help from *Only Angels Can Wing It*, Liz Curtis Higgs, Thomas Nelson Publishers, Tennessee, 1995. Used by permission of publisher.

Asking for Time Together from *If Teacups Could Talk*, Emilie Barnes, Harvest House Publishers, Oregon, 1994. Used by permission of publisher.

They Want Me For One Reason from *When You Can't Come Back*, Dave & Jan Dravecky, Zondervan Publishing House, Michigan, 1992. Used by permission of publisher.

Be A Student of Your Children from *The Blessing*, Gary Smalley & John Trent, Thomas Nelson Publishers, Tennessee, 1986. Used by permission of publisher.

Take Time to Communicate from *Always Daddy's Girl,* H. Norman Wright, Regal Books, California, 1989. Used by permission of publisher.

A Boy Becomes a Man, Joan Hake Robie, *The Sunday News,* Lancaster, Pennsylvania, August 21, 1977.

Middle Man adapted from *Normal Is Just a Setting on Your Dryer,* Patsy Clairmont, Focus on the Family, Colorado, 1993. Used by permission of publisher.

The Paper Chase from *Only Angels Can Wing It,* Liz Curtis Higgs,Thomas Nelson Publishers, Tennessee, 1995. Used by permission of publisher.

We May Not Understand from *When God Doesn't Make Sense,* James Dobson, Tyndale House Publishers, Illinois, 1993. Used by permission of publisher.

Let Go of the Loss from *Can I Control My Changing Emotions?,* Annie Chapman, Luci Shaw, and Florence Littauer, Bethany House Publishers, Minnesota, 1994. Used by permission of publisher.

My Miracle Tape adapted from *Mama, Get the Hammer! There's a Fly on Papa's Head,* Barbara Johnson, Word, Inc., Texas, 1994. Used by permission of publisher.

The Death of a Saint from *Peace With God,* Billy Graham, Word, Inc., Texas, 1953, 1984. Used by permission of publisher.

Believe What God Believes About You from *Always Daddy's Girl,* H. Norman Wright, Regal Books, California, 1989. Used by permission of publisher.

Believing God for the Impossible from *The Secret Kingdom,* Pat Robertson, Word, Inc., Texas, 1992. Used by permission of publisher.

Come Home from *No Wonder They Call Him The Savior,* Max Lucado, Questar Publishers, Multnomah Books, Oregon, 1986. Used by permission of publisher.

Hoping For Good News from *How to Forgive Your Children,* Quin Sherrer with Ruthanne Garlock, Aglow Publications, Washington, 1989. Used by permission of author.

A Special Kind of Love adapted from *More Than A Carpenter,* Josh McDowell, Tyndale House Publishers, Inc., Illinois, 1977. Used by permission of publisher.

Assess Your Expectations from *Can I Control My Changing Emotions?,* Annie Chapman, Luci Shaw, and Florence Littauer, Bethany House Publishers, Minnesota, 1986. Used by permission of publisher.

Encouragement from *Your Personality Tree,* Florence Littauer, Florence Littauer, Word, Inc., Texas, 1986. Used by permission of publisher.

Call It Commitment &

I'm Learning from *Fit to Be Tied,* Bill and Lynne Hybels, Bill & Lynne Hybels, Zondervan Publishing House, Michigan, 1991. Used by permission of publisher.

Keeping a Promise adapted from *Carpe Diem,* Tony Campolo, Word, Inc., Texas, 1994. Used by permission of publisher.

Checking on the Job I Already Have from *Dr. Kaplan's Lifestyle of the Fit & Famous,* Dr. Eric Scott Kaplan, Starburst Publishers, Inc., Pennsylvania, 1995. Used by permission of publisher.

Is Anyone Listening? from *A Woman's Guide to Spiritual Power Through Scriptural Prayer,* Nancy L. Dorner, by Starburst Publishers, Pennsylvania, 1992. Used by permission of publisher.

God Had Granted Me the Desires of My Heart adapted from *When You Can't Come Back*, Dave & Jan Dravecky, Zondervan Publishing House, Michigan, 1993. Used by permission of publisher.

Together is Better adapted from *Locking Arms*, Stu Weber, Questar Publishers, Multnomah Books, Oregon, 1995. Used by permission of publisher.

Accountability adapted from *Seven Promises of a Promise Keeper*, Focus on the Family, Colorado, 1994. Used by permission of author.

A Mandate for Mentoring from *Seven Promises of a Promise Keeper*, Howard Hendricks, Focus on the Family, Colorado, 1994. Used by permission of publisher.

Giving to God from *Real Man*, Edwin Louis Cole, Edwin Louis Cole, Thomas Nelson Publishers, Tennessee, 1992. Used by permission of publisher.

Ups and Downs from *A New View From the Zoo*, Gary Richmond, Harvest House, Oregon, 1995. Used by permission of author.

A View of Heaven from *The Secret Kingdom*, Pat Robertson, Word, Inc., Texas, 1992. Used by permission of publisher.

Pao, Senhor? from *No Wonder They Call Him The Savior*, Max Lucado, Questar Publishers, Multnomah Books, Oregon, 1986. Used by permission of publisher.

One Step Back from *A Man's Walk with God*, Jack Hayford, Living Way Ministries, California, 1993.

Relax! from *How To Fail Successfully*, Jill Briscoe, Fleming H. Revell, New York, 1982. Used by permission of author.

Like Flying a Kite from *Peace With God*, Billy Graham. Word, Inc., Texas, 1953, 1984. Used by permission of publisher.

Underground Commitment from *Living Above the Level of Mediocrity*, Charles Swindoll, Word, Inc., Texas, 1987. Used by permission of publisher.

Pulpit Helps for various short anecdotal quotes and stories, AMG International, Chattanooga, Tennessee.

Contributors

Alma Barkman is the author of six books, the latest being *Purrables* (Starburst Publishers). A freelance writer for 25 years, she leads workshops for beginning writers. Contact: 583 Municipal Rd., Winnipeg, Manitoba, Canada R3R 1J2. (204) 895-2353.

Virgean L. F. Bosworth had a promising dancing and acting career when God stopped her pursuit through a 1972 motorcycle accident that resulted in brain injury and coma. She writes for two international head injury publications. Contact: 300 N. Chestnut, #302, Olathe, KS 66061. (913) 764-2642.

Dr. Lorrie Boyd is a Professional Speaker and co-author of the book, *Change Your Life With Humor.* Lorrie speaks on *Using Humor to Cope with Grief, Loss, and Change.* Contact: Boyd Seminars, 12555 Euclid St., Suite 25, Garden Grove, CA 92640. (714) 636-5457.

Julie Carobine has penned dozens of published articles and essays. She edits the newsletter of The National League of American Pen Women—Simi Valley, CA Branch. Contact: 10142 Fallen Leaf Court, Ventura, CA 93004.

Jeri Chrysong, a legal secretary, is a humorist, writes devotionals and is an award-winning poet. Contact: 19022 Hamden Lane, Huntington Beach, CA 92646. (714) 962-9709

Pat Clary, author, popular speaker, motivator and teacher is the President and Founder of The Women's Ministries Institute. Nationally and internationally, Pat encourages women to rise n shine for Jesus, dusting off their gifts and talents and using them for the glory of the Lord. Contact: The Women's Ministries Institute, 1605 E. Elizabeth, Suite U7, Pasadena, CA 91104. (818) 398-2291 x291

Jim and Sally Conway are co-directors of Mid-Life Dimensions Counseling Center and authors of many books, including *Men in Mid-Life Crisis* and *When a Mate Wants Out.* They speak extensively throughout the United States and are experts on the subject of the mid-life crisis of men and women. Contact: P.O. Box 3790, Fullerton, CA 92634. (714) 680-3660.

Teresa Daniels, an encourager and creative communicator for over 25 years, enjoys teaching the Word. She speaks, sings, and writes for her church, seminars, conferences and women's events. She also trains small group leaders through The Women's Ministries Institute. Contact: 3502 W. Magill Ave., Fresno, CA 93711. (209) 438-0176.

Danna Demetre, R.N., is a writer and a motivational speaker whose passion is to encourage individuals toward a life of greater balance. She has over 20 years experience in the medical and fitness fields and was a corporate marketing manager and professional trainer. Contact: 2063 Monarch Ridge Cir., Rancho San Diego, CA 92019. (619) 444-3400.

Nancy L. Dorner is a free-lance speaker, writer, retreat leader and director of Creative Directions, a Christian seminar service. She has written three books: *A Woman's Guide to Spiritual Power*, and *Glimpses of Grace* and Glory. Contact: 5030 Angling Rd., Kalamazoo, MI 49008. (616) 344-5852.

Dori Drabek has served in leadership as a pastor's wife and in various women's ministries for 20 years. As a speaker, God has fulfilled her dream to impart God's love to women of all ages and backgrounds. Contact: 2344 W. Carol Dr., Fullerton, CA 92633. (714) 526-7429.

Celeste Duckworth, in addition to her speaking and writing ministry, is passionate about sharing Jesus in her hair salon and the streets of her city. Contact: 630 N. Brierwood, Rialto, CA 92376. (909) 820-6306.

Tamera Easterday is a freelance writer and speaker who has dealt with cancer, physical disabilities and pain. She endeavors to assist others in learning how they can help friends and family who are hurting. Her advice is practical and based on the fruit of the Spirit. Contact: P.O. Box 887, Tehachapi, CA 93581.

Bill and Pam Farrel are co-authors of *Pure Pleasure: Making You Marriage a Great Affair* (InterVarsity Press). Bill is a senior pastor and Pam is a director of women's ministry. Pam and Bill are the co-directors of Masterful Living, a communications ministry. Contact: Masterful Living, 629 S. Rancho Santa Fe Rd., #306, San Marcos, CA 92069. (619) 727-9122.

Karin Lindholtz Fite teaches junior high English part-time and is continuing her education at Cal Poly. She and her husband are actively involved in marriage ministry at their church. Contact: 3823 Requa Avenue, Claremont, CA 91711. (909) 593-3304.

Cheri Fuller is the author of twelve books including *Home Business Happiness* (Starburst Publishers), numerous magazine articles, and is a university professor. She is a popular speaker at parents' and women's events and has appeared on *Focus on the Family*, ABC-TV's *Home Show*, and many other programs. Contact: P.O. Box 770493, Oklahoma City, OK 73177 or FAX (405) 749-1381.

Jeanette D. Gardner is a freelance editor/writer with more than 1500 articles in print and three books to be published in March, 1996. Contact: 4708 Delmar, Roeland Park, KS 66205-133. (913) 722-4601.

Ruthanne Garlock, Bible teacher and author, co-wrote with Quin Sherrer the bestseller, *A Woman's Guide to Spiritual Warfare* (Servant). She and husband John have taught for Bible schools and leaders' seminar in forty countries on five continents. Contact: P.O. Box 226048, Dallas, TX 75222.

Donna Clark Goodrich is the author of 12 books and over 600 articles, short stories, and devotionals. She also is a freelance editor and proofreader, and teacher at Christian writers seminars. Contact: 648 S. Pima St., Mesa, AZ 85210. (602) 962-6694.

Glenda Gordon is a writer and graphic artist. Contact: 2063 Mimosa Court, San Bernardino, CA 92404. (909) 864-8343.

Anne S. Grace has a B.S. degree in education from Radford University and is also a graduate of the Writers Digest School. Anne speaks for groups and writes devotions, inspirational articles, and awaits publication of her first book about living in the grace of God. Contact: 671 Spyglass Summit, St. Louis, MO 63017. (314) 434-8491.

Lille Diane Greder has inspired thousands nationwide with her personal story and concert, *From Ashes to Beauty*. Lille's refreshing speaking style combines humor, music and exhortation in her presentations. Contact: (805) 649-1805 for a brochure.

Dick Hagerman has had numerous magazine and newspaper articles published and is the author of *Eat, Drink, and Be Especially Joyful* (Provident House Publishers). A dentist of 37 years, Dick has also been a lay preacher and elder in the United Presbyterian Church. Contact: P.O. Box 365, Wendell, ID 83355. (208) 536-2187.

Judy Hampton makes her home in Brea, California. In addition to operating her own business, Judy is a featured speaker for retreats, conferences and Christian organizations, and is active in several ministries. Contact: 670 Oakhaven Ave., Brea, CA 92621. (714) 528-0704.

Adell (Dollie) Harvey, a country parson's wife, has had ten books published and is often called "The Evangelical Erma Bombeck." Contact: Box 130, Teton, ID 83451. (208) 458-4960.

June Hetzel has enjoyed the roles of classroom teacher, curriculum specialist, administrator, author, and editor. Contact: 241 W. Patwood, La Habra, CA 90631.

Liz Curtis Higgs, CSP, CPAE, has presented nearly one thousand humorous, "encouraging" programs for both Christian and business audiences in 44 states since 1986. She is the author of five books and is a Contributing Editor for *Today's Christian Woman* magazine. Contact: P.O. Box 43577, Louisville, KY 40253-0577. (502) 254-5454.

Mona Gansberg Hodgson, an award winning poet, author, editor, and speaker, has placed several hundred articles, poems, and short stories. Mona founded and directed the Central Arizona Christian Writers' Workshop for three years and is a contributing editor for *The Christian Communicator*. Contact: P.O. Box 999, Cottonwood, AZ 86326-0999.

Diana L. James is a professional speaker and writer in both secular and Christian markets. Her topics are designed to help people "Bounce Back" from set-backs and bad times. Contact: 86-P Calle Aragon, Laguna Hills, CA 92653. (714) 457-1213.

Pauline Jaramillo is a journalist and freelance writer. She has done volunteer work with various social service organizations, including food distribution centers. Her bilingual and bicultural (Spanish/English) ability enable her to function with ease in both cultures. Contact: P.O. Box 225, Rim Forest, CA 92378.

Sharon Jones is adept as an author and conference speaker at passionately encouraging today's Christian women and youth to put into action the truths taught in the Bible. In addition to her freelance work, she's Managing Editor of *Christteen* magazine. Contact: P.O. Box 1519, Inglewood, CA 90308. (213) 750-7573.

Dr. Eric Scott Kaplan, writer and featured speaker, is founder of six chiropractic and weight-loss centers and is national director of clinical operations for *Clinicorp, Inc.*. Kaplan is one of 40 who were chosen by *The President's Council on Physical Fitness and Sports* and *USA Today* to be featured in their national "Kids and Sports Hotline Series." His most recent book, *Dr. Kaplan's Lifestyle of the Fit & Famous* (Starburst Publishers), has been endorsed by such well-known personalities as Norman Vincent Peale, Tom McMillen, Gary Carter and Billy Cunningham. Kaplan travels throughout the nation speaking on motivation, communication and management. Contact: BigScore Productions, P.O. Box 7341, Lancaster, PA 17604. (717) 293-0247.

Pamala Kennedy is a national and international speaker and the author of *Where Have All the Lovers Gone?* (Thomas Nelson). She has been a pastor's wife for 26 years. Contact: 6511 LeFevre Dr., San Jose, CA 95118. (408) 267-5014.

Helen Hertha Kesinger is an inspirational writer of short stories and poems, sharing how God works through ordinary people. Contact 221 Brookside Dr., Paola, KS 66071-1111. (913) 294-2937.

June Cerza Kolf is the author of *When Will I Stop Hurting?*, *How Can I Help?*, *Teenagers Talk About Grief*, *Comfort and Care for the Terminally Ill*, and *Grandma's Tears*. She is available for workshops on helping others in crisis, starting grief support groups or to lead a session to help the bereaved. Contact: (805) 943-2742

Georgia Curtis Ling is an entertaining speaker and writer who touches the heart and tickles the funny bone as she shares stories about faith, love and life. She is a Southern gal, born and raised in Kentucky, a thirty-something pastor's wife, mother, and newspaper columnist. Contact: 4716 W. Glenhaven Dr., Everett, WA 98203. (206) 259-9136.

Sharon Marshall is founder and director of SCORE, an educational program validated by the United States Department of Education for accelerating achievement of high risk youth. Author, educator, and speaker, Sharon has written numerous educational materials and three books, *Justin, Heaven's Baby; Surviving Separation and Divorce;* and *When a Friend Gets a Divorce, What Can You Do?* Contact: CLASS Speakers at (619) 471-0233.

Dan Miller shares his inspirational story to churches, businesses, associations, schools, and students. *Focus on the Family* has broadcast his story in Spanish, French and Russian. Dan and his wife present seminars on how to be "Dreammakers, not Dreambreakers!" Contact: 2485 Alaska Ave. E., Port Orchard, WA 98366-8214. (360) 871-8446.

Kathy Collard Miller and **D. Larry Miller** write and speak as individuals and as a couple. Kathy is the author of 15 books, including *Healing the Angry Heart, Your View of God . . . God's View of You,* and the *Daughters of the King* Bible Study Series (Accent Publications). Contact: P.O. Box 1058, Placentia, CA 92670. (714) 993-2654. (See Copyright page for additional information.)

Elizabeth Nagy loves art, gardening, reading and sharing God's Word at women's Bible studies and through her writing. Contact: P.O. Box 390144, Anza, CA 92539.

Mary Nelson, editor for Accent Publications, has ghosted or co-authored five books and several magazine articles. Contact: 2621 S. Deframe Circle, Lakewood, CO 80228.

Jan Northington is a freelance writer and conference speaker. She is the author of *Separated and Waiting* (Thomas Nelson) and has written numerous articles. Contact: 2130 Sombrero Dr., Los Osos, CA 93402. (805) 528-2522.

Karen O'Connor is an award-winning author/speaker, known for her inspiring books and presentations on intimacy in relationships. Her journey from brokenness to restoration has made her especially sensitive to other people. She has appeared on national radio and television and leads women's retreats. Contact: 2050 Pacific Beach Dr., #205, San Diego, CA 92109. (619) 483-3184.

Star Paterson is a former social worker, counselor, and Women' Ministries Director. She enjoys teaching Bible studies and speaking for women's retreats and conferences. Contact: 709 50th St. S.E., Auburn, WA 98092. (206) 939-4357.

Lila Peiffer has written two novels, *The Secrets of the Roses* and *Rosehaven*, (Thomas Nelson). Contact: 4402 Prospect, Yorba Linda, CA 92686. (714) 524-1275.

Cora Lee Pless, a free-lance writer, has had articles accepted by publications including *Guideposts, Decision,* and *The Christian Reader*. Cora Lee enjoys teaching Sunday School and is available as an inspirational speaker. Contact: 127 Overhead Bridge Rd., Mooresville, NC 28115. (704) 664-5655.

Betty J. Price is the author of *101 Ways to Fix Broccoli and* co-authored with her husband Harvey, *ABC's of Abundant Living*. She has a unique music ministry as a Choirchime soloist that spans the world. Contact: P.O. Box 151115, San Diego, CA 92175-1115. (619) 466-9136.

Laura Sabin Riley is a free-lance writer and homemaker. She has published articles in *Decision* magazine and is in the process of writing a devotional book for stay-at-home moms. Contact: 10592 Del Vista Dr., Yuma, AZ 85367. (520) 342-7324.

Karen Robertson is a teacher, freelance writer, and professional speaker. *Easter Threads* is one of the many humorous and touching stories she includes in her presentation called, "Stand by Your Man." Karen just finished her first book titled *Raising Kids Right—Morning, Noon, and Night*. Contact: 33140 Claremont St., Wildomar, CA 92595. (909) 678-3030.

Joan Hake Robie, editor-in-chief of Starburst Publishers, is author of 15 books, including *Turmoil in the Toy Box II* and co-author of bestselling *Halloween and Satanism*. Joan has received a 4-star rating from Copley News Service for her radio interviews. She has appeared on TV shows such as Geraldo, Sonya Live, and Morton Downey. Joan is a speaker and conducts seminars. Contact: Starburst Promotions, P.O. Box 4123, Lancaster, PA 17604. (717) 293-0939.

L. C. Robie (Sky-Pilot) Robie, well-known evangelist, traveled extensively in the Central and Northeastern states. His ministry spanned nearly 70 years. He composed two gospel choruses and wrote several gospel tracts.

Becki Conway Sanders is a pastor's wife and has authored the book, *What God Gives When Life Takes, Trusting God in a Family Crisis.* She speaks frequently on suffering, God's will, and marriage for women's and youth groups. Contact: Mid-Life Dimensions Counseling Center, P.O. Box 3790, Fullerton, CA 92634. (714) 680-3660.

Linda Claire Scott is a freelance writer with over 200 articles accepted in 55 different publications. She has an elementary teaching degree and has tutored reading and math for ten years. Contact: 5247 Honeywood Lane, Anaheim, CA 92807

Jessica Shaver writes opinion, poetry, stories, devotionals and humor for newspapers and magazines. She holds a Master's in English literature and teaches at writers' conferences. Her book *GIANNA* is the triumphant story of a baby who survived being aborted. Contact: 186 E. Cameron Place, Long Beach, CA 90807-3851. (310) 595-4162.

Christi Anne Sheppeard has found that frustration and pain are not strangers as she continues the fight to turn the tide of her life history of abuse and loss. Hers is a message of encouragement and endurance. Contact: 700 E. Washington St. #230, Colton, CA 92324.

Quin Sherrer has co-authored six books to help women pray more effectively. One with Ruthanne Garlock, *A Woman's Guide to Spiritual Warfare* was a bestseller among Christian paperbacks. Quin had vast newspaper and magazine experience before writing Aglow's bestseller, *How to Pray for Your Children.* She serves on the U.S. and International board of directors for Women's Aglow Fellowship. She and her husband, LeRoy, live in Colorado Springs.

Patricia Smith is director of P.A.S.S. (Practical Application of Scriptural Submission), a ministry of encouragement for today's Christian woman. She has been involved in women's ministries for nearly 20 years, is a conference speaker and writes a monthly newsletter, *Peace in the Pressure Cooker.* Contact: P.A.S.S. Ministries, P.O. Box 27307, Tempe, AZ 85285-7307. (602) 966-1983.

Betty Southard is a popular international speaker, Bible Teacher and author of *The Grandmother Book.* She is also the Minister of Caring for a large television ministry and serves on the teaching staff of Christian Leaders, Authors, Speakers, Seminars (CLASS). Contact: 10 Blanchard, Irvine, CA 92715. (714) 856-9073.

Ruthie Lindal Swain does editorial work in Chicago and music teaching in Colorado Springs. Contact: 2115 Nolte Dr., Prescott, AZ 86301. (520) 445-8977.

Lavon Illum Swink has ministered with her husband, Carl, many years in pastoral home ministry and evangelism. She is a seasoned Bible teacher. Contact: 111 Regier St., Elbing, KS 67041. (316) 799-2350.

Marcia Van't Land is the author of *Living Well With Chronic Illness* and is available for speaking in the Southern California area. Contact: 12648 Ramona, Chino, CA 91710. (909) 627-2024.

Ruth Van't Land wrote her poem when she was a junior high school student. Ruth enjoys taking her mom on "wild wheelchair rides." Contact: 12648 Ramona, Chino, CA 91710. (909) 627-2024.

Teresa Vining is a freelance writer from the Kansas City Area. She writes for businesses and Christian organizations and has had her short stories and articles published in Christian and secular publications. Her most recent project was a teen Bible study curriculum for Promise Makers Ministry. Contact: 1438 N. Lucy Montgomery Way, Olathe, KS 66061. (913) 764-4610.

Fred H. Wevodau is a former Air Force pilot, cross-cultural minister, committed dad and international builder of men. His stories have their diverse beginnings in the skies of Viet Nam, college dorms, an all-too-real family and the streets of the world—but they all come from the heart and end in God's Word. Contact: The Navigators, 2525 Ivy Place, Fullerton, CA 92635. (714) 528-1727.

Carol Wolff is a home schooling mom. Contact: 2199 Gordon Ave., Menlo Park, CA 94025.

Jeanne Zornes is a widely published writer and speaker whose book credits include *When I Prayed for Patience . . . God Let Me Have It!* (Harold Shaw). Contact: 1025 Meeks St., Wenatchee, WA 98801.

Future *God's Vitamin "C"*™ Books

We would like to include your exciting, "tug-at-the heart" and thought-provoking stories in future editions of our *God's Vitamin "C"* books. We invite you to submit them, enclosing an S.A.S.E. (self-addressed stamped envelope) on the topics of:

- Women/Mom
- Men/Dad
- Couples
- Children
- Grandparents
- Students and Graduates
- Christmas
- Angels, Miracles and Heaven
- Happiness
- Kindness
- Virtues
- the Workplace
- those in the Helping Professions (nurses, teachers, ministers, etc.)
- general categories (spiritual life, Christian living, families, etc.)
- humor

Each submission should be no longer than 1,000 words. Please send typed, double-spaced manuscripts, along with a computer disk if you have it available. Also enclose biographical information on yourself.

You may also submit your favorite cartoons, quotes and poetry. (Please be sure to provide the source.) Send to:

Editorial Director
Starburst Publishers
P.O. Box 4123
Lancaster, PA 17604

Other Books by Starburst Publishers
(Partial listing—full list available on request)

God's Vitamin "C" for the Spirit
—Kathy Collard Miller & D. Larry Miller

Subtitled: *"Tug-at-the-Heart" Stories to Fortify and Enrich Your Life.* Includes inspiring stories and anecdotes that emphasize Christian ideals and values by Barbara Johnson, Billy Graham, Nancy L. Dorner, Dave Dravecky, Patsy Clairmont, Charles Swindoll, H. Norman Wright, Adell Harvey, Max Lucado, James Dobson, Jack Hayford and many other well-known Christian speakers and writers. Topics include: Love, Family Life, Faith and Trust, Prayer, Marriage, Relationships, Grief, Spiritual Life, Perseverance, Christian Living, and God's Guidance.

(trade paper) ISBN 0914984837 **$12.95**

God's Chewable Vitamin "C" for the Spirit

Subtitled: *A Dose of God's Wisdom One Bite at a Time.* A collection of inspirational Quotes and Scriptures by many of your favorite Christian speakers and writers. It will motivate your life and inspire your spirit. You will *chew* on every *bite* of **God's Chewable Vitamin "C" for the Spirit.**

(trade paper) ISBN 0914984845 **$6.95**

The World's Oldest Health Plan   —Kathleen O'Bannon Baldinger

Subtitled: *Health, Nutrition and Healing from the Bible.* Offers a complete health plan for body, mind and spirit, just as Jesus did. It includes programs for diet, exercise and mental health. Contains foods and recipes to lower cholesterol and blood pressure, improve the immune system and other bodily functions, reduce stress, reduce or cure constipation, eliminate insomnia, reduce forgetfulness, confusion and anger, increase circulation and thinking ability, eliminate "yeast" problems, improve digestion, and much more.

(trade paper-opens flat) ISBN 0914984578 **$14.95**

Dr. Kaplan's Lifestyle of the Fit & Famous   —Eric Scott Kaplan

Subtitled: *A Wellness Approach to "Thinning and Winning."* A comprehensive guide to the formulas and principles of: FAT LOSS, EXERCISE, VITAMINS, NATURAL HEALTH, SUCCESS and HAPPINESS. More than a health book—it is a lifestyle based on the empirical formulas of healthy living. Dr. Kaplan's food-combining principles take into account all the major food sources (fats, proteins, carbohydrates, sugars, etc.) that when combined within the proper formula (e.g. proteins cannot be mixed with refined carbohydrates) will increase metabolism and decrease the waistline. This allows you to eat the foods you want, feel great, and eliminate craving and binging.

(hard cover) ISBN 091498456X **$21.95**

A Woman's Guide To Spiritual Power   —Nancy L. Dorner

Subtitled: *Through Scriptural Prayer.* Do your prayers seem to go "against a brick wall?" Does God sometimes seem far away or non-existent? If your answer is "Yes," *You* are not alone. Prayer must be the cornerstone of your relationship to God. "This book is a powerful tool for anyone who is serious about prayer and discipleship."—Florence Littauer

(trade paper) ISBN 0914984470   **$9.95**

Angels, Angels, Angels   —Phil Phillips

Subtitled—*Embraced by The Light...or...Embraced by The Darkness?* Discovering the truth about Angels, Near-Death Experiences and other Spiritual Awakenings. Also, why the sudden interest in angels in this day and age? Can we trust what we read in books like *Embraced By The* Light?

(trade paper) ISBN 0914984659   **$10.95**

From Grandma With Love   —Ann Tuites

Subtitled: Thoughts for Her Children Everywhere. People are taught all kinds of things from preschool to graduate school, but they are expected to know instinctively how to get along with their families. Harmony within the home is especially difficult when an aging relative is involved. The author presents personal anecdotes to encourage caregivers and those in need of care. Practical, emotional and spiritual support is given so that all generations can learn to live together in harmony.

(hardcover) ISBN 0914984616   **$14.95**

Migraine—Winning the Fight of Your Life   —Charles Theisler

This book describes the hurt, loneliness and agony that migraine sufferers experience and the difficulty they must live with. It explains the different types of migraines and their symptoms, as well as the related health hazards. Gives 200 ways to help fight off migraines, and shows how to experience fewer headaches, reduce their duration, and decrease the agony and pain involved.

(trade paper) ISBN 0914984632   **$10.95**

Purrables   —Alma Barkman

Subtitled: *Words of Wisdom From the World of a Cat.* This book was derived from the antics of the family cat, Sir Purrcival van Mouser. The author has taken anecdotal material used in a weekly humor column and combined it with Scriptural truths from the book of *Proverbs.* **Purrables** is an inspirational self-help book with a unique slant. Sir Purrcival van Mouser draws the reader into consideration of spiritual truths as they apply to everyday living. The humorous behavior of the cat is used to draw a parallel with our own experience or attitude, and the application is summarized by an appropriate proverb. **Purrables** especially appeals to anyone who loves a cat and would therefore enjoy reading truth from a different *purrspective.*

(trade paper) ISBN 0914984535   **$6.95**

Books by Starburst Publishers—cont'd.

Parenting With Respect and Peacefulness   —Louise A. Dietzel

Subtitled: *The Most Difficult Job in the World*. Parents who love and respect themselves parent with respect and peacefulness. Yet, parenting with respect is
the most difficult job in the world. This book informs parents that respect and
peace communicate love—creating an atmosphere for children to maximize their
development as they feel loved, valued, and safe. Parents can learn authority
and control by commonsense, interpersonal, and practical approaches to
day-to-day issues and situations in parenting.

(trade paper) ISBN 0914984667   **$10.95**

Beyond The River   —Gilbert Morris & Bobby Funderburk

The first novel of *The Far Fields* series, **Beyond the Rive**r makes for intriguing
reading with high spiritual warfare impact. Set in the future and in the mode of
Brave New World and *1984,* **Beyond The River** presents a world that is ruined
by modern social and spiritual trends. This anti-utopian novel offers an
excellent opportunity to speak to the issues of the New Age and "politically-
correct" doctrines that are sweeping the country.

(trade paper) ISBN 0914984519   **$8.95**

Winning At Golf   —David A. Smith

Addresses the growing needs of aspiring young golfers yearning for correct instruction, positive guidance, and discipline. It is an attempt not only to
increase the reader's knowledge of the swing, but also sets forth to inspire and
motivate the reader to a new and rewarding way of life. **Winning At Golf** relays
the teachings of Buck White, the author's mentor and a tour winner many times
over. It gives instruction to the serious golfer and challenges the average golfer
to excel.

(trade paper) ISBN 0914984462   **$9.95**

Purchasing Information:

Books are available from your favorite Bookstore, either from current stock
or special order. To assist bookstore in locating your selection be sure to give title,
author, and ISBN #. If unable to purchase from the bookstore you may order
direct from STARBURST PUBLISHERS. When ordering enclose full payment
plus $3.00 for shipping and handling ($4.00 if Canada or Overseas). Payment in
US Funds only. Please allow two to three weeks minimum (longer overseas)
for delivery. Make checks payable to and mail to STARBURST PUBLISHERS,
P.O. Box 4123, LANCASTER, PA 17604. Credit card orders may also be
placed by calling 1-800-441-1456 (credit card orders only), Mon-Fri, 8 AM–5 PM
Eastern Time. **Prices subject to change without notice.** 01-96